THE
QUIVERING
TREE

Sylvia Theresa Haymon was born in Norwich, and is best known for her eight crime fiction novels featuring the character Inspector Ben Jurnet. Haymon also wrote two non-fiction books for children, as well as two memoirs of her childhood in East Anglia.

The Ben Jurnet series enjoyed success in both the UK and the US during Haymon's lifetime: *Ritual Murder* (1982) won the prestigious CWA Silver Dagger Award from the Crime Writers' Association. *Stately Homicide* (1984), a skilful variation on the country house mystery, was praised by the *New York Times* as a 'brilliantly crafted novel of detection . . . stylish serious fiction', and favourably compared to the work of Dorothy L. Sayers.

AN EAST ANGLIAN CHILDHOOD VOLUME 2

S.T. HAYMON

THE QUIVERING TREE

propolis

First published in 1990 by Constable

This edition published 2024 by Propolis Books

The Book Hive,
53 London Street,
Norwich, NR2 1HL

ISBN 9781916905160

These memoirs - written in the 1980's and recalling events of the 1920's -
vividly reflect the language and attitudes of the time towards class, race and
gender. The publisher acknowledges that in our more enlightened times
some of these may cause offense, but asks that they be treated as accurate
reflections of historical events.

Cover by Niki Medlik at **studio medlikova**

For Rebecca, Sarah, Jessica and Naomi

INTRODUCTION
by
Esther Freud

In this, the second of her two memoirs, crime writer S.T.Haymon
refers her readers regularly to the first – *Opposite The Cross
Keys* – a jubilant recreation of a year in her Norfolk childhood,
when, aged eight, she enjoyed extended stays in the rural home
of Maud, her maid. In *The Quivering Tree*, the now twelve-year
old Haymon is once again attempting to escape her family: a
remote mother, described as 'kind,' a father who was at least
'always pleased to see her,' and siblings, grown up by the time of
her clearly inconvenient birth. At the start of this book however,
her father is dead, and her mother is making plans to move to
London. Sylvia has been ill, no longer the 'unconquerable' girl
we'd come to know, but the thought of leaving her beloved
Norfolk reignites her fighting spirit. 'I informed my mother that
I would not be going with her to London. . . . I loved everything
about Norwich and could not see my way to exchanging such a
paradise for an overgrown ant heap with too many people and
no country or sea for miles.'

Chandos House is to be her new home. It is inhabited by two
mistresses from her school: Miss Gosse – shiny, boot-button eyes,
snub-nosed as a spaniel – and Miss Locke, with her boyish figure

and Peter Pan crop of hair. Chandos House is not the lodgings she'd have chosen, but the result of an intervention by the fearsome headmistress, Mrs Crail: 'Between her bark and her bite there was nothing much to choose. You could catch rabies from either.' Mrs Crail, it soon transpires, has placed her at Chandos House with the sole hope of causing trouble. And trouble is what ensues.

Elegant, disturbing at times and darkly funny, Sylvia is thrown into an adult world, unaware – how could she be otherwise? – of the true nature of the relationship between the Misses Gosse and Locke. Jealousies and secrets, tricks and threats are as perplexing as all the talk of love. Love that bears no relation to any kind she'd known before.

She is also at the mercy – at least where food is concerned, and food for Sylvia is of great concern – of the whims of the hulking, alcoholic housekeeper Mrs Benyon, who on occasion appears behind her as she practises the piano and sings in a voice, 'deep and powerful. A voice with teeth in it. It took the song by the throat and shook it, the way a terrier shakes a rat to show it who is master.' Here Haymon's skill for creating characters is in full force, and soon we are as immersed as young Sylvia in the daily intrigues and characters of the house: The mistresses, their bluntly outspoken friend Miss Malahide, and the gardener Joey Betts, small and knobbly with legs bent out of shape by a former life as a jockey. Betts is a friend to Sylvia when she most needs one, and with whom she enters into an unlikely alliance: his theory that racing tips given by a girl still 'pure' (making Sylvia blush...) are more likely to result in wins, means there is money to be gained if and when she picks a winner. And money can be exchanged for food.

Caught between childhood and adolescence, with only *The Quivering Tree* outside her window to confide in, it is no surprise that Sylvia finds herself increasingly, unfamiliarly, in tears. Her mother is in London, and with her, Maud, and she doesn't feel she can return to the sanctuary of *Opposite the Cross Keys*, because that is in the past and she must move forward, mustn't she? Half-starved and confused by the attentions of the predatory Miss Locke, who pinches her bottom and kisses her mouth, she is forced – when her head begins to throb and blood inexplicably trickles down her leg – to turn to the manager of Goat Lane Chemist, Mr Spencer, who with infinite tact and sweetness instructs her in the use of a sanitary towel, with its strings, loops and hooks. 'Are you absolutely certain your mother never said a word to you?' Even Maud's response, when she'd previously asked about the brown wrapped parcels, was unhelpful. 'What are they for?' 'What you think? For you to ask silly questions about!'

Everything is changing. Even the familiar landmarks of Norwich – the Cathedral, the Agricultural Hall, the black angel on the top of the memorial in the cattle market – all look different now Sylvia no longer belongs here, Chandos House being in the suburbs. When she encounters once well-known faces, they don't know whether to commiserate over the death of her father or be jolly. Not being sure, they move on.

Sylvia's isolation feels complete as she stares at the pictures in the window of the Haymarket Cinema, men and women kissing, or looking as if they were about to. Kissing, at least this kind Sylvia knows, is to do with 'Love with a capital L', something which – like Einstein's Theory of Relativity – she imagines she'll get around to learning about later. So it is with annoyance that she finds herself blushing when a boy she hardly knows appears at her side and asks if she'd like to see the film. He is blushing too, but when she tells him that she wouldn't he doesn't give up, and Sylvia knows this is because once, with her unthinking interest in History, she'd mentioned she admired his name, Robert Kett – the same as the great Norfolk rebel hero who'd been hanged from the battlements of the castle in 1549.

Undaunted, Robert shows up at Chandos House, and not knowing how else to entertain him, Sylvia invites him to meet the unaccountably bad-tempered donkey Bagshaw, who live in a field behind the garden. Smitten, he brings him an unrisen sponge cake from his mother's kitchen and caught between childhood and pubescence their friendship blossoms, resulting one afternoon in an innocent and raucous game, slamming drawers and shouting, their laughter so loud it brings them to the attention of Miss Locke. Her swift and violent reaction will not be forgotten.

This is a darkly sophisticated story, flash full of humanity, the vulnerabilities of its characters artfully managed. We see deceit, blackmail and abuse. . . but there is love here too. Not the straightforward love which suffuses the pages of its prequel, but a darker and more unnerving kind that makes *The Quivering Tree* as gripping as it is surprising.

CHAPTER ONE

'Don't ring,' my brother Alfred admonished me. 'Wait till I've brought in the rest of the stuff.'

He went back down the narrow path to the gate and out to the car. The house was built a long way back from the road, and the sound of the traffic, already distant and dreamlike, was further masked by a rustling noise which came from a large untidy tree at the side of the porch. There was no wind, and it was hard to decide what the leaves were making such a fuss about.

Alfred need not have worried about my ringing the doorbell betimes. Now that I had actually arrived at Chandos House I was in no hurry to gain entrance. On the contrary. The longer it was put off the better. I propped my school attaché case, my shoe-bag, my music case and my bundled-up tennis racquet, hockey stick and lacrosse stick against the suitcase Alfred had already deposited on the front step and moved back on to the path, to get a better look at the exterior. I didn't take a very good look in case somebody looking out of a window saw me and came to the door whilst I was unsupported by Alfred's presence.

The house was Edwardian, of less importance than, unseen, its name might have suggested, but not without a certain consequence: solid, the nearest dwellings on either side an affluent distance away. Unfortunately, my dead father had taught me, young as I was, to be an architectural snob and before darting back into the protective shadow of the porch, itself a foolish irrelevance of pseudo-Tudor held up by outsize skittles painted a turgid green, I curled up my lip at the narrow bays, the bricks no number of centuries would ever mellow, the general mean-spiritedness of the place that, incredibly, for the next two years, was to be my home. Though tears came into my eyes at the prospect, another part of me was not displeased.

How unreal my possessions looked, parked on that alien doorstep! My music case had the St Giles address tooled into the leather. My mother and I had watched it being done with red-hot dies, an advertisement of my place in the world, never to be removed. 'Last you a lifetime,' the man who did it had promised, and my mother and I had nodded approvingly, for who could ever imagine living anywhere else? But now – St Giles? Where was that? It might as well have been on the moon. The tennis racquet, the hockey stick and the lacrosse stick had the air of ritual objects belonging to an alien cult into which I had yet to prove myself worthy of initiation. The suitcase wasn't mine, not mine particularly, that is. It was a family object, like most of the things that, up to that moment, had surrounded me, cushioning and confirming my existence. But where was the family now, apart from my father, trapped in the cemetery and deprived for ever of his armchair, his newspapers, Caruso records and all the other things that made life worth living?

Alfred came crunching up the path with my box of books, and plunked it down next to the suitcase. He wasn't looking too happy himself, but whether it was sadness at our imminent parting or because the coarse pebbles of which the path was made were scratching his beautiful brogues I couldn't tell, and he went back to unstrap my bike from the running-board of the Morris Oxford before I had time to ask. The thought of the Morris Oxford made the tears well up in earnest. After all, it wasn't as if I were parting from my brother for good. I would be seeing him from time to time, even though our relationship would be completely changed (but then, everything was changed, wasn't it – not only that), but the car, never again. Alfred had announced that he was going to turn it in for a sports model, an Alvis or a Riley or an MG, something that went better with his plus-fours and his ukelele and the girls with red lips, long cigarette-holders and bobbed hair streaming in the wind he often took along as passengers. The fact that his fiancée, Phyllis, didn't smoke and that whenever she came out in the Morris Oxford with us Alfred had to pull up every few miles so that she could get out to be sick, made me privately wonder whether I would ever be called upon to be bridesmaid at that particular wedding.

I waited on the porch, tremulously reflecting that by rights there ought to be a place where motor-cars which had served their masters well could be turned out to grass like old horses, instead of being sold down the river like so many Uncle Toms. How could the new owners, whoever they might be, be expected to learn our Morris Oxford's little ways and tolerate them, as we had, as endearing expressions of personality? How could they, for example, appreciate that, though the set of celluloid windscreens looked identical, in fact only a particular one fitted a particular door, and you could go blue in the face to no purpose trying to fit the ratchets of one into holes where it did not choose to go? We had always been meaning to mark the windscreens in some unmistakable way, but somehow had never got round to it, and now, as with everything else, it was too late. Anyway, with time it hadn't proved necessary, because we had come, little by little, to recognize certain intimate marks of identity, such as the stain on the one that belonged on the front passenger side where Phyllis had been sick on the black belting that surrounded the celluloid before Alfred had come to a place where it was safe to stop.

If only I were older, I thought, I could have kept the Morris Oxford myself and gone driving all over Norfolk in it, the way we had before my father died. Only, children couldn't get driving licences and though, to my way of thinking, at twelve I wasn't a child any longer (particularly as the experience of losing a parent was a very ageing thing) I wasn't a grown-up either. I wasn't anything. This doleful reflection cheered me up wonderfully, and when Alfred came back with the bicycle I was able to greet him with an encouraging smile.

'You can always use that Cherry Blossom polish with the dye in it. I bet it'll cover up the scratches so you'd never even know they were there.'

'What?' Alfred stared. He propped the bicycle against the privet hedge that, on one side, edged the path from the house to the road. 'We'll have to ask where this goes.' He came back to the porch and put an arm round my shoulder. 'Know what?' he said. 'I'm going to miss my little sister.'

The bell was still clanging somewhere deep in the house when Miss Gosse opened her front door, which was rather unnerving, both because I wasn't used to doorbells which kept on ringing when the need for their services was patently past, and because Miss Gosse herself was such a surprise.

I knew her, of course. I'd have been pretty thick not to, considering that she had been teaching me mathematics, or trying to, for more than a year. I even prized her funny, olive-skinned face with its shiny, boot-button eyes and its snub nose as one of the alleviations of the school day; the black hair parted in the middle and drawn tightly back from her forehead into an intricately plaited knot which was more like one of those fancy bread rolls than a bun, except there weren't any poppy seeds, naturally.

My new landlady's head, then, presented no problem: it was the rest of her. In school, like all the other mistresses, Miss Gosse wore her black college gown, such a soaring symbol of authority as it billowed along the corridors that one scarcely noticed the body beneath, unless it was as big as a barge like the body of Mrs Crail, the headmistress. I knew Miss Gosse was short – not much taller than myself, I now discovered, so greatly had I sprung up in the half-term I had been away from school – but until the moment I entered Chandos House for the first time and saw her in a blouse and skirt, no gown, no dignity, I had never noticed that her sturdy little legs were much too short for her sturdy little body, almost dwarfish.

As one who, not out of vanity and without giving a lot of thought to it, had always taken it for granted that I would grow up beautiful, because beautiful was the best thing to be and only the best was going to happen to me, I felt a stab of fear to see Miss Gosse the way she was. Not that I was afraid short legs were catching, nothing silly like that; only that they proved you could never be sure. For all I knew, Miss Gosse had never wanted to be a maths mistress at all, but a chorus girl with lovely long legs that went far up her thighs, and look what she had been landed with instead.

At school we – that is, the other girls in my form and I – often filled in dull moments with arguing as to whether Miss Gosse looked more like a Pekinese than she did a King Charles spaniel, or vice versa. Sometimes, just to stir things up, I would maintain that it was a pug of whom she was the spitting image. In my heart, however, I was a King Charles man through and through. At St Giles we had briefly had a King Charles spaniel puppy whom I had loved passionately in the short time before it had dashed out into the street and been run over by a tram. There were times, during maths, as I sat trying to take in parallelograms or quadratic equations or whatever was the flavour of the day, when Miss Gosse, standing in front of the blackboard with a stump of chalk in her hand, would turn her head in a certain way, and instantly grief for the lost puppy would overwhelm me, so close was the resemblance between her and my darling Tirri.

Occasionally, Miss Gosse would notice my distress and misinterpreting its cause, tell me kindly that, if only I concentrated, all – parallelograms, quadratic equations, the secrets of the universe – would be revealed. She was a great one for concentrating. Standing wedged with my luggage in the narrow hall of Chandos House, a knobbly hallstand nudging my back in an unfriendly way, I found myself willing her to concentrate on tea. Now that I had recovered from my illness, my appetite had recovered tenfold, and I was ravenous. Breakfast at St Giles that day had been of the sketchiest, and lunch non-existent with the moving men hovering, itching to whisk everything in the house away to London, the last remnants of food in the larder included. Disgorged at last by an empty house which would already have seemed a total stranger were it not for the discoloured rectangles left on the wallpaper that showed where our pictures had hung, we – the three of us, my mother, Alfred and I – had driven to the station with ages to spare before the train left for London: plenty of time to go and get something to eat if only the two grown-ups had given a thought to it, which they hadn't, and I didn't like to bring up the subject, it seemed so crass when my mother was in such a state.

It was funny. For as long as I could remember, my mother had mourned the cruel necessity which had made Norwich our home. London, I was instructed, was not only bigger, it was better in every possible way, a place where life was lived to the full as against the mere vegetable existence which was all that went on in the benighted provinces, or at any rate in the benighted province of East Anglia. She was forever, as she put it, 'popping up to town' to spend a few days with one or other of her four sisters resident in the capital, either as a temporary escape to the full life, or even just to buy a new hat because London hats were, by definition, infinitely superior to those on sale in Norwich, even in posh shops like Bunting's or Chamberlains. When I asked her once why she had ever married my father and come to live in Norwich in the first place, if she disliked the city so much, she had opened her beautiful brown eyes wide and replied that everyone made sacrifices for love, an answer I found unsatisfactory in the extreme, since it in no way corresponded to my juvenile fantasies as to the nature of that mysterious quality.

But now that the moment of parting had come – almost come, rather, for a notice at the platform barrier announced a forty-minute delay – she paced to and fro, from the bookstall to the booking office and back again, tormenting herself over and over with the despairing question: was she doing the right thing?

Her indecision confused me beyond what had already become the normal confusion of those months following my father's death. How could it not be the right thing to go and live in London since that was what she wanted to do, and there was nothing now to stop her? After all, two of her children – my sister and the younger of my two brothers – were already living and working there; and Alfred, also a grown man, was going to be married as soon as, in the light of our bereavement, it was considered decent to do so. As for myself, I was taken care of, wasn't I, so why the eleventh-hour agony? It couldn't be because of my father that she thought she ought to stay where she was, because he was no more in Norwich than he was anywhere else except heaven, where he was bound to be, having been a sweet and lovely man.

All the same, I couldn't help wondering if my mother's last-minute second thoughts might not be on account of my father after all; if it didn't make her uncomfortable to think of him up there close to the throne of God, looking down all the time to see what she was up to, and thinking that she couldn't wait to be off the minute the coast was clear. I know his new address made *me* feel awful. Alive, my father had been exquisitely scrupulous about according his children their own private living space, mental and physical – but dead! The last thing I wanted was for him to burn in Hell, but oh! it was intolerable, knowing him in heaven and privy to absolutely everything that went on – everything! When, intending comfort, people told me not to grieve, that night and day he was watching over me, I wanted to shout, 'He isn't! He isn't!' Whenever I went to the lavatory, I would whisper fiercely as I pulled down my knickers: 'Don't look! Don't look!'

Even Alfred, my unfailingly kind brother, looked and sounded a little frayed after a half-hour of repeated assurances that yes, my mother was doing the right thing. I could tell by the way he scanned the railway lines converging in the distance that, like me, he was willing them to produce a train moving slowly over the points into Norwich Thorpe station. I'm not sure that, even as he reminded her that her sisters – our aunts – would be there in force at Liverpool Street to meet her, he did not send up a little prayer to the god of the London and North-Eastern Railway: 'Hurry up, for Christ's sake!'

Maud, our maid,* was already ensconced in the new house, ready to let in the movers and tell them where the furniture and everything and everyone else was to go. In the meantime, George, Aunty Kay's chauffeur (she was the rich one), resplendent in his grey uniform and peaked cap, would drive the reunited sisters in the Seabrook to Aunty Kay's house where she would be able to relax, have a meal, put her feet up, until word came that the house was ready for her reception, down to the last hairpin.

The reference to a meal really did for me. Up till then I had been playing a private game to make time pass and divert my mind from my mother's and my own sufferings. Every time we

---

* For more about Maud, see *Opposite the Cross Keys* (Propolis, 2024)

approached the bookstall I strained to see how much I could read of the front pages of the newspapers displayed there, how many story titles on the covers of the magazines, the *Strand*, the *London, Argosy, Happy Mag*, before my mother turned on her louis heels and it was time to trail back to the booking office once more. Now, my hunger smote me with such force that if I hadn't seen with my own eyes that the larder there was bare I would have cut across Alfred's optimistic affirmations that of course she was doing the right thing with: 'No, you're not! Let's go back to St Giles and never leave it again, ever!'

CHAPTER TWO

Driving away from the station, out of town by the Sprowston Road, a long pull-up past dingy houses which seemed to have nothing to do with the beautiful city centre where I had lived and had my being, I had felt too battered by my mother's emotions to feel any of my own, conscious only of the great void which throbbed inside me, expanding and contracting, *glug, glug*, like one of those volcanic mudholes they went in for in New Zealand.

'Was the train late?' Miss Gosse now inquired. 'We'd expected you earlier. What a pity you've missed tea!'

It was my introduction to the life of a lodger, a life where meals materialized only at pre-stated hours, and if you were late, hard cheese. No offer to make a fresh pot, no bringing back to the table of what was left of the bread and butter: between whiles, no hot snacks on tap in the kitchen, no larder overflowing with little somethings to keep you going until it was time once more to sit down to a proper meal. I had missed tea. How I missed it!

Alfred looked at me worriedly. After all, I was only just well again. Dr Parfitt had emphasized that I had to be careful, whatever that might mean. Afraid he might say something, I tugged surreptitiously at his jacket. Making demands, I knew instinctively, even if he didn't, was no way to get my new lodging life off to a good start.

A large square woman came into the hall through a door at the far end. As she reached the slash of light which came through the glass panels in the front door, I could see that she wore a long-sleeved overall with a design of purple and white shrubbery which echoed in a truly remarkable way the marbled pattern of her skin. Marbled not only described her complexion but also the extraordinary immobility of her features. When she spoke it was *snap*! Her lips moved the way a lizard moved, almost too fast to be seen before they froze again. Only a slight quiver of the heavy jowls, a tremor that never let up completely, gave the game away that she hadn't just that moment arrived on the boat with the Elgin marbles.

'This is Mrs Benyon, our housekeeper,' said Miss Gosse, smiling. And, turning to the woman in question: 'And this is Sylvia, our little guest.'

Guest! I thought bitterly, not taken in for a moment. A fine guest who didn't even qualify for a cup of tea!

Mrs Benyon looked at me without noticeable warmth and demanded, in a tone that was more London than Norfolk: 'Horlicks or Bovril?'

The question took me aback, both because it was unexpected and because I hated both drinks equally.

'We all have a mug of either Horlicks or Bovril at eight o'clock,' Miss Gosse explained with a touch of coyness, as if confessing to something a little on the naughty side. 'Mrs Benyon needs to know which you prefer.'

I knew better than to say neither, thank you just the same. I said Bovril, not becase I liked the one any better than the other, but because the few times I had had to drink the stuff it had at least arrived with a couple of cream crackers in the saucer.

The housekeeper pointed to my sports equipment which, for want of anywhere else to put it, Alfred had propped against the hallstand.

'That,' she pronounced, 'will have to go under the stairs. The rest –' and she looked at my brother meaningly – 'will need to be carried up.'

Alfred sprang forward with offers of assistance, but I could see the woman had made him nervous. So handsome, so good-humoured, he was used to people smiling at him. Disapproval threw him out of his stride. He grabbed at the bundle. As he did so the lacrosse stick twisted in the same unpredictable way it often twisted on the playing-field; banged against a brass tray which stood on the bit of hallstand which jutted out in front of the central mirror, and knocked it to the floor. Some letters ready for the post which had been placed on the tray slid across the linoleum.

As Alfred and I, stammering apologies, scrabbled red-faced to pick them up, I lifted my head to see the housekeeper looking across at Miss Gosse with a glaze of satisfaction on her marbled face. As loud as words, the look proclaimed: 'What did I tell you?'

'Accidents will happen.' Miss Gosse smiled, but she sounded a bit nervous herself. In the few moments I had lived in Chandos House I had learned that Mrs Benyon was a very powerful person.

My room at Chandos House was so small that Alfred, going ahead with the suitcase, made the mistake of assuming it was some kind of anteroom, with the proper bedroom somewhere beyond. It was, in fact, built over the hall and was of comparable proportions, only slightly smaller, part of its space having been snaffled by the first floor landing. Once he had realized that was it, my brother was forced to put the suitcase on the bed, which I could tell immediately Mrs Benyon, wheezing up the stairs behind us to keep an eye on what we were up to, didn't like one little bit, only there was nowhere else to put it, if we were to be able to move about the room at all. As it was, the box of books had to go under the bed, which wasn't such a bad idea considering how the latter dipped in the middle.

The only other furniture was a straw-seated chair on which were a box of matches and a green metal candlestick fitted with a white candle, plus, in front of the window, a tall, narrow chest of drawers with a mirror perched on top, too high to see into, except on tiptoe. A shallow niche, fixed up with a rail and curtained off in the same faded chintz as hung on either side of the window, served as a wardrobe. I could tell just by looking at him that Alfred – not out loud: he wasn't going to risk offending Mrs Benyon, whose important position in the household he had noted, just as I had – thought it was a poky little room, but I loved it on sight, taking its smallness as a positive virtue. I saw myself curled up inside it as in a chrysalis, snug as a bug in a rug until the moment came – as come it must – for me to fly free towards the sun, a butterfly on iridescent wing. In the meantime, it *was* dark, though: darker than I cared for, owing to a branch of the untidy tree outside spreading its bulk clear across the window. Its leaves, pressed against the glass like nosy urchins, were almost completely round, with shallow, rounded teeth that did not look at all aggressive. The leaf stalks were ones you could be sorry for, they looked so weak and defenceless. No wonder the leaves shivered and quivered, afraid of dropping off altogether.

It was so dark that Alfred looked round for the electric light switch. The housekeeper, divining his intention, actually chuckled, the marble, though only momentarily, turning into rubber before resuming its accustomed rigidity. 'You'll look a long time for one o' them in this house. We only got gas here.'

'Gas!'

We both of us looked up at the light dangling in front of the window, and sure enough, there it was – a gas mantle with a beaded frill and two little pulleys with rings at the ends for regulating the flame, or so I supposed; also a further box of matches on top of the chest of drawers. We were astonished. No doubt in 1930 there were in Norwich homes besides this one where electricity had not yet penetrated, but only the cottages of the poor, surely: not houses like Chandos House.

'Old Mr Gosse didn't hold with it,' Mrs Benyon condescended to explain. 'Said it wasn't natural, all those wires going every which way. One day we'd be struck by lightning, sure as eggs are eggs.'

'I'm surprised he thought gas any safer. Does Mr Gosse still live here?' Alfred wanted to know.

'Passed over eleven years come November. But Miss Gosse wouldn't go and do something he wouldn't want her to. She knows what respect is.'

'Quite!' Alfred agreed hastily, but I could see that my big brother was worried about me, about lighted matches, escaping gas and all that. Since my father's death he had increasingly taken on the paternal role. 'Think you can manage to light it, Sylvia, and turn it off properly?'

'Of course I can.' I added, at my most winsome: 'If I can't, I'm sure Mrs Benyon will show me how.'

Mrs Benyon didn't say she would, she didn't say she wouldn't. She paced heavily out of the room, throwing over her shoulder as she went: 'When you got that case empty, bring it down so's it can go in the shed.'

'Shed reminds me,' Alfred said after she had gone, her footsteps deliberate on the lino of landing and stairs, seeming not to fade away in the distance the way footsteps could normally be relied on to do, 'I've got to find out where your bike goes.' Instead of going, however, he stood eyeing the gas fitting with undiminished distrust. 'I don't like it. Suppose you have to go the lav during the night?' During my illness I had been obliged to go only too often.

'There's always the candlestick. That's what it's for, I suppose.'

'I still don't like it.' But my brother's face brightened. 'I know what! You can have the torch out of the car. I put new batteries in only last week. I'll go and fetch it.' After another worried pause: 'What I ought to do is drive back into town and rustle you up something to eat. The shops'll be shut, but I'm sure Mrs Coe wouldn't mind fixing you up with a few sandwiches if I ask her.'

'It would take far too long.' The Coes, the friends with whom Alfred had arranged to stay, lived almost as far across the city as it was possible to be and still be in Norwich. Besides, whatever could I say if they found crumbs? It would look awful. 'I'm all right, really I am. But the torch is a lovely idea.'

'If you're sure.' Before he went downstairs Alfred bent over and kissed me. 'I'll see to the bike at the same time.' Whilst he was away I sat on the bed in my little room, enjoying the loveliness of it. When my brother came back he looked marginally happier.

'Bike's round at the back. There's an enormous garden – fruit trees, vegetables, everything, and fields back of that. It's really the country. You'd never know from the road. You'll get fresh air, fresh garden produce, soon put the roses back in your cheeks.'

He handed over the torch, pressing the catch as he did so. In the light the room looked even better, so that I was sorry when he switched it off again, so as not to waste the batteries. He had also brought two squares of chocolate which he had found in the little cupboard in the car's dashboard. 'Beggars can't be choosers.'

The chocolate was plain Bournville, which I didn't care for normally, and fuzzy with a pelt of car fluff. Just the same I wolfed it, fluff and all, and felt even hungrier to be reminded of what food was like.

'Another thing you won't believe,' Alfred went on. 'I asked Miss Gosse for the number so I'd know where to get you, and she said they weren't on the phone! Papa and the wires again – can you credit it? She says there's a very nice call-box at the crossroads, wherever they are, so it's no inconvenience to be without one. Quite the contrary. "Privacy is a great boon, don't you think?" Boon! That's what she actually said!'

I wanted to tell Alfred to stop worrying. Because I was so much younger than the rest of them, my family were always worrying about me, quite unnecessarily. As it was, he went on, insisting: 'Promise you'll ring me every Saturday morning without fail – and any other time if you need anything. You've got the office number, and the Coes'.'

'You know I have. You made me write them down in my diary.'

'Well, then. Always make sure you've got pennies with you for putting in the box.' A sudden thought: 'How much money have you got, anyway?'

I felt in my blazer pocket, took out my money and counted it in his presence, even though I knew beforehand exactly how much there was.

'Ninepence. A threepenny bit and six pennies. It's all arranged for Miss Gosse to give me a shilling pocket money every Saturday.' I was, and sounded, quite pleased about this because up to that time I had only been getting sixpence; but Alfred did not appear to share my satisfaction in my enhanced financial status. Taking out his wallet, he extracted a pound note which he put down on the bed beside me. 'Put that away somewhere safe. You have to have something in hand. When you've used it up, let me know and I'll give you another.'

'A pound! Thanks!'

Alfred and I looked at each other with a mixture of love and exasperation on both sides. For myself, I was very glad to have such a lovely man for my brother, but suddenly I couldn't wait for him to go so that I could get on with the rest of my life.

'I suppose I ought to start unpacking,' I suggested diplomatically.

CHAPTER THREE

This is how I came to be living at Chandos House in the first place.

A few days after my father's death I fell ill. I had diarrhoea, I couldn't keep a thing down. I suppose I must have picked up a germ somewhere: any other time that would certainly have been the verdict. Happening when it did, Dr Parfitt, our GP and a foolish old man, said it was grieving. I think he said it primarily because he was terrified of germs himself and grasped at any excuse for not making a proper examination in case he caught something. He grew his yellowish-white moustache down nearly to his chin on the grounds that it trapped germs before they had a chance to get into his mouth and make him ill the way they had made his patients. I used to wonder how he ever managed to eat his meals through such an obstruction, until my mother, one morning, sent me round to his surgery early, after she had been up all night with one of her throats. Then I found out. I was to pick up a bottle of his pink medicine, the kind he prescribed for everything above the waist.

Dr Parfitt came to the front door himself, his napkin still tucked between two buttons of his waistcoat, and his moustache neatly parted in the middle, the swags of hair held in place on either side with two of his wife's hairpins. Even so, he had got a little of the yellow of his egg on the left side. His lips, seen for the first time, were moist and very red. I never saw them again.

Whilst diarrhoea and vomiting seemed pretty unromantic ways to register grief, not to be compared to the broken hearts I enjoyed reading about in Maud's copies of *Peg's Paper* and in the novels of Ruby M. Ayres, it was a diagnosis I did not dare to question, lest people should think I was not particularly upset my father was dead, which I was. Dr Parfitt treated me, not with the sympathy one might have expected in the circumstances, but with an irascibility which, looking back, I can understand. Manifesting as I did symptoms both above and below the waist I was a problem. Was the pink medicine indicated, or the blue? I am surprised he did not consider prescribing a cocktail of the two, but this, apparently, was contrary to all good medical practice – his, at any rate. In the event, he opted for neither. Instead, I was instructed to drink milk, milk and more milk – ugh! – in all probability the very stuff which, in its then unpasteurized state, had been the cause of the trouble in the first place.

I lost weight, I had to stay away from school, I hardly dared put a foot out of doors for fear I might suddenly need to go to the lav in a hurry. The fact that my mother's sisters were already actively house-hunting in London on our behalf did not make me feel any better.

My family was almost too understanding, treating me, to my way of thinking, altogether too much as if I were one of those delicate children one was always coming upon in books intended to make you feel religious. Unlike those little horrors, I was – even with a father already in residence – nowhere near ready for heaven. Anyone who wanted it was welcome to my place in the queue.

When I began to be a little better, my sister Maisie took a holiday from her job in London and came down to Norwich to keep me company and cheer me up; to take short walks with me, and then longer ones as my bowels gradually moderated their antisocial behaviour. One sunny day we took the tram that went to the Earlham Road terminus, opposite the cemetery, and then walked the rest of the way to Earlham Hall, a house which had once been the home of the Gurneys and now belonged to the Council. In the garden behind the house was a rock garden which, in spring at any rate, was one of the wonders of the world, a honeycomb of paths and mini-canyons where you could walk, if you were a child with small, careful feet, drenched in scents and spices, half-drowned in waves of colour, with insects on gossamer wings for company and bees zigzagging from flower to flower too busy even to notice you were there.

The Gurneys, so I'd been told, were Quakers, people who were expected to go about in drab clothes and live in a very plain and boring way. Gardens not being a sin, seeing that God himself had planted the first garden of all, the Garden of Eden, I could only think that they had planted their garden at Earlham Hall to make up for the dreariness they had to put up with in every other department. There were peacocks in the garden too, but whether they had been put there by the Gurneys or the Council, I couldn't say.

On the day that I went to Earlham Hall with my sister, she sat on a bench with a book in her hand, supposedly reading, but actually keeping an anxious eye on me as I clambered about the rockery. I wished people wouldn't fuss so. I went up some roughly hewn stone steps between clumps of pinks and catmint to a little gravelly plateau where, as I knew from earlier visits, I could be monarch of all the flowery kingdom. As it happened, just as I reached this eminence, a peacock, stepping daintily, came up the further side and we met in the middle, neither of us minded to give way and the bird snaking its head from side to side as if it wasn't at all glad to see me.

My sister called out, 'Careful he doesn't peck at you!' as if I could have done anything to prevent it, had it had a mind to, except beat an ignominious retreat, which, for some reason I could not put into words, was unthinkable. Anyway, she need not have worried. With a slatty noise like someone letting down a Venetian blind, the peacock opened its fan and stood there unmoving, the delicate fronds at the tip of each Argus-eyed quill swaying gently in the soft breeze.

What happened next wasn't a mystical experience, an epiphany or anything high-flown like that. It was probably due to the sun and the buzz of insects combined with the hallucinating effect of the light slanting off all that peacock-blue threaded through with emerald and gold. Suddenly I felt drunk – not on the horrid milk that had been forced down my rebellious gullet week after week, but intoxicated by the glorious surprises, the amazing possibilities, that went with being alive. My father was dead, my lovely family life had fragmented like the pieces inside a kaleidoscope, never to fall again into the same pattern, yet just the same – not to mince words – I was happy! I could feel the world turning, myself with it, and not just round and round either, but up and down at the same time like the horses on the roundabout at the Whitsun Fair, the steam organ blaring until, with nostrils flaring and a triumphant whinny, my painted charger wrenched itself free of the revolving carousel and with one mighty leap flung itself into the sky, heading for the stars.

Beneath the frozen crust of grief an abiding sense of joy flowed strongly. For a moment – the peacock standing there as if it could not have cared less – I savoured that joy undiluted. For a moment. Then guilt flowed in, polluting the virgin spring. How could I dare to be happy with my father, as they said, scarcely cold in his grave? It was treachery, even if confusing, since at the same time as being cold under the earth he was warm as toast in heaven. I pictured my dreadfully all-seeing father – by the minute growing less and less like the parent I had known and loved – looking down from the celestial city disappointed in me. *Is that all I mean to you?* he could be saying. *A dose of diarrhoea, a token sick – and after that, everything in the garden is lovely?*

Racked by warring emotions, I must have shown on the surface something of the internal conflict, for my sister gave up pretending to read; shut her book and stood up.

'What is it, Sylvia?'

At that moment the peacock, slowly and carefully as if it took a bit of doing, turned its back on me. Like a piece of stage scenery not needed for the next act, the blue and the emerald and the gold – magnificent viewed from the stalls, canvas and chipboard behind – revolved majestically. It wasn't the first time that I had seen a displaying peacock from the rear, the tatty underside of the tail feathers, the rump perched foolishly on ungainly legs, but it was the first time that I consciously comprehended, so to speak, the global absurdity of the rear view; realized that,

God be praised, there was always something, someone, to prick pretensions and put the world, the real world, together again.

I burst out laughing with the relief of it – though a laughter which may have had in it some element of hysteria because my sister advanced to the bottom of the rockery steps, face uplifted in concern.

'What is it?' she asked again. 'Are you sure you're all right?'

'Yes,' I answered, when at last I had got my breath back and the peacock, fan re-folded into a court train, had swayed itself off like an affronted dowager. 'I'm fine!'

CHAPTER FOUR

Later that same day, I informed my mother that I would not be going with her to London. I loved my school, my music lessons at Miss Barker's, the castle, the Market Place, I loved everything about Norwich and could not see my way to exchanging such a paradise for an overgrown ant heap with too many people and no country or sea for miles.

There was also, absurd and compelling, a further consideration which I hardly acknowledged, even to myself. Whilst I knew quite well that heaven was all over, up there behind the sky – the sky of London as well as the sky of Norwich – I was equally certain that my father's particular corner of it was situated straight up from St Giles, a fact that, squirming beneath his pitiless surveillance, I might well have taken as a point in London's favour: he would surely have difficulty picking me out from seven million people. Only, how, in London, was I ever to find *him* when I needed him, as I so often did? How, at such moments, amidst all the big city noise, could he sense that silent tide of longing which spread out like a tidal wave through the universe seeking him?

My mother's reaction was what, at the age of twelve, I should have expected.

'What do you mean, not going? You can't stay here on your own!'

I did not see why I could not do exactly that, and I proceeded to say so. With some smugness I pointed out that *I* would never dream of trying to stop *her* from going to live where she wanted, so why, when it came to me, was she acting the exact contrary, without charity or any regard for my own heartfelt desires?

'You'll have to pay my board and lodging,' I conceded, 'but then it costs you money to keep me at home. I don't see why I can't go into lodgings, the same as Alfred.'

'Alfred isn't twelve years old.'

When I suggested that in some ways I was a fitter candidate for lodger than my brother, since I knew how to launder my own underwear, which was more than he did, to say nothing of sewing on buttons and darning socks, my mother's defences began to crumble, the way they usually did when I saw fit to mount a sufficiently determined attack. It's possible – I don't know, I don't wish to do her an injustice – that the prospect of a London life which, except during the school holidays, did not have to make room for an unruly, demanding child, had suddenly appeared seductively on the horizon. My mother was too old, I had been born too late, too long after my siblings. Though I knew nothing of how children were begotten, I felt instinctively that I must have been a slip, an error of judgement. Not that my father had ever appeared other than delighted by my existence, and my mother had always been very kind.

Once I had accustomed her to the idea in principle, the persistent obstacle remained: what would people say? Although she was leaving the city and, to hear her speak, had not the slightest intention of continuing her Norwich acquaintanceships across the 110-mile-long divide, the thought that people might speak ill of her, accuse her of abandoning her child to the problematic good offices of a landlady, was something she found difficult to contemplate.

'I suppose I could always speak to the Kings or the Harrisons,' she said at last. 'They might be willing to take you.'

But I did not want to, I categorically refused to be 'taken'. I did not see myself living with people who were sorry for me because I was a little orphan Annie. If anyone was going to do the taking, I wanted it to be me. I had a strong sense of moving, not just into a new house but into a new life which I must enter unencumbered by any of the old furniture.

Next day I went to see the person who, after some thought, I had nominated in my mind for the post of landlady. Her name was Mrs Curwen and she lived on the slope of St Clement's Hill, bang opposite the Secondary School where I was a pupil in Form IIIa. She also taught there: botany. In those days, teachers in the State system had to give up their posts when they married, so I imagine that Mrs Curwen was a widow – I certainly never saw any husband about – and as such, a proxy spinster as it were, had been allowed back into the maiden fold. She couldn't possibly have been divorced, because the Council or the school governors or whoever was in command would never have countenanced such a woman teaching the young. And she couldn't have been a courtesy Mrs, as Mrs Crail, the headmistress, was reputed to be, the way cooks and housekeepers at that time often were for status' sake, because she had a little daughter about seven years old.

Mrs Curwen seemed to me a good choice on several counts, not the least of which was the proximity of her house to the school, a nearness, I reckoned, equivalent to an extra half-hour in bed in the mornings. Secondly, I liked her. She blushed a lot, which made her look prettily rosy, and she spoke with a stammer which, in some way, seemed to bring her down to a child's level instead of, like most of the other teachers, being perched on top of some invisible Mount Sinai whence they issued commandments incised on tablets of stone.

Thirdly, I liked botany, everything about it, and especially the seriousness of the botany exercise books with their blue-lined pages interleaved with beautifully heavy plain paper for drawings and diagrams. I loved the names into which botany was buckled as into magical armour, names that belonged in spells, like Oenotheraceae and Caryophyllaceae. The spells themselves, which went by names like Baer's Hypothesis of Photosynthesis, were very potent and enough to send delicious shivers down your spine. I sensed too that Mrs Curwen liked me as a person, not just the way teachers usually liked children who were good at their particular subjects; and finally, I had deduced, from the way her daughter often wore dresses, not only with hems that had been let down leaving the stitch marks showing where the old turn-ups had been, but often with borders of another fabric altogether added on to them to make them last longer, that her mother could do with a bit of extra money.

I waited until I could be sure everyone had gone home from school – I didn't want to bump into anyone I knew, to whom I would have to explain about the diarrhoea and so on – and then I went to call on Mrs Curwen, who was surprised to see me, but welcoming. Her home had a friendly untidiness, with dented cushions on the couch and toys strewn about the floor. She gave me tea and fairy cakes with chocolate icing on them, which I thought a good omen so far as her cooking was concerned. As soon as I had explained the purpose of my visit her daughter, who was called Viola and who was present, began to jump about, crying, 'Oh, do let her come, Mummy! Do let her come!' Mrs Curwen went very red, and stammered a lot: but in the end she said that she didn't see why not.

When it came down to business, Mrs Curwen was totally inadequate. She hadn't a clue how much to charge for my board and lodging, and I needed to know so that I could tell my mother. After a great deal of stammering she came out with a pound a week, which I didn't think enough, and said so. Now that I was convalescent, I warned her, and my appetite coming back, I was eating like a horse, and she had better make it twenty-five shillings, just to be on the safe side.

So it was decided – or so I thought. Until a week later, that is, when my mother received a note from the school secretary, requesting her attendance at the school, to speak to Mrs Crail.

Mrs Crail, the Secondary School headmistress, looked remarkably like a pig, which was not necessarily a disaster since pigs normally, whatever their intrinsic nature, have faces which look extremely good-natured, with cheeky little snouts and mouths that are turned up at the corners in a perpetual smile. Mrs Crail always held her head thrown back a little, perhaps to lessen the number of her double chins, unless it was due to the weight of the large bun of lack-lustre hair she wore wedged into the nape of her short neck. The really dreadful thing about her was that, notwithstanding the way her piggy mouth turned up in its perfect crescent and the way her small eyes constantly half-closed themselves as if in the throes of irrepressible mirth, you only needed to be in the same room with her, even with the central heating on, to feel it growing colder by the minute, a new Ice Age on the way.

Smiling, crinkling her eyes, speaking in low, genteel tones, she disseminated sarcasm, venom, and a total hatred of children – even of those who tried to toady up to her, which I suppose was something in her favour, if not much – until the very air seemed poisoned, unbreathable. To parents summoned to her presence – no parent who had instigated such a meeting did so twice – her manner was insufferably patronizing, a masterpiece of bullying disguised under the heading of doing what was best for your child. My mother returned from the ordeal pale and shaken, uncertain as to what had actually been said to reduce her to that condition. She was uncertain of everything except of having been instructed that Mrs Curwen was no fit person to whom to entrust her daughter, and that she was not to do it on pain of – my mother couldn't quite remember what, only that it didn't bear thinking of. That the *diktat* had to be obeyed went without saying.

Appalled that Mrs Crail's writ should run with equal force outside the gates of school as within, I demanded: 'Didn't you ask her why?'

'She smiled at me,' my mother responded weakly, 'and I didn't like to.'

A few days later a letter came to say that Mrs Crail had arranged for me to board with Miss Gosse and Miss Locke who shared a house somewhere up the Sprowston Road. It came as no surprise. If, in her wisdom, she had booked me into the local brothel, assuming Norwich boasted such an amenity, I am pretty sure my mother would not have dared to raise an objection. The cost of my accommodation was to be thirty shillings a week as against Mrs Curwen's twenty-five.

I grumbled: 'Probably the extra five shillings is for Mrs Crail's commission.' Gone my vision of last-minute dashes across the road as the morning gong was going. 'And it's probably half-way to Wroxham.'

'It can't be all that far.' I could see that, the prospect of London resuming the foreground of her thoughts, my mother was rapidly losing interest in the conversation. 'If Miss Gosse and Miss Locke can bike it every day, I'm sure you can.'

CHAPTER FIVE

A few minutes before eight I turned off the alarm on my clock which I had set to make sure I shouldn't be late down for my Bovril, and sat on the edge of the bed waiting and watching for the long hand to reach the twelve. Though it was still light out of doors, my room was already dark, and I was glad that I had completed my unpacking without having to cope with lighting the gas mantle; something I knew I would have to get used to, but not just yet, whilst I was hungry and strange and new. Bovril was supposed to give you strength, so the advertisments said. I hoped it would give me courage to conquer the alien force hanging from the ceiling.

I had hung up my clothes behind the curtain, and put away everything else in the chest of drawers, including Alfred's pound note which I tucked in among my handkerchiefs inside the sachet embroidered with my initials which I had made at Eldon House, the private school where you learned to be a little lady but did not, unfortunately, get an education, which was why I wasn't there any longer. The empty suitcase waited by the door to be returned downstairs. As for the books, I dragged the box under the bed free of the dip in the mattress, and, reaching in at random, brought out the dozen which came out easiest. It would be quite exciting, changing over, say, every other week: greeting old favourites after an interval, discovering afresh the pleasure of reading them.

The ones I was able to arrange on the shelf over my bed were something of a commentary on my life up to that point; and, for a moment, I wondered nervously whether it was wise to leave them out on show for anyone who came by to see. Was it even possible that Mrs Crail, having been instrumental in bringing me to Chandos House, would make a formal inspection of my quarters? Then I thought, momentarily brave in my new persona: *Let her come! See if I care!*

The truth was that my family – or, at any rate, my father and my brother Alfred – had passed on to me an obsessive and indiscriminate passion for the printed word, which was such a passport to treasure that (whilst they might unwillingly concede that some books were worthier than others) they could not find it in their hearts to condemn anything that came in printed form as being entirely without merit. Having learned to read well before I went to school, and having from the first been given the freedom of the St Giles bookshelves, I read *The Old Curiosity Shop*, *The Sheikh*, and *Mrs Strang's Annual for Girls* with equal respect and enjoyment. I thought most of Kipling quite as good as Ethel M. Dell and both very nearly the equal of *The Naughtiest Girl in the School*. The very thought of all the books in the world still waiting to be read was dizzying. I realized that I didn't have a moment to waste if I was to get through them all before it was time for me to die.

In my Chandos House bedroom, waiting for the clock hand to move – perhaps because I was now living with schoolmistresses, or perhaps because I was hungry – my resolution wavered. I sensed that, so far as literature was concerned at least, the time of joyous anarchy was past. Unless, perhaps, whilst I had been ill, I had been growing up without knowing it, and knew already, without being told, that Ethel M. Dell was *not* as good as Kipling, whatever another part of me might think. Either losing my nerve, or just to be on the safe side, I rearranged my meagre shelf: took down *The Way of an Eagle*, *The Sheikh*, and the small bundle of *Peg's Papers* which I had rescued from Maud; shoved them back in the box out of sight, and replaced them with *Ivanhoe* and *Huckleberry Finn*.

Two minutes before eight I stepped out on to the landing, bringing the empty suitcase with me. A dim light was burning, a gas bracket, turned down low, creating shadows which were not friendly. It seemed to me that there were a great many doors, all of them painted brown, all of them shut, a contrast with St Giles which made me momentarily tearful before I reminded myself to welcome the bad feeling since it balanced out the happiness and made the latter morally OK. I wondered which was Miss Gosse's door and which Miss Locke's. I hoped Mrs Benyon's door was not too close to mine.

Miss Gosse was waiting in the hall, going through the letters on the brass tray to make it look, I think, as if she wasn't waiting at all but was there on private business. She smiled up at me with a touching anxiety as I came down the stairs. I warmed to her because I could tell by her expression that she was doing her best, and I hoped she would warm to me similarly, because so was I. I should have liked to ask her if she would have wanted me for a lodger even if Mrs Crail had not told her she had to have me, like it or not, but I was afraid the chances were that as an honest woman not used to lying, she would reply 'No'. After all, she and Miss Locke had each other for company. They had to put up with children all day long at school, and it stood to reason they wouldn't have wanted one at home as well, outside working hours. It was different for Mrs Curwen who had a child to look after anyway, so one more wouldn't have made all that much difference. Miss Gosse and Miss Locke would almost certainly have been better pleased with a dog – a King Charles spaniel, perhaps, to match Miss Gosse's bright bulging eyes and her puggy little features.

I wondered what had happened to Miss Locke.

Miss Gosse took the suitcase from me and set it down at the side of the hallstand, next to my school case and my shoebag. As if she had read my thought she said: 'Helen – Miss Locke – has gone to the concert at St Andrew's Hall. She won't be back till late. You'll see her in the morning.' On the way down the hall towards the back of the house, she added: 'When I saw your music case I thought, *oh good!* You and Miss Locke will be able to play duets together.'

'I hope I'll be good enough.'

'Much better than me, that's certain! I'm afraid there are times when Helen – Miss Locke – quite loses patience with my clumsy fingers. I hope this won't make your head swell, Sylvia, but the staff all agree that nobody plays for prayers better than you do.'

The praise, sweet to my ears, brought a lump to my throat.

'Do they really?'

'Miss Malahide always says, the way you play us out, though our feet are obliged to march for the sake of decorum, our spirits go to our classrooms dancing.'

Miss Malahide was the art mistress, whiskered, leathery, and demonstrably barmy. Reduced to life size, I followed Miss Gosse down the hall almost to the end of it.

'We shall have to take you on a conducted tour.' She smiled as she opened yet another shut door. 'In the mean time, this is the dining-room.'

I went through the door and exclaimed, 'How pretty!'

Miss Gosse looked pleased. I could see she thought I meant the room, and I knew better than to put her right. In fact, the room was nothing much: dull beige paper almost hidden under framed photographs of rocky places, bleak and treeless and without people; a round dining-table covered with a brown cloth, an old-fashioned sideboard holding toast racks and cruets and a bottle of HP sauce, and a piano of which I knew instantly to expect the worst, since its front was made of a kind of fretwork with faded mauve satin showing through the holes. Somebody had placed my music case at the side of it. It leaned against the yellowish wood nonchalantly enough, but I transmitted a silent apology to the music books within, or rather to their progenitors, to Mozart and Beethoven, to Ivor Novello and (my taste in music being as eclectic and indiscriminating as my taste in literature) to whoever it was who wrote 'The Birth of the Blues'.

'Go on,' Miss Gosse urged. 'Try it out, just to see what you think of the tone.'

I raised the lid from the yellowed keys and, without sitting down on the stool covered in worn burgundy velvet, pounded out the first few chords of 'Three-Fours' by Coleridge-Taylor, my show-off piece, which I loved because it sounded so difficult when in fact it was almost as easy as 'Chopsticks'.

Miss Gosse exclaimed, 'There! I knew you'd like it!' I did not say that, on the contrary, I thought it sounded like a string of old tin cans. One thing was certain: I was never going to sound like Moisevitch on that. But then, who was I kidding? I was never going to sound like Moisevitch on anything, not even the Steinway in St Andrew's Hall; which was why, without having discussed it with my mother, I had told Miss Barker, my music teacher, that I would be discontinuing my lessons once I had moved. Though I had said it was too far to come all the way to Earlham Road twice a week, I would have come ten times the distance if there had been a dog's chance that I would sound like Moisevitch at the end of the journey. Miss Barker had been quite put out – not only, I am pretty sure, because of losing the money from my fees. I had passed several Royal Academy of Music examinations and had won the medal at the Norwich Music Festival for piano solo under twelve, playing one of Bach's French Suites, so she had expectations of me. There was even the possibility – she had dangled the dream in front of me as one proffering a golden apple of the Hesperides – that I might one day become a music teacher like herself if I went on practising.

That was before my father took me to hear Moisevitch, which he did not long before he died. It was meant to be a treat, which it was, and an incentive, which it definitely was not, because I, who had previously – even if, out of superstitious dread, the actual words remained unspoken – thought myself capable of everything, almost, learned with the opening arpeggios that not only would I never be a concert pianist but that to be a music teacher was an unacceptable alternative. This last, to be truthful, did not exactly make me feel sad. On the contrary. So many roads through life beckoned delightfully, it was almost a relief to find one blocked, one choice less.

I stopped showing off with Coleridge-Taylor, closed the piano lid carefully, ashamed of Miss Gosse's undeserved praise and at the same time glad of it.

'Miss Locke *will* be pleased!'

When I had exclaimed 'How pretty!' what I had meant was the garden. The single good thing about the Chandos House dining-room was its french window which gave on to a lawn with lovely old untidy fruit trees growing out of it as if they had just that moment risen from deep down in the earth and were stretching their gnarled limbs in an ecstasy of light and air. Behind the trees were flowerbeds and shrubberies and vegetables, with a glimpse of fields beyond. Unlike the rest of the house that I had seen so far, the dining-room was bright with sun, so light that at eight o'clock in the evening there was still no need for gaslight to drink our Horlicks/Bovril by. The garden was permeated with the golden warmth of evening. A blackbird sang in an apple tree. A shimmering veil of midges hovered above the grass.

Miss Gosse said, 'We often eat here with the window open in the summer. Would you like to have it open now?'

I said that I should like it very much. Just at that moment Mrs Benyon came in with a tray with two mugs on it. She put the tray down on the dining table. My heart twanged with sorrow as I saw that there weren't any cream crackers.

Miss Gosse said: 'Would you mind opening the french window, Mrs Benyon?' And, to me, in explanation: 'I'm afraid the bolt's a bit high up for me.'

Mrs Benyon looked out at the garden as if she couldn't abide the sight of it. She said: 'Mosquitoes,' in her heavy, flat voice and went out of the room without doing anything about the bolt.

'She's quite right, of course,' Miss Gosse said brightly. 'Mrs Benyon, as you'll discover, is the practical one of our little household. Are *you* practical, Sylvia?'

Not too sure, but anxious to make the reply which would do me the most good: 'I – I think so.'

'Capital!' exclaimed Miss Gosse. 'That makes two of you!'

I went upstairs again carrying hot water for my bedtime ablutions. Upon Miss Gosse's instructions I had gone through another door, this time the one at the end of the hall, the door into the kitchen, large, red-tiled expanse with the same aspect and consequently – though the window was much smaller and obstructed by some pot plants that were mottled rather like Mrs Benyon – some of the same light which had transformed the dining-room. I could hear the blackbird still singing.

'If you don't see Mrs Benyon, knock on the door next to the dresser. That's the door to her bedroom. She will have your hot water ready.'

Relieved in some way I could not have explained that the housekeeper and I were to sleep on different levels, I went into the kitchen and found her on the point of emerging from her bedroom door, one she made haste to shut as soon as she saw the intruder into her domain. Hungry and emotionally stressed as I was, her hostility confused me. So far in my life, so far as I could tell at any rate, most people seemed to like me – at least they acted as if they did. As a result, I had not yet encountered enough of the other kind to have evolved the right technique for dealing with them. That was why I always found myself struck dumb in the presence of Mrs Crail, for instance, and it was exactly the same with Mrs Benyon. She floored me with her utter lack of love, not a speck of it showing through the thick crust of her withering indifference. I wondered fleetingly whether the housekeeper, as the headmistress was reputed to be, was another of those courtesy missuses, and if a certain prickliness might not be a common factor among women who pretended to be married when they weren't. I also wondered if Mrs Benyon might be thinking that she ought by rights to be paid extra now that she had one extra to housekeep for, and Miss Gosse had made no offer in that direction.

This latter thought made me feel more sympathetic towards her, and I might have ventured something in my sweetly winsome vein about doing my best not to be any extra trouble; only, as I watched her filling the shining copper hot-water can from the outsize kettle which stood steaming on the range, I saw that she filled it to the very brim, deliberately, dangerously full, and gave up all hope of a truce. Rightly or wrongly, I felt convinced that she intended me to spill some of the scalding water on the hall lino or the stairs, if not on to myself, so that then she could complain to Miss Gosse: 'See what you've lumbered me with!'

Disguising my mistrust with elaborate gratitude, I took the can and with slow, careful steps made my way out of the kitchen and along the hall to the foot of the stairs. Before I ever set foot on the first tread, my hands felt trembly. I knew I would never make it.

I had to make it.

After a quick glance back to make sure both the kitchen and the dining-room doors were shut, I set the can down, opened the front door as quietly as I was able, picked up the water again and emptied a good half-canful on to the roots of the tree that quivered outside my window. Steam rose from the soil which didn't matter as there was nobody to see it, and if it killed the tree, too bad, the noisy thing. I was back indoors in a trice, making my demure way upstairs, full of a glee which momentarily overlaid what might have been a sudden, agonizing pang of homesickness, but could just as easily have been a renewed, a raging, apprehension of my empty stomach.

After all that, I didn't even wash. I didn't seem to have the strength, let alone the inclination. I put the plug in the bathroom basin, poured in the water, added some cold, and waited a little before letting it out: in a strange place you never knew what bathroom noises might resound through the house, and who might be listening out for them. Miss Gosse had told me to leave my sponge bag hanging from the mahogany towel-stand where I would find the towels set aside for my use – skimpy things, a small hand towel and another slightly larger, each stiff as a board. Before I hung the sponge bag up I carefully dampened my sponge and wetted the bristles of my toothbrush in case anyone thought to check up on me. I also unfolded the larger towel and mucked it about a bit so that it looked used.

Back in my bedroom it had become really dark and a little

scary. Nobody had shown me how to light the gas mantle and I was afraid to try uninstructed. I didn't fancy lighting the candle either. Instead, I switched on the torch and undressed by the light of that. The leaves outside the window were noisier than ever. Either the hot water had been a stimulus or the wind had got up and was jigging them about even more than they ordinarily bestirred themselves. I turned the torch on them and watched them for a little. They quivered like those people in the Middle Ages who were always coming down with the ague. I flashed the torch on, then off, then on again, thinking that to anyone outside in the road – a passing radio operator, say, on shore leave from his ship – it could have looked like Morse code. Calling on my limited knowledge, I sent three shorts, three longs, three shorts, beaming into the darkness – SOS – wondering whose help, if anybody's, I was calling for.

I got into bed and slid instantly, cosily, down to the middle. It could have been a sailor's hammock, slung from beam to beam. There and then I fell in love with that bed, the feel of my book box nudging my buttocks through the thin mattress, the thought of the books I was brooding like a hen on a clutch of eggs. Would I awaken to find that a new Zane Grey had hatched out during the night, or perhaps a hitherto unknown play by one W. Shakespeare? I realized that, despite everything, I was still happy, the stream still forging ahead strongly.

Could the dead people in heaven see in the dark? I hoped not, but you never knew. I certainly did not want my father to lose any sleep on my account. He had always said he needed his eight hours. But just in case there was anybody up there hoping for news, I pulled the covers over my head and said out loud: 'Don't worry! I'm all right!'

I wasn't, you know. All right. Not for long, anyway, though longer than I had thought, waking up, as it seemed to me, no more than five minutes later: until I looked at my clock numbers, shining green in the blackness, and discovered it was ten minutes past eleven.

Hunger was what had awakened me, together with the certainty that without food, instanter, I should not last out the night. Hunger and a revelation. I had been dreaming, sort of, of Miss Barker and Ludwig and Amadeus and Ivor, and of straining in vain to remember the names, one on each side of the printed music, of 'The Birth of the Blues'. Though I didn't manage to recall either, I did remember something else.

I remembered that inside my music case, along with the great composers, there was a whipped cream walnut, purchased on my way home from my last music lesson and then – difficult as it was to believe – overlooked in all the hoo-ha of moving. Fully awake now, I pictured it in the case as clearly as if I could have reached out and taken it in my hand, its chocolate smell by now tempered with a *soupçon* of cowhide, but none the worse for that; its taste, conceivably, made even more ambrosial by a week spent sandwiched between 'Rondo alla Turca' and 'An die ferne Geliebte'. Fears of waking up the household, of having to explain to Miss Gosse and, much worse, to Mrs Benyon, faded in comparison with the prospect of biting off the gleaming walnut which crowned that mini-pyramid, of nibbling the swirled chocolate to get at the delicious goo within. Alive with anticipation, I scrambled up the slope that led out of bed, felt for my torch, and gingerly opened the bedroom door.

The landing light was out which was a relief, the darkness encouraging me to feel myself invisible. And I was lucky. Either the floorboards of Chandos House did not squeak like those of St Giles, or, in years of practice circumventing Maud when about my private business, my feet had acquired a sensitivity to making choices which enabled me to get down to the ground floor with hardly a sound. As I neared the dining-room, a noise from the direction of the kitchen first froze me to the spot with horror before making me, albeit silently, giggle with relief. It was Mrs Benyon, snoring.

Noiselessly I turned the white china knob on the dining-room door, noiselessly entered and crossed to the piano. Although the out of doors at the back of the house was presumably as dark as the out of doors in front, it did not seem so. My awareness of the french window, of its wide expanse of glass deluded me into the conviction that I could see grass and fruit trees and a gentle sky.

I opened the music case and tenderly removed the whipped cream walnut, so filled with exultation as to forget completely to take, as I had intended, a quick peep at 'The Birth of the Blues' so as to satisfy myself once and for all who in fact had been responsible for that masterpiece of jazz. I had already decided that I would bite off the walnut at once, to fortify me for the return journey, the nut and no more. The rest would have to wait until I regained the haven of my hammock-bed.

The walnut was so glorious I could have exclaimed aloud, praising God for nuts. And would have, probably, if somebody standing in the open doorway, had not got in first, in a voice veined with a familiar undertone of mockery: 'Well, I must say! What a little pig!'

Miss Locke taught history. This was particularly apt since she was the only person I had ever seen whose forehead and nose, in profile, were precisely in line, the way they were in gods and goddesses from Ancient Greek temples. Presumably the Ancient Greeks thought such a profile a sign of beauty. In my judgement, for what it was worth, whilst it may have been OK on gods and goddesses fresh from Mount Olympus, it was pretty off-putting in a human being, especially one in authority. It made Miss Locke look censorious, which I didn't think she was, particularly. The thing, however, that made her face a difficult one to come to a decision about was that the two halves, upper and lower, did not really belong together. They reminded you of the faces in those jokey books which have their pages divided horizontally, making it possible to combine brows and chins you would never ordinarily dream of putting together.

The Ancient Greeks, I am pretty sure, would not have been best pleased with a classical brow and nose that modulated, as the history mistress's did, via a small round mouth filled with small teeth, to a chin that pointed forward and upward, a little like Punch.

Just the same, met by night in the dining-room of Chandos House, slim-armed in her sleeveless shift of greeny-blue, she was undeniably beautiful, holding a candlestick with a lighted candle in it and the light thrown up on to her face. It made her eyes deep-set and mysterious and contrived to etch a honey-coloured aureole round the edges of her short brown hair. Unusually for schoolmistresses of that time, Miss Locke wore her hair cut like a man's. Not exactly an Eton crop, which was beginning to go out of fashion anyway, it looked so ugly from the back, but more like something you might expect to see on a faun or a satyr, or a poet of the Romantic period. The hair, curly, with a natural spring to it, fitted the shape of her head like a cap, one that stuck to the edges of her face as if carved there. Her exposed ears were unusually small, the kind Ethel M. Dell and *Peg's Paper*, I shouldn't be surprised, meant by shell-like, not meaning a crab or even a whelk, I felt sure, but something dainty and delicate not to be picked up on Cromer beach. Had I thought about it, or been a bit older, I might have guessed that Miss Locke must be a history teacher with exceptionally good qualifications for Mrs Crail to put up with a hair-do like that.

I knew that I was much too old to cry, but cut off from my walnut in mid-bite, I had no alternative. I howled: burst out that I hadn't had anything to eat since breakfast and not much even then: that I wasn't a pig, whatever she said, just dying of hunger, that was all.

'Be quiet, you little fool!' Miss Locke ordered. 'You'll wake up Mrs Benyon.'

She had only to command once. Then, with a finger to her lip, she led the way into the kitchen where, whilst I watched incredulously, half-certain it was all a dream, she opened the larder door, took a loaf out of an earthenware crock set on the floor, and brought it to the scrubbed deal table where a bread board and bread knife waited as if against just such an emergency. The housekeeper's snores continued with unabated gusto as Miss Locke cut two slices, real doorsteps. Putting back the loaf, taking care to replace the lid of the crock without noise, she returned to the table with a jar of strawberry jam, which she spread generously over the bread.

'Won't Mrs Benyon notice?' I whispered.

'Her?' Contemptuously, barely keeping her voice down: 'She'll think she ate it in her sleep. Let me see now –' Miss Locke pondered, more to herself than to me. 'We'd better not take a plate –' Then: 'I know!'

She took a handkerchief out of her pocket, a sensible-sized one, not the lacy kind my mother went in for, not a bit of use for wrapping hunks of bread and jam in.

'No crumbs, mind!' Miss Locke scooped every last crumb off the bread board into her cupped hand before popping her little haul into her little mouth. She aligned board and knife exactly as they had been before, and returned the pot of jam to its shelf. She handed me the handkerchief-wrapped booty, which I received too overwhelmed even to say thank you. 'That at least should make sure we don't find a corpse in the morning. Up you go now – quietly!'

If I nearly disobeyed this injunction, she had only herself to blame for it. Half-way up to the landing, going slowly and carefully so as not to create crumbs which might give us both away, I became aware of Miss Locke's footsteps on the stairs behind me, going faster than I. The next moment, she pinched my bottom.

'Hurry up, slowcoach!' she hissed in my ear, edging past.

On the landing she waited until I had completed my own ascent, gone to my room and shut the door. A little later, standing on the thin chenille rug that lay between my bed and the chest of drawers, the bread and jam, wrapped and untasted, still in my hand – the whipped cream walnut, set down on the bed for a moment, had slid down into the dip in the middle – I heard a door opening and guessed that Miss Gosse had been awakened by the sound of Miss Locke's footsteps on her way to her own bedroom, and had got out of bed to speak to her. I heard only the sound of voices, not what was said. I heard Miss Locke laugh – at least I think it was her – and say something or other, and then I heard a door shut.

I sat on my bed in the dark to consider that nobody had ever pinched my bottom before. I did not consider it at all nice.

A schoolmistress!

I unwrapped the bread and jam and ate it all up in indignant bites that must have interfered with my digestion, for I could feel the bread stuck somewhere at the back of my breastbone. Then I went to bed. Only when the alarm went off at 6.45 did I remember the whipped cream walnut in the dip, and for a dreadful moment thought that I had gone to sleep on top of it. Visions of melted chocolate and goo stuck to the sheet made me wish never to wake up again. When, albeit reluctantly, my eyes insisted on opening on their own account, I saw that in fact the whipped cream walnut had fallen on to the floor and was still edible. My spirits rose, readying for what the new day might hold, not only by way of breakfast but by way of everything.

Just to be on the safe side, though, I polished off the whipped cream walnut before I went down to the dining room. Which, considering that breakfast turned out to consist of a mingy bowl of cornflakes and one triangle of toast – only one! – was just as well.

CHAPTER SIX

The Sprowston Road sloped gently but unremittingly down to the city, a fearsome freewheeling joy as my Hudson gathered momentum with a fine disregard for a child's hands desperately squeezing its unresponsive brakes. The bicycle, which had belonged to my sister Maisie before she had grown up and gone to work in London, weighed a ton, or something not far short of it. Knowing nothing of bicycles, my parents had purchased the vehicle – it seemed a kind of *lèse majesté* to call it anything less – following their general principle that what was solid and heavy must, for that very reason, be superior to what was hollow and light. Downhill, it gave gravity a new meaning. Uphill it equalled a hellish ache in the calves; and even as, in a shocked way and suppressing an impulse to scream, I enjoyed the first part of my first ride from Chandos House to school, my legs were already anticipating the anguish of the ride back.

A journey which had to be undertaken four times a day, what was more. After breakfast, to my consternation, there had been no packet of sandwiches proffered for putting into my school case before it was strapped to the bike carrier. Was it possible that my frugal hostesses dispensed with lunch altogether?

'We prefer to have our main meal at midday,' Miss Gosse had mercifully explained. 'So much healthier, and as we have an hour and a half there really is ample time so long as we (I could tell she meant "you") don't hang about chatting.'

Shooting the slope not quite out of control, I heard a bicycle bell behind ringing like mad. It was Miss Locke trying to catch up with me.

'Next on the right!' she shouted.

I could have done with more notice. As it was, I shot across the bows of a United bus which luckily had better brakes than mine, up a turning which, with the illogic of geography, rose from the gentle planes of the Sprowston Road like the motte of Norwich castle. Momentum carried me up the first few feet of this precipice, after which the same gravity that an instant earlier had lent wings to my flight grabbed me by the rear wheel so fiercely that I had, more or less, to fall off and push – just at the moment, too, when Miss Locke and Miss Gosse sailed past, Miss Locke making nothing at all of the gradient and Miss Gosse's stumpy legs pumping away merrily nineteen to the dozen.

Pushing the Hudson up the hill was almost as hard as actually riding it. I wanted to call out to the pair disappearing in the distance that I was a convalescent, it wasn't my fault; but they had vanished round the curve of the motte, on to the plateau which ended at the school gates. By the time I myself had arrived at the latter, it was to find their two bicycles parked smugly side by side in the reserved racks, and they themselves, no doubt, at their leisurely robing in the Staff Room. For my especial benefit the gong was well into the unctuous ululation which meant time was running out and prepare to meet thy Maker – or rather, Mrs Crail, which was infinitely worse.

I dashed to the cloakroom, hung up my shoebag, tore off my panama and blazer, changed my shoes even though there wasn't time for such fussiness, except that to put a foot still clad in an outdoor shoe to a school floor was a capital offence. I ran to deliver the letter which alone would readmit me to the sacred portals – Dr Parfitt's letter which certified that I was fit to return to my studies provided that, for the remainder of the term, I was excused gym, games, and, by implication, any other dangerous physical pursuit such as racing to get into the Assembly Hall for prayers ahead of the headmistress.

Miss Reade, the school secretary, had her office next door to the headmistress's room. As I knocked, waiting to be told to enter, Mrs Crail emerged from next door in all her glory, Bible in hand, gown filled with some celestial thermal that was bearing her along, if not aloft, everything in place but the halo.

'Back at last, Sylvia!' At sight of me her little eyes disappeared in one of her crinkled smiles. The voice was like a dose of salts. I knew better than to expect any expression of gratification at my restoration to health. 'Let us hope in more conciliatory mood. No more threats of revolution, I trust, to make us all tremble in our boots.'

She really was an old devil the way she nourished herself on the remembrance of ancient grudges. English was her subject and donkeys' years ago, working through some exercise in *Marriott's English*, we had been instructed to come up one at a time to the blackboard and inscribe thereon any one word whose sound – sound, mark you – we thought among the most beautiful in the language. Despite this emphasis on purely aural values, most of the first girls to go up to the board under Mrs Crail's sneering, smiling gaze, wrote words like *Mother* or *Baby*, or *Jesus* which, to my way of thinking, was not only soppy in the extreme but directly contradictory to what was being demanded of us. The textbook specifically enjoined us to ignore meaning. The sound was all.

Pondering in the time available what should be my own contribution, I hit on the word *Evolution*. Mouthing it silently, I relished the way it rolled over the tongue, like chocolate fudge sauce. By the time it came to my turn to perform, I had made a slight alteration to my first draft. Not *Evolution* but *Revolution*. *Revolution really* rolled. One little 'r' made all the difference.

When I had written the word on the blackboard in my best print, I stood back and regarded my handiwork with a certain modest satisfaction. Even in chalk *Revolution sounded* good. Mrs Crail who, making her own rules, had commended the *Mothers* and the *Babies* and the *Jesuses*, looked at *Revolution* and smiled and smiled; following upon which she told me what she thought of the company I kept, obviously consisting of anarchists, Bolsheviks, and the descendants of those abominable Frenchmen who had cut off the heads of Louis XVI and Marie Antoinette. A ritual erasing of the infamy, she took hold of the dampened felt pad we used for cleaning the blackboard and rubbed the offending word out. This pad, never damp enough, was by mid-morning always full of powdered chalk. You had to know how to use it, gingerly, and even then you were lucky not to get chalk dust in your hair and your mouth among other places. Since Mrs Crail always appointed blackboard monitors on whom the duty – and the powdered chalk – customarily fell, it could not be said that she was unaware of the drawbacks of the blackboard eraser. In the warmth of the moment she had just forgotten.

Revolution disappeared in a shower of chalk dust which, settling on Mrs Crail, found plenty to settle on. When at last, breaking an intolerable silence, I muttered haltingly – in Mrs Crail's presence I was seldom able to express myself in any other way – that all I had meant by *Revolution* was wheels turning round, not the guillotine or anything like that, she gave me twenty-five lines for impertinence.

Actually, obeying the instructions of the eponymous Mr Marriott, I hadn't meant anything. Not that it would have made any difference to have said so, the little episode being merely a continuation of the malign fate which from my first entry into the school had gone out of its way to foul up any relationship I might have had with its headmistress.

To quote another instance.

In St Gregory's Alley, a pedestrian way tumbling downhill from Goat Lane to St Benedict's, an undistinguished building advertised itself as the local headquarters of the ILP, initials whose meaning I had never thought to probe until, passing by one day, I noticed that, following some refurbishment of the premises, its facade was now emblazoned with the words, 'INDEPENDENT LABOUR PARTY. FREE READING ROOM AND LIBRARY. OPEN TO ALL.'

Unable to resist such an invitation, I went inside, only to be disappointed. The library, so far as I could see, consisted of two bookcases filled with dejected-looking books with titles that for the most part I could make neither head nor tail of. The sole occupant of the room, an equally dejected-looking woman who sat at a card table with a box file on it, regarded me with such distrust that, if only to establish my standing as a member of the literate classes, I felt impelled to pull out a book at random and bring it over to her with my best smile, which for all the good it did me I might as well have saved for a more propitious occasion.

'I'd like to borrow this one, please.'

Having printed my name, my address, and the name of my school on one of her cards, she let me have it eventually, reluctantly. It was clear from her manner that she did not expect any *cachet* to accrue to the ILP from its having secured my custom. The book clasped to my chest, I walked out of the building bang into Mrs Crail, who just happened (of course!) to be descending St Gregory's Alley at that fateful moment. The title of the book, which (of course!) just happened to be turned outward for anybody to read was: *Father Gapon: Martyr of the Russian Revolution.*

Mrs Crail took Dr Parfitt's letter from me, and opened it. Perusing the contents, her smile grew even jollier than usual.

'There are seven weeks left of term,' she announced at the end, as if telling me something I didn't know. 'How your doctor can predict the state of your health in seven weeks' time is beyond my imagining.' Handing the letter back as if divesting herself of something subtly unclean: 'Tell Miss Reade you are excused games for the next three weeks. *Three* weeks. I hope I have made that clear?' I nodded dumbly. 'Thereafter, failing a fresh letter, you will be required to join in all normal school activities, the same as everybody else.'

'Don't let it worry you, dear,' comforted Miss Reade after the headmistress had sailed away, smiling. 'Her bark is worse than her bite. She's all right, really.'

Across the arc of the years I still have to say that I don't think Mrs Crail was all right, really; and as between her bark and her bite there was nothing much to choose. You could catch rabies from either. It may be vanity which convinces me that she did not hate the sight of me the instant I first came within range of those smiling eyes. It was only after I had settled into the school and let down my guard that the rot set in. It was then that she made the shocking discovery that I was an enthusiast, a category of persons which, along with clever dicks, she seemed to regard as having been put on earth to try her, her especially. What she clearly aimed for in her school was a pleasing mediocrity on the part of all concerned, staff and pupils alike. No difficulties, no surprises. 'You!' she would exclaim, jabbing a pudgy forefinger at the miscreant who had dared to be difficult or surprising, and smiling all over her face as she returned an essay marked with a big blue 'R' (for 'Repeat in the Detention Room after school'). '*You* are a clever dick. A little less cleverness next time, *if* you please!'

Mrs Crail taught English – her own tunnel-vision version of it, that is. Not the incomparable jewel-box of language, the treasure-house of literature my father and my brother Alfred had encouraged me to recognize it to be, but English as a pinched, sectarian cult devoted to the worship of an obscure deity called the Syllabus. According to its inflexible tenets, as promulgated by its high priestess, one did not inquire of a poem, 'Is this good?' or, for that matter, 'Is this bad?' but only 'Is it in the Syllabus?' If the answer to the question was no, then, even if its beauty took you by the throat or its unique insights transformed your life, thumbs down. Cast it into that outer darkness reserved for quotations that would never be required in an examination paper.

As an enthusiast, I found myself – to my sorrow, for I would truly have preferred a quiet life to one poised forever on the brink of catastrophe – unable to keep my mouth shut. If only Mrs Crail had taught arithmetic, say, I could gladly have stayed mum from the beginning of the lesson to the end of it, and she could have marked me down as a model citizen. But how to stay silent when you had just that minute discovered 'Christabel'? *Not in the Syllabus!* Or 'The Rubáiyát of Omar Khayyám'? *Not in the Syllabus!* Or Oscar Wilde? *NOT IN THE SYLLABUS!*

CHAPTER SEVEN

There was a lot of window glass about in the Secondary School. Seen from the bottom of St Clement's Hill, the swell of the land lending importance, the two-storey main building looked fairly imposing, although its pomp and circumstance in fact housed nothing much but cloakrooms and office with, above, the labs positioned strategically where their bad smells could waft away on the breeze to the houses on the other side of the road, without distress to the sensitive nostrils of the budding young academics below. Out of sight behind this somewhat meretricious facade, the classrooms arranged around two quadrangles divided by the Assembly Hall were bungaloid and open-air, the brain-children of an architect who must either have hated little girls or could never in his own youth have attended a school constructed on such principles.

Admittedly, in summer the long narow rooms, tall windows taking up one long side, folding doors the other, had a lot going for them. Thistledown and the occasional butterfly drifted through: house-sparrows, surreptitiously encouraged by trails of crumbs, popped in and out to relieve the tedium apparently inseparable from getting an education. In winter, on the other hand (to say nothing of the other foot), the school raised the finest crop of chilblains in East Anglia, if not the entire British Isles. In the proclaimed cause of reducing the incidence of piles contracted by sitting on radiators with nothing between young bums and their sizzling convolutions except school bloomers, underfloor heating had been installed, the pipes unfortunately at a depth which, whilst they may have contributed to keeping the magma beneath the earth's crust pleasantly warm, on the surface had to be taken on trust, of which there was not a lot about.

Keep both feet firmly on the floor at all times was the standing, not to say sitting, order, *and you'll be all right, glowing with health.* Certainly, the mercury dropping like lead, the ink thickening in the inkwells, our noses glowed as we strove unavailingly to discourage down-dropping mucus from its ambition to form a stalactite, and our chilblained toes grew itchy to the point where pain became an exquisite torture, almost enjoyable. 'Are your feet firmly on the floor, girls?' sounded despairingly from mistresses themselves prowling to and fro like caged animals in the space between blackboard and desks in the interest of keeping their own circulation from calling it a day.

The school rule was that when the temperature, as registered on the thermometer attached to the frame of the folding doors, showed something sub-arctic – fifty degrees Fahrenheit is the number which intrudes itself on my recollection (though I may be mistaken: it could have been 273° Absolute) – windows were permitted to be shut, doors unfolded to form a fourth wall against the encroaching ice. As a result of this dispensation, in cold-getting-colder weather very little work got done, the mistresses' little promenades bringing them on transparently disguised ploys to check the thermometer, the pupuls' energies concentrated in a fierce communal act of willing the temperature down.

'Don't breathe on it!' Maria Veronese, whose genes were tuned to a warmer clime, would plead when Miss Adams, our form-mistress, who was short-sighted, put her face close to the glass when taking a reading. 'You'll warm it up!'

What busy bees we were once the crucial number was passed, running for the long hooked poles that slammed the windows shut, hauling the doors along their metal trackway like sailors in *HMS Pinafore*. The quadrangles were alive with activity. We could have murdered Alice Boulter, the form half-wit, for screaming out as if it were good news: 'It's going up, Miss! The temperature's going up!'

Back at school in mid-summer, I could afford to be nostalgic about the joys of winter. Rightly or wrongly, and even though in my absence my desk in the front row had been given to Peggy Coates because she had begun to wear glasses whilst I was not there to defend it, I sensed a welcome in the place. About my schoolfellows, my erstwhile best friends, best enemies, I was less sure. I was after all, as I was humbly ready to acknowledge, guilty of three unforgivable crimes. I had been ill, I had been associated with a death, and now, as if those two were not enough, I was living with some of Them – the Them on the other side of the great divide which separates the teachers from the taught. Not one of the girls asked if I were feeling better, or said she was sorry about my father, but then I had never been so barmy as to have expected them to. Alice Boulter, the dope, wanted to know if Miss Locke wore pyjamas or a nightie in bed at night. Both, I answered: one on top of the other. This reply raised a titter and warmed the atmosphere a little, not much.

As it happened, my personal position in Form IIIa had always been on the equivocal side. Through no fault of my own, and no particular cleverness either, I had gone straight from the First to the Third Form, which meant that, separated from my contemporaries, the children with whom I had entered the school, I found myself among others who were a full year older and had already established their own pecking order.

French had been my downfall. I was the only girl in my year to come from a private school, and French – a subject at that time not taught at all in State primary schools – was one of the few things Eldon House had taught me – taught me by the medium of a genuine Frenchwoman, what was more, so that it not only was French, it actually sounded like it. Madame Bradley was married to an Englishman and powdered her face dead white like a Pierrot's, with black outlines round her eyes. She had worn gauzy, wide-brimmed hats in class as well as tight-fitting dresses that fastened all the way down her back from nape to hem with little buttons covered with matching fabric. It was a marvel to us how day after day she could sit on all those buttons and never once move a buttock. It had given us a high opinion of the French, a race which otherwise, I am practically sure, we would have regarded with suspicion and contempt. We felt privileged to have her for our teacher, an admiration which carried over into our work. Thanks to those buttons, we had felt she was somebody worth trying for.

When Miss Parsons, my French teacher at the Secondary School, found out how much French I knew, she set in motion a personal campaign for my advancement – one that, given Mrs Crail's prejudice against excellence of any kind, would have got nowhere if the object of her endeavour had been anybody but me. By then, however, the battle lines of my relationship with the headmistress had already been drawn up; and, aware of how much I hated the proposal –I never, in all my time at the school, learned the art of dissembling in that piggy presence – Mrs Crail smiled and smiled and said what a good idea.

Peggy Coates's glasses, instead of the usual metal, were framed in mock tortoiseshell, which made her look like Harold Lloyd. They were the latest thing and she was besotted with them, to say nothing of being as pleased as Punch to have my seat in the front row. Just the same, her glance of triumph slid off me uneasily as if, my father being dead, I too was putrescent, beyond the grave, which was odd because suddenly I had never found myself so confident, so aware of life, as I was at that particular moment. The realization came to me that it was a legacy from my father – all the life he no longer had need of.

Because a gift like that wasn't something to be frittered away on trifles, I went up to Peggy and said: 'I don't see why you needed to take my desk.'

'My eyes, dummy!'

'Your eyes,' I pointed out – quite amiably, I like to think – 'have got glasses on them, making them as good as new, if not better. If not, you'd better go back to your optician and complain. If you didn't have glasses I wouldn't say a word. But as you *have* –'

Leaving the girl appalled at my cheek I went up to Miss Adams and asked if I could please have my desk back. After all, Peggy Coates had glasses, whereas I had to make do with my two unaided eyes, such as they were. Our form-mistress, who was a gentle soul, looked flustered. She obviously had not viewed the matter in the light I indicated; but my calm sense of justice carried the day and Peggy Coates, near to tears and spilling her books and papers as she pushed angrily between the ranks of desks, was returned to the second row from the back whence she came.

At lunch Miss Gosse inquired: 'Well, Sylvia? Were you glad to be back?'

'Very.'

CHAPTER EIGHT

I must have been getting used to the bike ride because I arrived back at Chandos House only a minute or two after Miss Locke and Miss Gosse. Admittedly, my knees trembled and my calves felt like jelly, but I managed it; to be rewarded with the most delicious smell of roasting meat rolling down the hall and quite overlaying the ground base of polish and imperfectly suppressed mildew which seemed normally resident there.

'Run up and wash your hands, dear,' Miss Gosse called over her shoulder, already on her way to the dining-room. 'We're ready to start.'

Run I could not, even after having been called 'dear', but I hoisted my aching bones up the stairs as fast as I was able. Half-way to the landing I heard Miss Locke's brisk step behind me. Forewarned by what had happened upon our last encounter there, I shrank back against the dado, my rear protected, and let her pass. As she did so, she reached out with her long thin fingers and tweaked my nose.

'There!' she laughed, continuing on her way to her bedroom without pausing for an answer. 'Is that better?'

Well, it was and it wasn't. Speaking for myself, I felt confused by teachers who tweaked you *anywhere*.

Lunch – or dinner, as Miss Gosse insisted on calling it – was lovely. Not just the food. Breakfast had been too hurried a meal for anything but its scantiness to have made much impression on me; but at lunch I noted and enjoyed the happy atmosphere, the way Miss Gosse and Miss Locke were obviously content with each other's company. It wasn't anything particular that they said, just something you felt, something that even Mrs Benyon's dour presence going to and fro from the kitchen could not dampen. When Miss Gosse carved Miss Locke's meat she carefully – you might almost say lovingly – cut out the fat because, I suppose, she knew that Miss Locke didn't care for it. And when Miss Locke got up from the table to get the mint sauce which Mrs Benyon had left on the sideboard, she gave Miss Gosse a little pat on the head as she passed her chair, just the kind of pat you might give a King Charles spaniel.

Sitting opposite Miss Locke as we ate our meal, I saw her, really saw her for the first time. At school, in converse with any of the teachers it was unthinkable to look them directly in the face. One might as well have ventured to engage eyeball to eyeball with Medusa. Instead, one directed one's gaze a little to the right or a little to the left, or, better still, down at one's feet, so that at best one garnered a general impression only, which might or might not be accurate.

Now, with only the table between us, I realized for the first time that Miss Locke was not nearly so young as I had thought her. That boyish figure, that Peter Pan cap of hair, had misled me. Was she young at all, in fact?

Whilst it was true that I was at an age when all grown-ups, to my pitiless eye, were bogged down in varying degrees of senility, I could at least see quite well that Miss Locke was not young in the way Phyllis, my brother's fiancée, or any other of my brother's girl-friends, was young. Her complexion had a used look as if – in good condition, mind you, donated by one careful owner – it had been picked up secondhand at a good-class jumble sale; and her face, whilst free of wrinkles, had something written there which, although I could not decipher it, I knew was not to be found on the face of the genuinely young.

It could, of course, have been simply that Miss Locke was clever, a history teacher with a degree – I had lived long enough to be aware that knowledge, delicious as it was to possess it, was, like all self-indulgences, ageing – whilst my brother's female acquaintance, including my future sister-in-law, were one and all, in the arrogant judgement of childhood, brainless ninnies with nothing on what they hopefully called their minds but boys. All the same, looking at Miss Locke across the table – surreptitious, darting glances of which, in all probability, she was perfectly aware – I couldn't help thinking that a little brainlessness, a touch of boy-mania, would have improved that Ancient Greek profile, that narrow nose whose nostrils looked scarcely wide enough to accommodate a good blow.

I watched a little anxiously as Miss Gosse carved my portion, hoping she hadn't any ideas about cutting out my fat the way she had Miss Locke's, because there was little enough to the solitary slice as it was, fat and lean combined. In fact, the food on all three plates, taken together, scarcely equalled what in St Giles would have been considered adequate for one. By now, though – and that was something – I was pretty sure that Miss Gosse was not stingy by nature, simply that Chandos House had its own standards of what constituted enough to eat. Had we, in St Giles, been, all unaware, a family of guzzlers? I did not think so but it was hard to decide. In a single day my past life, *cuisine* and all, had, along with dinosaurs and the Battle of Waterloo, receded into a shadowy past where nothing was truly real except the *pastness* of it.

The lamb tasted as good as it smelled, the peas and new potatoes from the garden sheer poetry – but oh! the insufficiency! Though I did my best to make my food last as long as Miss Gosse and Miss Locke did theirs, it was gone in a trice. So far from assuaging my hunger it merely whetted my appetite. I began to doubt that, during my stay at Chandos House, I should ever have time to think of anything else besides eating.

Yet why, just the same, when Miss Locke, looking up from her plate and observing mine already empty, said: 'I shouldn't be surprised, Lydia, this child would like a second helping,' and Miss Gosse, astonished but willing, had picked up the carving knife and fork again, did I stammer, red in the face: 'Oh no, really, thank you, I've had loads'?

At teatime, on the other hand, I could hardly believe my eyes. I had already been told by Miss Gosse that during the school week I should, as a general rule, take my tea on my own, since both she and Miss Locke preferred to do their marking of homework at school rather than have to ferry piles of exercise books to and fro. As, on that particular afternoon, there was to be a staff meeting in addition, I arrived back at Chandos House, ravenous as usual but, give or take Mrs Benyon, looking forward to a quiet time that would, as it were, enable me to take my bearings uninterrupted before I settled down to my own homework: read a book, play the piano perhaps, explore the garden; do the small, nosy things that, hopefully sooner rather than later, would convert lodgings into a home.

I went upstairs and prised *Beau Geste* out of the box under the bed. Legionnaires cut off in the desert, not an oasis for hundreds of kilometres, *mon colonel*, not so much as a mouldy date to stave off the pangs: altogether an apt choice for making me count my blessings as I munched the single slice of bread and butter and the solitary bun which, on the basis of past performance, were the sum of my expectations.

Instead, on the dining-room table, my unbelieving eyes were dazzled by the sight of a large dish loaded with triangles of bread and butter sliced with a delicacy to bring tears to the eyes, plus half a currant cake already cut into pieces, which must mean it was expected all to be eaten. A glass bowl filled with a home-made strawberry jam full of the bumps of whole fruit, none of your shop mush, completed a tea that dreams were made of.

Only, how much was my share? Obviously, tea had been laid out for the three of us. I tried to count the pieces of bread and butter, in order to ascertain how much I might take with a clear conscience, but the dish was so full that, for fear of breaking tender slices which might not be mine, I was forced to desist.

Drooling at the chops, I waited a little in the hope that the housekeeper would come into the dining-room and issue me with my instructions. Nothing happened, and at last I could bear it no longer; went timidly into the kitchen where I found her adding a teapot to a tray already set with a slop basin, sugar bowl, milk and hot-water jug.

Not so much as looking at me, Mrs Benyon said in the flat, glazed voice which went so well with her glazed eyes, her mottled-marble complexion: 'Can't be kept waiting a minute, can you? Regular little madam. Let me tell you, miss, whatever it may have been like where you come from, here we won't all jump to your tune.'

I countered, stammering the first excuse I could think of: 'I – I thought I could save you the bother of bringing in the tray –'

'Very kind of you.' The tone conveyed no kind of thanks. 'But as it happens, I don't encourage interlopers in my kitchen any more than I do black beetles.' Saying which, she picked up the tray and, with a heavy tread that positively cried out for the Dead March in *Saul* as an accompaniment, bore it out of the room, abandoning me so definitively that, starving as I was, I could have wished I had the willpower to go upstairs to my bedroom and stay there and keep your rotten old tea.

Not being made of the stuff of which martyrs and masochists were made, I followed the woman meekly back to the dining-room, stifled my impatience until she had set down the tray at the side of the incomparable feast. 'Please,' I whispered then, unable to stay quiet a moment longer, 'could you please tell me how much is for me?'

Mrs Benyon turned on me her frozen glance and observed icily: 'It's your stomach, not mine.'

'I mean –' hunger emboldening me – 'I don't want to eat Miss Gosse's or Miss Locke's by mistake.'

'I should hope Miss Gosse and Miss Locke get their bread and butter and cake fresh cut.' The housekeeper spoke as if I had insulted her. Yet, as her tidings of great joy sank in at last, I could, almost, have embraced her.

'You mean, it's *all* for me? How kind you are!'

'Not kind at all,' declared Mrs Benyon, still aggrieved. 'So don't you go thinking any such things. If there's one thing I can't stand it's false pretences. And if there's another thing I can't stand and never have, it's kids.'

I protested, with that winsomeness of which I was half-proud, half-ashamed: 'I won't stay one for ever, you know.'

The housekeeper turned away from the table; gave me a coldly appraising once-over. 'Two years an' a bit, Miss Gosse said. You'll still be a kid when you get out of here. Either that, or –' She broke off.

'Or what?'

'You go on like that at home?' Mrs Benyon demanded without much interest. 'No wonder they wanted to get rid of you.'

'They didn't want anything of the sort!' I cried, beyond either politeness or policy. 'It's what I chose to do! That is, I wanted to go and stay with Mrs Curwen, only Mrs Crail –'

'So she's the one waved her magic wand! I might've guessed!' The housekeeper's lower jaw moved a fraction from right to left and back again, from left to right, at the same time that her glazed eyes snapped open and shut three times, for all the world like a china doll bent forwards and backwards again to make her eyelids work. I felt surprised not to hear their dull clunk as they fell into place. It took a little while to realize that Mrs Benyon was laughing.

'Well, I never!' she declared. 'The artful old so-and-so!'

I ate up all the tea, except for the last piece of the cake, which I wrapped up in my handkerchief; ran upstairs and hid under my pillow for later. It was the first time since arriving at Chandos House that I felt able to address myself to anything without having my thoughts or actions subverted by a supervening preoccupation with food. I was able to take stock of my situation and to decide that, taking one thing with another, I was still happy.

School that afternoon had been a double period of art, which I always enjoyed as much for the room in which it took place as for Miss Malahide the art mistress's instruction. The Art Room was situated at the northern end of the north quad, a lofty room with no open-air nonsense, but with tall, north-facing windows which – to my way of thinking, at any rate – admitted a light unlike any other. Even on the greyest day the light drew an outline of surpassing delicacy round everybody and everything within its four walls, making them separate in a way nothing else in the world was separate, inviolate even when they appeared, superficially, to be touching. Just to be there, to know that even though you yourself were not properly placed to reach a judgement, your own body must be a similar masterpiece inscribed on the Art Room air, was a life-enhancing experience even if you couldn't draw for toffee.

If, on the other hand, you weren't into life-enhancing, there was always Miss Malahide.

Miss Malahide had pepper-and-salt hair cut in a square bob and whiskers to match. She had a way of throwing her head back, tossing her mane as you might say, her whiskery muzzle protruding, which made her look very like a lion, fierce but not frightening; just as the crazy way she talked sometimes astonished you with a sanity that was as reassuring as it was strange. Perhaps because she was an artist, perhaps because she didn't rate a gown like the other mistresses, she wore, summer and winter, a voluminous black cloak which she was given to flinging over her shoulder with theatrical gestures that used to make us put our hands up to our faces to cover our giggles. Not that we need have bothered, probably. She wasn't the kind to take offence. In fact, for all her eccentricities, she was, I think, of all the women teaching at the school, the single one that we recognized as a complete human being, someone to be believed in as we believed in ourselves.

It was funny. The girls of Form IIIa treated what happened in the outside world as real – which of course was what it was. That was why, since my return, they had quite understandably gone off me for bringing things like illness and death into the cosy, make-believe sanctuary of school where getting your sums right or winning your netball colours was what counted. With the mistresses it was exactly the reverse. School was the one reality; whatever happened outside was a fantasy it didn't do to take too seriously. That was why, with one exception, they treated my return to the fold with the utmost insouciance, concerned only with the logistics of how I was to make up work missed during my absence. Beyond a cheerfully perfunctory inquiry, the reason for my temporary dropping-out of the community was not their business.

The exception was Miss Malahide.

'Pa died, did he?' At my reluctant nod – every time I assented to the proposition of my father's death it seemed that I killed him anew – 'Loved him, did you?' A further small nod. I was aware of the girls' sardonic glances. 'Pity, that. Take your seats, girls – not like a herd of bison, *if* you please, but quietly, prayerfully, as befits one's demeanour in a temple of the arts. As I was saying –' continuing the conversation in a smooth, unbroken line like those she was apt to sweep across our drawing paper with a BB pencil to show us how something ought to be done, and then blame us for taking ten minutes to rub the soft smear out – 'a pity you loved him. Now my pa, bless him, was a complete monster. Couldn't say so at the time, of course, but we were all so delighted to see him go, I can't tell you. After the funeral we went for a bang-up tea at Gunter's and then on to the panto: *Dick Whittington*. Glorious! My ma was a new woman. Married again as soon as the year was out – but would you believe it? Blow me if the second wasn't as bad as the first, if not worse! A good woman, but not a penn'orth of judgement. Tell your ma from me, don't be in too much of a hurry.'

The possibility of my mother remarrying was so patently ridiculous that I laughed out loud.

'That's right,' said Miss Malahide approvingly. 'Cheer up – you can't cheer down!'

Because I had been away for so long she let me choose what we should do that day, and I said 'Models', although it brought, as I knew it would, groans from the rest of the form. Models wasn't drawing from life, as one might have expected, but drawing arrangements of large cylinders, pyramids and cubes which, with their smooth white surfaces and cool, unambiguous shadows, were like music by Bach or God. At the end of the lesson Miss Malahide marked mine G for Good, which I hoped wasn't just her being kind, though I was afraid it probably was.

CHAPTER NINE

The garden was another country – lovely, but not at all what I had meant by staying on in Norwich. Even as I gazed about me in admiration, I yearned for the Market Place, the castle, the cathedral, the vibrating pulse of that centre which, for all of my life up till then, had enfolded and defended me the way its ancient walls had once enfolded and defended the entire city.

Nothing was left of the walls except for some lumps of masonry sticking up through the pavement like dragons' teeth looking for a very clever dentist. Thanks to the good offices of Mrs Crail, nothing was left of me either, marooned as I was on the shirt tails of the city, in neither town or country, a nothing place for nothing people.

Luxuriating in the complacent discontent that goes particularly well with a good tea, I wandered beneath the fruit trees, sloshing my shoes through the fallen blossom; past herbaceous borders where lupins and peonies and bearded iris took precedence. I skirted a netted enclosure of currant and gooseberry bushes, and came to the vegetable garden.

The vegetable garden was enormous, taking up by far the largest part of the land available: not so much a garden as a regimental parade-ground, ranks of this and that and the other in the vegetable line standing to attention into the far distance. How could Miss Gosse and Miss Locke with their birdlike appetites – even with Mrs Benyon added to the equation – put away such tonnage of food? Even assuming Mrs Benyon spent her days pickling, bottling and preserving, what did they do with it all?

On a sanded space outside a greenhouse filled with tomato plants a man was sitting on a wooden bench in the sun, reading a newspaper. All about his feet the ground was covered with punnets and punnets of strawberries, neatly fitted into crates of slatted wood. The man, who was small and knobbly, not young, with bow legs whose curvature, in their corduroy breeches, was noticeable even when he was sitting down, looked up from his paper and announced, not asked: 'You'll be the gal, then, what her ladyship's taken in.'

Not pleased at all with the way he put it, I admitted repressively that I was indeed boarding with Miss Gosse.

'Tha's what I said.' The man tilted back the peak of his cloth cap which had been pulled down against the strong light. He inquired matily: 'How the ol' goats treating you, then?'

Dropping the repressive bit since, to tell the truth, I was delighted to have come upon someone, anyone, to talk to, I replied that they were treating me very well, thank you.

'S'long as you don't let 'em start taking liberties,' the man admonished. 'Best advice I can give you. Start as you mean to go on.' I should have liked to ask what particular liberties he had in mind, but, as usual, was shy about asking. Picking up his paper again, the man looked at me in a peculiar way, pale-blue eyes narrowed, before inquiring: 'You pure, gal?'

At this surprising question the red flooded into my cheeks, I couldn't think why, except that 'pure' was one of *those* words, whatever *those* words might be. I had reached the point in life where, although I was as completely ignorant of matters sexual as on the day I was born – more ignorant, probably, for how could one possibly undergo that particular transmogrification without picking up a few hints along the way? (knowledge unfortunately mislaid in all the stress of learning to be a baby) – I was at least grown up enough to recognize my ignorance. There was, in IIIa, a small raffish group of girls that the rest of us knew, somehow, were not ignorant. We also knew, somehow, that this knowledge which they alone of their classmates possessed was in some way connected with boys. In the evenings, when they should have been indoors doing their homework, they hung about on street corners, not exactly talking to boys but with boys circling them under the street-lamps like moths about a flame, except marginally more cautious, not getting close enough to get burned. These girls turned up their noses at me because I was a swot and because I came from a private school talking posh, and I turned up my nose at them because they completely failed to understand how exciting it was to learn things – the kind of things you learned at school, that is, not out in the streets under the street-lamps.

The fact that I, normally so inquisitive, not to say nosy, made absolutely no effort to inform myself of what it was that they knew – indeed, went out of my way to avoid inadvertent enlightenment – I can only put down to a deliberate if subconscious suppression, a reluctance to hear something which would take me into areas where I was not yet ready to venture.

The man insisted: 'Well – are you?' 'I – I think so,' I stammered.

He gave me another of his looks; then, apparently satisfied, handed me the paper he had been holding.

'Get an eyeful o' that, then –' indicating with a dirt-encrusted fingernail where I should look – 'an' tell me what you fancy.'

It wasn't like any newspaper I had ever seen at St Giles: a kind of sporting sheet, printed on pink paper, with races listed according to venue and starting times, and the names of the horses entered for them.

I cast my eyes down the lists without really seeing them; wondering, though once more too shy to ask, what on earth being pure could possibly have to do with horse races.

As if reading my thoughts, the man explained: 'It's what you might call a scientific experiment. Somethin' I heard. Bloke on the Cattle Market – gipsy, he were – tol' me the best way to be sure of a winner is to get a young gal what's a virgin – (another of *those* words! My face flamed afresh) – to pick it out fer you.' He finished kindly: 'Not that I'll be casting 'spersions on yer morals, gal, if it don't work. You know what them gippoes are.'

I returned to the racing sheet confusedly: relieved when a familiar name stood out, my brother's.

'King Alfred,' I pronounced, with sudden confidence.

'King Alfred?' The man repeated the name unbelievingly. 'Get away! That refugee from the cat's meat man!' He took back his paper and frowned at the relevant line. 'Thirty-three to one! You aren't having me on, by any chance?'

'King Alfred!' I repeated, pleased with the regal sound of it. The reward for my racing tip was a punnet of strawberries which I didn't want to accept because – though I did not say so

– I wasn't sure they were in the man's gift to bestow. Full up as I was with my gorgeous tea, the sacrifice was not all that great.

'Go on!' the man insisted. He thrust the fruit at me so that I had no choice between taking it or getting strawberry stains on my school uniform. 'Stick it up yer bloomers if yer think *they're* going to say anything – which they won't, take it from me. I'm the one in charge of this here garden. Without me, as they know very well, it'd be a wilderness you could wander about in fer forty years an' no Promised Land at the end of it, either.'

'It *is* an awfully big vegetable garden for so few people –'

'Tha's on account of old Mr Gosse. Never knew him myself, before my time. Foreigner. Gossi his name was, afore it was Gosse. Bet you never knew that! Frog or Eytie, something like that. Always thought another war were just round the corner, so they tell me, an' wanted to be sure he wouldn't starve when the Jerries come marching up London Street into the Market Place.'

'Really?' I was glad to learn something of Miss Gosse's family history. It made me feel less a stranger at Chandos House. It also made me understand how Miss Gosse came to look the way she did with her dark skin and hair, her black boot-button eyes. 'Does Miss Gosse think the same about the war, then, that she keeps on growing so much?'

'Never heard her say, one way or the other. Only she'll never change nothing her daddy did, I know that.' The man folded away his paper, put it in his jacket pocket and got up from the bench in a way that indicated the audience was over. Sorry to be constrained to break off the only social intercourse that had come my way, I offered to help him carry the strawberries up to the house, only he said no; so I announced my intention of going down to the bottom of the garden in order to complete my tour of inspection.

From where we stood, I could make out a gate at the far end. Where did it lead?

'Jest a track along the back o' the houses, an' a field the other side, got a donkey in it. If you go down there, mind out. It's a right ole devil.'

I couldn't understand how a donkey could be dangerous, but I said I'd be careful. With my best private-school manners I told the man how glad I was to have made his acquaintance, and that I hoped to see him again soon.

'Mondays, Wednesdays, Fridays, my days here.' The man looked at me. 'Bugger as burnt the cakes, weren't he?'

'What? Oh – you mean King Alfred. Yes he did, though it's probably only a legend.' Even as I spoke I recognized the schoolroom prissiness that probably drove my class-mates barmy.

'Like thirty-three to one, eh? In case you want to know,' the man added, as I took my first steps away from him, 'the donkey's name is Bagshaw.'

'Is it? Why is it called that?'

'Because that's its name, what you think? Which reminds me – you never asked me mine.'

'I didn't like to –'

'Pah!' he spat in disgust. 'Some people'd shit theirselves if a mouse farted.'

I made the effort and inquired haltingly, 'What is your name, please?'

'Joey Betts,' he answered, enormously pleased with himself. 'What else?'

The track at the back of the garden was a delicious place, secret and spicily aromatic with the hawthorn, honeysuckle, sweetbriar and bramble that made up the untidy hedge on either side. There wasn't a proper gate into the field opposite, which was grass mostly and some spiky weeds: only a few strands of barbed wire. I could not see any donkey.

I stood there with my strawberries, but only for a moment. Through a gap between the wires a dove-coloured head with enormous teeth whipped out of the shelter of the hedgerow and attached itself to the punnet. For a second or so we struggled for possession, a good many of the strawberries jolting out on to the ground in the process: but my adversary had the advantages of strength and surprise. The teeth withdrew, taking the punnet with them.

The donkey ate the fruit first, and then the punnet, which it seemed marginally to prefer; then gave me a hard look which signalled plainly: 'That all?' I picked up some berries that had fallen on the path beyond reach of his questing head and threw them – it didn't seem very polite but his teeth were *very* large – into the field behind him.

The donkey did not deign to go after them; merely shrugged his head – a head that was disproportionately large in relation to his body – in a way that amply conveyed he did not think much of me. It was a head you almost expected him to take off presently and there underneath would be a couple of pantomime men coming up for a breath of air.

The animal, however, did not take off his head; only leaned his neck on the barbed wire in a way that frightened me. I expected to see blood spurting from his jugular any minute, but it was only strawberry juice, followed by saliva. When it was clear that no more strawberries or punnets were on offer, Bagshaw spat at me.

'That bloody critter in't one to waste his spit where it ain't appreciated. Sure sign he likes you,' Joey Betts said consolingly when I came back into the garden feeling sticky and rejected. 'We got a tap here, you want to use it.'

He turned on a stopcock at the side of the greenhouse and provided me with a bar of orange soap and a towel, both proffered with a kindness which made tears come into my eyes. Rightly or wrongly, I felt that I had found a friend.

'Put a sock in it,' he said in a friendly way whilst I washed and dried my face, sniffing between times. 'If I was to turn on the waterworks for every time that Bagshaw spewed me in the kisser, I'd've drowned in me tears twice over by now. If you don't mind me saying so, you take things too personal. Bagshaw's got problems, poor ole bugger. All day long, no one to talk to, no one to care a brass farthing if he's dead or alive. Wonder is he don't go clean off his rocker, let alone a little harmless spit what don't hurt nobody.' Taking back his toilet articles, the gardener draped the towel over the back of the bench, and gave me a sudden sharp look. 'Reckon you could do with a bit o' love yerself, gal.'

'Oh no!' I protested, my eyes filling again despite all my efforts to discourage them. 'Everyone's been very kind.'

'Kind!' Mr Betts exclaimed ferociously, and spat to one side himself, as if averting the evil eye. 'Gawd keep us from kind!'

Soon I was telling the knobbly little bow-legged man almost everything. How Maud and my mother had gone to London and how I had refused to go with them. How, because everything was changed, I didn't feel that I could go any more to Salham St Awdry to visit Maud's family, as I used to,* because it would be like stepping back in time and time had to go forward, hadn't it? – it had to.

I told him how I had wanted to lodge with Mrs Curwen, only Mrs Crail had put a stop to it. I told him how at lunch Miss Locke had said she thought I would like another slice, which I would have done, ever so; yet somehow, when I'd been asked directly, I had felt compelled to say no, I was full up thank you: could you understand a thing like that? I told him, whimpering a little, how happy I was, how I couldn't help it, even though in the circumstances it was awful. I also told him how unhappy I was because my father was dead.

'Snuffed it, did he? When was that? An' how old are you?' When I had answered his questions Mr Betts cocked his head to one side and regarded me with a quizzical eye. 'Twelve years to have yer dad by yer! Some people don't know when they're lucky! How long d'yer think I had mine?' The man looked at me with bright-eyed anticipation, as if we were playing a game and it was my move. 'Go on – have a guess!'

Just to say something, I said twenty years; whereupon the gardener shook his head triumphantly.

'Dead wrong! T'weren't twenty seconds! T'weren't twenty nothing! Never had no dad except technically, as you might say. Bugger lit out afore I were even born, what you think o' that? But do you see *me* weepin' an' wailing' like I'd backed the winner of the Thousand Guineas an' then lost the bloody ticket? You do not! So what you on about, what's had twelve glorious years?'

* See *Opposite the Cross Keys*

Back indoors and feeling the need for celebration, I opened the music stool and found a pile of sheet music, old-fashioned songs with fancy print on the title pages as well as pictures of ladies who stuck out front and back simultaneously, as if they couldn't make up their minds whether they were coming or going.

I enjoyed playing songs. It was like a game, compressing the three lines of music – the two of the accompaniment plus the single stave which carried the melody – into a recognizable version of a piano piece, something that didn't need a singer to make sense of it for you. I picked out one because of its exotic title – 'Indian Love Lyrics' – and because the lady on the cover was dressed up in Indian clothes, though anyone could tell at a glance that she wasn't Indian; besides which, she stuck out in the same places as the ladies in all the other pictures, something – though without having any proof, my geography lessons with Miss Howell not having covered this particular point – I felt sure genuine Indian ladies did not do.

I played the introduction, pleased with my choice, even pleased with the piano, whose jangly tones had what I could easily imagine to be an authentic Indian sound. I had a vision of jangly bangles tinkling around slim brown Indian ankles.

Framed in the dining-room door, Mrs Benyon sang:

'Pale hands I loved beside the Shalimar,
Where are you now? Who lies beneath your spell?'

The housekeeper's voice was not exactly musical, but not negligible. Not at all like my father's records of Tetrazzini and Galli-Curci, but not like the ladies who sang in charity concerts either. It was deep and powerful, a voice with teeth in it. It took the song by the throat and shook it, the way a terrier shakes a rat to show it who is master. Mesmerized by the sheer volume of sound I almost stopped playing, except that I was afraid to, especially when the singer advanced into the room with her slow massive gait that was like a statue moving; approached the piano and put her hands on my shoulders, her head pushed forward a little to peer at the text. Abandoning the melody line for the accompaniment pure and simple, I soldiered on, thinking how very different Indian love songs were from English ones.

'Pale hands, pink-tipped, like lotus-buds that float
On those cool waters where we used to dwell
I would have rather felt you round my throat
Crushing out life than waving me farewell.'

Mrs Benyon's breath, curling round my cheeks, smelled sweet, much too sweet for comfort. As she stood there, puffing it out over my shoulder I felt myself positively drowning in its dreadful sweetness, which was no perfume I recognized – that is to say, not lavender water, Parma violets nor eau de Cologne, nor that Evening in Paris scent Phyllis went in for and which I always felt – not that I would have dreamed of mentioning it – smelled like cat's litter slightly the worst for wear. With that smell wafting about me, hitting the piano front which promptly batted it back into my face, I could easily have brought my tea up, except that I was hanged if I was going to be parted from the only decent meal that had come my way since coming to lodge at Chandos House.

I hurried to the end of the song as fast as I dared, and then stood up, dislodging the podgy hands from my shoulders as if by accident: full of a desperate admiration as I edged towards the french window, seeking air.

'How marvellously you sing!' I gasped, I gushed. 'You ought to be in opera!'

'Opera!' Mrs Benyon looked as if I had insulted her. 'I hope I got something better to do with my time.'

'Do you sing in the church choir?'

'I do not!'

'The chapel, then?' I persisted, unwilling to let go this possible key into the closed life of this closed woman. I hated not knowing about people.

'I don't sing anywhere!'

'Except here,' I corrected winsomely, my lungs recharged. 'I'll always be happy to accompany you.'

The housekeeper was looking annoyed. It was strange that such flat, immobile features could convey emotion, but they could, to perfection.

'How many times I got to say I don't sing anywhere, ever?'

'But we just –' I stammered.

'But we just what?'

'Sang. "Pale hands I loved" – you know –' I managed feebly.

'Pale hands I what?' Mrs Benyon drew herself up and I saw that she too stuck out front and back like the old-fashioned ladies on the song sheets – except that you could tell by the look in her eyes, whatever the others might or might not have known, she knew all right whether she was coming or going.

Both at the same time, it wouldn't have surprised me.

CHAPTER TEN

On Saturday morning the sun shone, birds sang. The leaves outside my bedroom window quivered excitedly, or so it pleased me to imagine. 'Food!' I distinctly heard them rustling, as I hurried through my dressing. 'Lovely food!'

I ran downstairs, anxious to put away my meagre breakfast without delay; get off to the city and on with the task of stocking my private larder. The thought of putting myself into a position where I no longer felt compelled to think about food all the time intoxicated me. I was high on hopes of, at last, contriving to fill the churning crater which seemed to have taken up permanent residence in my innards. Mrs Benyon's teas, during the week, had been extraordinarily variable in quantity, the magnificent opulence of the first afternoon never repeated, and subsequent teas ranging between fair and two desiccated triangles of bread without so much as a smidgeon of butter between them. I had given up trying to puzzle out whether it was some inadvertent blunder on my part which determined my allotment on any given day. Like Jehovah, and equally unknowable, the housekeeper at Chandos House was that which she was, stony as marble and unpredictable as Fate.

By the time the weekend actually came round I had, in my dreams, spent Alfred's pound note twenty times over. Every idle moment had been taken up with a writing of lists, with a weighing of pros and cons of great moment. Penny for penny, did monkey nuts fill you up better than shortbreads? Were doughnuts to be preferred to sticky buns, and which of the two went stale first? Was chocolate, however delicious, a better buy than almond brittle which, given an iron determination, you could suck practically from one week to the next before the last sliver dissolved on the tongue? How long before apples went soggy and Cornish pasties grew mould? Would Dutch cheese, when Mrs Benyon came into my room to dust, give itself away by the smell?

My choice of cache being strictly limited, I had nominated the book box under the bed as my hiding-place. If I hid the food under a good thick layer of books, the housekeeper would never know.

Or would she? I decided, quite calmly, without any crass upsurge of anger, that if she did, I would kill her.

Tremulous with anticipation, I took my seat at the breakfast table; smiled into the smiling faces of Miss Locke and Miss Gosse. Miss Gosse was dressed in a green Aertex shirt and a white skirt, Miss Locke actually wore trousers. There was a different, a weekend, atmosphere – no school gong, as it were, lurking over the horizon, ready to sound off with its horrible, triumphant sound. Instead, leisure, pleasure, food. Food! It was going to be a lovely day.

Miss Gosse handed me my shilling pocket money, happy to do so, I could see, even though it wasn't her own money she was giving away. Money seemed to make her less shy; the way, I had often noticed, it did with a lot of people. She informed me that Saturday, beginning at noon, was Mrs Benyon's time off – that she had every Saturday afternoon, as well as alternate Sundays, when she had the whole day. It did not necessarily mean that on such days she left the house, the choice was hers: simply that, at such times, in or out, her services were unavailable under any circumstances. On Saturdays, cold collations would be left out for whoever wanted them, to be taken or not as desired. On Mrs Benyon's Sundays, of which, incidentally, tomorrow was one – Miss Gosse paused in her exposition of Chandos House ways to remark comfortably: 'But then, you'll be spending your Sundays with your brother, won't you?'

I blushed scarlet. What had my mother, a woman incurably addicted to saying whatever she thought her listeners would be best pleased to hear, led my landlady to believe? That I should never be hanging about the premises to trouble the schoolmistresses' sabbath peace?

For some reason I found it impossible to say outright that actually I had no plans to spend my Sundays with Alfred: in fact, quite the contrary. I hoped he wouldn't think I was sulking, that I was jealous of Phyllis, which I wasn't, not in the least. I loved my brother, I wanted him to be happy. I was a great believer in happiness. I simply had not the words to explain to him or to anybody else that the death of my father had made me realize, as perhaps my brother himself did not, that, in the natural way of things, the time had come for us go to our separate ways, each waving lovingly to the other across an ever-widening distance. Freedom came into the equation somewhere, though I was not sure how: my father free of life, myself at last free to live, nobody's daughter or dear little sister, but the irreducible me. Sometimes they seemed bleak alternatives rather than choices. At others, I wanted to jump up to the sky with the excitement of what was in store for me.

As it was, I managed to get out that I needed to go into the city that morning to make some small purchases; and finally, hot with effort, let it be known that, shopping apart, I had no plans to go anywhere, Saturday or Sunday. It was my intention to stay home catching up on as much as I could of the school work I had missed during my absence. Amid my stumbling and stammering, it was with surprise and some elation that I heard myself calling Chandos House home.

Miss Gosse looked taken aback, I thought, but pleased in her shy way, as if she too had noticed the word. Miss Locke, intent on forcing her napkin back through its ring, her straight nose and brow inclined over her task, glanced up to comment mockingly, 'A model child!'

She made me blush all over again, of course: at that time almost anything could set me off. Miss Gosse said, smiling affectionately at her friend: 'You mustn't mind Miss Locke, Sylvia. She's a great tease!'

I ran upstairs, put on my blazer and opened the left-hand drawer of the chest of drawers to take out Alfred's pound note.

It wasn't there.

It wasn't anywhere. I had tucked the money inside the folds of the handkerchief Alfred had brought me back from Switzerland. With its blue gentians embroidered round the edges it was my favourite, and I had selected it especially. I could not possibly have been mistaken.

On the chance, nevertheless, that I *was* mistaken, I pulled all the handkerchiefs out of the sachet, pulled out everything in the drawer, everything in all the drawers. Then I levered out each one in turn and examined the space behind, coated with fluff and a dead ant or two. On the chance that the note had dropped down to the floor, I squeezed myself into the narrow space between the chest of drawers and the window. There was so little room to move that when I turned round my nose pressed up against the window, up against the quivering leaves, only the glass between us. I could tell by the way the leaves stared at me that *they* knew. They knew who had stolen my money.

As I did myself, for that matter. Who else could it have been? I slid the drawers back into place, slammed the handkerchiefs and clothes in all anyhow, and sat down on the bed to consider what I was going to do about it. Actually, I knew even before I sat down what the answer would be.

Nothing.

I saw myself crossing the landing, going downstairs, along the hall and through the door into the dining-room, to tell Miss Gosse and Miss Locke that their housekeeper had stolen a pound note from my drawer when she had come into my room to tidy it up or make my bed – *I saw myself, my eye!* Either they wouldn't believe me, or they would – which, if anything, would be worse. In the latter case they would feel obliged to sack the woman, send away the servant upon whom all their creature comforts depended. Bad as it was to steal – they wouldn't be able to deny that, that was something at least – I was the one who would come in for the real blame, the tale-bearer who, taken up with her own selfish concerns, had turned their cosy world upside down.

Either way I would have to go. Go to ghastly London, to that ghastly house – I had never seen it, but I knew exactly how it must be. And only a matter of minutes before I had called Chandos House home.

It was! It was!

I dug deep into my blazer pocket to finger the ninepence that was there untouched, and my shilling pocket money. I picked up my last and definitive shopping list from the top of the chest of drawers, crumpled it up and threw it into the wastepaper basket. I wondered fleetingly if, when I telephoned Alfred as promised, I shouldn't tell him what had happened, and decided that I couldn't possibly. For a second or two I thought about my dead father, just long enough to hope he had something interesting on in heaven that morning and so wouldn't be looking down and getting upset about what had happened to me. In case, however, he *was* looking, I put on the best face I could contrive to show how well I was coping with the disaster. Not even crying – at least, not so that you'd notice.

I went down the road to the call-box at the crossroads and got through to my brother at his office. We spoke for a very short time, not because he was not glad to hear from me – the warm concern in his voice almost broke down my defences – but because Saturday morning was his busiest time of the week. I could hear a blur of noises in the background, phones ringing, typewriters tapping, a richness of living that made me long to be grown up and out in the mainstream instead of timorously on the bank, barely dipping a toe in the water. Alfred took down the number of the box so that he could phone me back and it wouldn't cost me another tuppence, which, in the circumstances, was something to be grateful for. He said he needed to make arrangements as to the best time for picking me up next day, taking me over to the house of Phyllis's parents. There were plans to take a boat out on the Broads – would I like that? Or was there something else I would rather do? When I announced my intention of staying indoors at Chandos House to do schoolwork he sounded quite proud of my conscientiousness but upset that my weekend would contain no fun. The high regard my brother placed on fun was one of the things I loved him for, even if, sometimes, it made me feel that I was the grown-up and he the child.

I promised to telephone at the same time next week.

'Are you sure you've got everything you want?'

'Everything,' I answered, fingering the coins in my pocket; and we said goodbye even before the first tuppence ran out.

I had already decided that one-and-seven was not worth going into Norwich for. Nineteen penny bars of chocolate or, alternatively, nine whipped cream walnuts and a penny change over sounded a glorious abundance when you said it, just like that; but spread over the gut-crimping hunger of a week or more, it was nothing. I had often read in stories of high adventure that when there was only very little to eat over a prolonged period you could get used to it if you persevered, the way heroes in adventure books invariably did, because your stomach shrank. By the time I figured that I could, with a fair degree of credibility, apply to Alfred for a further subvention, my stomach could very likely have shrunk so much I wouldn't need any more money for food after all.

Not noticeably cheered by these consolatory musings, I set off back to Chandos House, though not by the way I had come. I didn't want to risk running into Miss Gosse and Miss Locke and having to explain that I had changed my mind about going into town. I couldn't feel certain of being able to preserve the necessary smiling exterior without cracks, of not letting the cat out of the bag about Mrs Benyon in a sudden irrepressible caterwaul that I had been robbed. Instead, I turned into the Catton Road and walked down it looking for the opening to the path that led along the backs of the Wroxham Road houses. Other things apart, it was something to do on a day that now stretched arid and undernourished till bedtime. I would go and commune with Bagshaw. We could at least be miserable together.

In the event, I almost overshot my objective. Head-on to the road, a van was parked in the entrance to the track, taking up practically its full width and masking its very existence: a white van with plenty of rust showing and one headlamp hanging out on a cable like an eye from its socket. As I drew abreast a man came round from the back, scarcely able to squeeze into the driving seat through the meagre slit that was the utmost he could get the door open. A wild rose in the hedgerow reached down and playfully scratched a thorny signature across the raddled coachwork.

The man, who was young, had two front teeth missing and could have done with a shave, saw me and grinned cheerfully through the open window.

'Lucky I didn't bring the Rolls.'

Once I had signified that I wished to turn into the track he said: 'Jest goin', lovey. On'y came in fer a leak'; started the engine and nosed the van out into the road. From behind, the vehicle, if that were possible, looked even more disreputable than from the front, the double doors tied together with string and looking ready to burst open at any moment. I watched it trundle up to the crossroads and turn right for the city.

The track all my own, I trailed along slowly, feeling frail and not in a hurry to get anywhere. The brief human encounter had made me feel better than I had felt before, but the path put me down. Under a sun already hot and promising hotter, amid a buzz of insects whizzing about like ballet dancers and a frenzy of blossom, of fruit and seed, it had no time for me. Left out, affronted, I found a stick and took out my spleen on some nettles that edged the path, only to have one of them get its own back by stinging my knee badly.

I saw a few strawberries which I must have overlooked the day before, lying on the rutted ground looking fresh and undamaged. Restraining the impulse to guzzle them myself, I picked them up to give to Bagshaw. The donkey, who was standing, head down, at the further end of the field, looked up morosely when I called his name, thought about it, and finally came shambling over. When he neared the barbed wire I steeled myself to thrust my hand through the gap unflinchingly, holding out the berries, only to have them butted out of my palm as if by a billy-goat, in what I could only interpret as an access of indigestion. Perhaps Bagshaw had found out the hard way that strawberries and donkeys did not mix, unless it was the punnet that was the trouble. I did not know; only that neither of us was in any mood to comfort the other.

It would have been too much, in the mood I was in, to have given prior thought as to how I was to get back to Chandos House through the bolted door at the bottom of the garden. Examining it now, the difficulties did not seem insuperable. There were battens to afford footholds, and the spikes at the top, whilst nobody could have called them inviting, were not so unchallengeable that, cautiously and taking care not to get your knickers caught on the points, you couldn't expect to lift your legs over, one after the other, in safety;

Conscious of the donkey watching me with the pleased, anticipatory expression of a bystander hoping for an accident to happen, I began the ascent, not so much climbing the door as scrambling up it. As nobody was about and my mother had made a particular point of my taking care of my clothes, I took off my blazer and dress and left them neatly folded for recovery later; tackled the door with teeth gritted in a determination which, after several abortive tries, took me to the top.

I was concentrating on the delicate business of negotiating the spikes when the voice of Mr Betts inquired from below: 'Gettin' into training for Everest, are yer?'

The surprise and, even more, the embarrassment of being discovered *en déshabille* made me nearly lose my balance.

'But you said you only came in on Mondays, Wednesdays and Fridays!'

'Then I said wrong, didn' I? Come to give the lettuces a water, if you must know.' The man squinted up at me, shading his eyes against the sun. 'You can do yerself an injury up there, won't please your ma nohow. Get yourself down, do, an' come in through the gate like a Christian.'

Decently back into my clothes, I came up the garden to find the lettuces watered and Mr Betts sitting on the wooden bench near the greenhouse with a copy of his sporting paper open by his side.

'Bin hopin' to run into you, as it happens,' he greeted my arrival, dipping his hand into his trousers pocket and bringing out assorted change. 'Mustn' ferget to pay me debts, must I?'

'But you don't –' I began, only to be brought up short, mesmerized by the miracle of what was happening. The gardener, having selected two half-crowns, returned the rest of the money whence it had come; took hold of my hand and placed the beautiful silver coins in the middle of my palm before folding my fingers over them.

'Commission,' he said, by way of explanation; and when I continued to stand there, staring down at the money and bemused by the wonder of it: 'Commission on King Alfred, dummy! That gippo knew what he was on about.' Mr Betts looked at me curiously. 'No need to carry on like you never seen dough before.'

I managed 'Thank you! oh, thank you!' when what I wanted to do was fling my arms round the bow-legged little fellow in gratitude and glee: tell him what infamy Mrs Benyon had perpetrated on me and how, thanks to him and that lovely racehorse, I could now go flying down to Norwich and buy food, five shillings' lovely worth of it. I shouldn't die of starvation after all.

Only of course I said nothing. I didn't dare. Not that I thought for a moment that Mr Betts would give me away by saying something to the housekeeper if I put him on his honour not to. Simply that the mere act of launching the tell-tale syllables on to the air was fraught with peril. I could see them drifting across the garden like thistledown, drifting through the open kitchen window to reconstitute themselves in silken whispers of 'Thief!' and 'Burglar!' that would bring Mrs Benyon out into the garden with marble, implacable tread to exact some revenge too awful even to conjure up in imagination.

Mr Betts picked up his paper and thrust it at me.

'What do you fancy fer today, then?'

I dropped the two half-crowns into my blazer pocket and looked where he directed. None of the horses' names rang any particular bell the way King Alfred had. In the end I picked out a horse called Grecian Vase because the Grecian bit reminded me of Miss Locke's forehead and nose, in one straight line. Seized by a sudden misgiving, I asked Mr Betts timorously whether I would be required to pay *him* commission if the horse failed to win.

''Course you will, gal, what you think?' Then, eyes twinkling. 'Take my advice. Get yerself into Norwich double quick an' blow every bleedin' penny while you got it to spend. Then, when I come asking for it back – well, I'll have to go on askin', won't I?'

CHAPTER ELEVEN

Everything was going right, not just the five shillings. Leaving by the back way I found yet another strawberry lying on the path, one that I could eat with a clear conscience now that I knew they didn't agree with donkeys. Next, aware of something pouching out the breast pocket of my blazer (it couldn't be breasts since I possessed none worth speaking of), I discovered half a packet of mauve-coloured Scholars' Tickets which cost a shilling for twelve and could be used by children of school age for a ride on the trams, any distance for a penny. As a result of this lucky find I willingly walked the mile or so down to the tram terminus and caught the tram which swayed along dreary Magdalen Road before bustling past the cheap shops in Magdalen Street, until it came to Fye Bridge and the river. Suddenly we were in *my* city, the city I knew and loved: the cathedral, the Agricultural Hall where every year at the Ideal Home Exhibition there was always a yellow and blue parrot on the Sharp's Creamy Toffee stand; the black angel on the top of the memorial in the Cattle Market to soldiers killed in the Boer War – black, I assumed, because there were so many black men in Africa: the Castle, the gunsmith's on Orford Hill with a full-size stag perched high up on the outside:

the hairdresser's shop in the Royal Arcade called Madame Pfob: the pith and core of my universe, complete. At Orford Place, where all the tram routes met briefly before taking their separate serpentine ways round the houses, I scrambled down the stairs from the top deck, impatient to submerge myself afresh, to be part of it all over again.

No.

After the first ecstatic moments spent deciding in which direction to go, wanting to go in every direction at once, the truth dawned. Living in the suburbs changed you, turned you into somebody else. I no longer belonged: foreign country. I seemed to be moving among hordes of people I used to know but who now were separated from me by a sheet of glass, invisible but shatter-proof, through which the living clamour of the city arrived flat and muted. Several people greeted me, cordially but with a certain awkwardness, as if, given the choice, they would have preferred not to have run into me. They seemed uncertain as to whether or not it was time to stop being commiserating and time to start being jolly. All in all, I was a problem, and they soon moved on thankfully to less complicated encounters.

I bought biscuits and fruit drops, whipped cream walnuts and a Lyons Swiss Roll, but my heart wasn't in it. At Palmer's, in Davey Place, I bought a loaf of bread and six currant buns, and was suddenly so transported by the gorgeous yeasty smell of the place that I came outside and stood by the shop window until I had devoured three of them, too quickly either for comfort or manners. Those were not days when persons of breeding ate in the street. Two girls I used to know at Eldon House School passed by with their noses in the air. You could tell, by the way, whilst pretending not to have seen me, their eyes slid sideways in delighted outrage at my uncouth behaviour, how much they thought I had come down in the world in every possible way since going to a municipal secondary school after having gone to a private one.

I went back into the shop and bought three more buns to replace the ones I had just wolfed. The woman behind the counter had a kind face. Perhaps, through the window, she had seen the mini-drama enacted outside. Anyway, she gave me, for nothing, a paper carrier-bag with string handles, usual price tuppence, to put my purchases in.

I wandered over to the Haymarket cinema to look at the pictures of coming attractions. If it had been open so early in the day I would gladly have spent ninepence out of my remaining money to go inside just to sit in the friendly dark, even though the film that was on looked nothing much. Next week's attraction was *The Broadway Melody*; the glazed cases stuck to the cinema walls were filled with chorus girls kicking up their long legs, in between pictures of men's and women's faces kissing each other or looking as if they were just about to do so.

My parents had taken me to the cinema from a very early age. No one, so far as I could tell, had ever censored what I saw, and so I knew a lot about kissing in films, which I did not need to be told was altogether different from other kinds of kissing, especially kissing at children's parties which, at that time, was the kind I knew most about. Postman's Knock, for instance, where you got called outside the door and found a boy on the other side knowing he had to kiss you and you to kiss him before he could get away, back into the room with the others. Well, kiss in a manner of speaking. What you actually did, both of you, was position your cheeks vaguely in the vicinity of the other's; purse your lips and then unpurse them with a little sucking noise, after which it was OK to draw apart, glad that was over. The great thing was not the so-called kiss, which was distinctly icky, but to be called out, to be chosen out of all the multitude. It showed you were in demand.

Young as I was, I was not too young to understand that the way the big faces on the cinema screen came together, their edges melting so that you could scarcely tell where one face ended and the other began, was not just, nor even principally, about kissing. It was about Love, Love with a capital L, one of the things that lay in store for me when I was grown up, along with lots of other things like high heels and understanding Einstein's Theory of Relativity. Whilst I often wished I could understand Einstein's Theory without having to wait that long, so far as the high heels etc. were concerned I was in no hurry. On the contrary. I thought high heels silly, and boys much the same: each an alien species going its separate wobbly way, one I felt – as yet, anyway – under no urgent compulsion to follow.

Feeling as I did, it was a source of some annoyance to me that, during the past few months, on the few occasions when I had come into actual contact with a boy, I had found myself willy-nilly blushing and sounding silly, unless, indeed, I found nothing to say at all, which was even worse. Now, outside the Haymarket, as if, activated by the long legs and the big faces on the walls, my unwelcome thought had conjured up one of the disturbing species out of the air, as at my side Robert Kett asked: 'You going to see it?'

'Shouldn't think so.'

After a long pause, as if a good deal of effort was involved in the saying of it: 'If you want to, I'll pay.'

Me, ungraciously: 'No thanks.'

Why were we both so ridiculously red? I could feel the heat of my own redness; see Robert Kett's, which, I was pretty sure, looked marginally worse than mine on account of all the freckles which dotted its surface. It was small comfort.

Robert Kett was a boy who had a cousin in IIIa. She was called Sybil, not a particular friend, just someone to whom, in my unthinking enthusiasm for history and with no ulterior motive, I happened once to say that it must be thrilling to have a name like Robert Kett, the name of the great Norfolk hero and rebel who had been hanged from the battlements of Norwich castle in 1549, 'like a ham hung up for winter store', as one of the bystanders had put it pithily, dreadfully. The authorities of the time had never taken the body down, leaving it to the crows and as a reminder to the citizens of the city of the price of rebellion. It was fifty years, so the story went, before the last poor remnants fell to the ground for the dogs to scavenge, which would have made it the reign of James I. The very thought of the end of Robert Kett was enough to bring a lump to my throat. Even in the reign of King George V, four centuries on, I could still, when the light was right, glancing up at the Norman keep, brutish on its hill, fancy I saw the pitiful skeleton still dangling there, and feel sad and proud to be alive in Norwich, part of Robert Kett's story.

A lot of Norfolk people called Kett must have been proud of their lineage because there were several Robert Ketts about in Norwich. In the great man's home town of Wymondham his namesakes, for all I knew, could be numbered by the dozen. Sybil who, like Henry Ford, thought history was bunk and didn't give a fig for the great rebel even though he might have been her very own ancestor, told her cousin that I was crazy about his name, a statement which, so far as I could guess, slid easily into the assertion that I was crazy about its bearer. A week later, with all the self-importance of a pander, she brought me a letter.

> Dear Sylvia,
>
> This is to let you know I am crazy about you too.
> I would like you to be my girl friend. We could go for walks and all that. I think you are pretty.
> Yours sinserely,
> Robert Kett, Sybil's cousin, I saw you at Dorothy Bell's party, remember?

It was my first love letter, in one way tremendously reassuring as evidence that one day real people, not wet, freckled boys, would fall in love with me. In the mean time, however, the very suggestion that I could be crazy about somebody who – no matter how illustrious his lineage – looked so little like Ronald Colman, my current favourite, was deeply offensive. Although afterwards, off and on, I was sorry for it – there was, after all, status in possessing a boyfriend, whatever he looked like – I gave Sybil my reply to deliver to the lovesick swain:

> Don't talk rot and there is only one S in sincerely.

Robert Kett and I parted amicably, the embarrassment level markedly reduced on both sides. I am sure he was relieved I had said no to going to see *The Broadway Melody*, and not just because he had saved himself ninepence. Like Tamino in *The Magic Flute* he seemed to believe he had undergone some ordeal and emerged with a good pass. I think it crossed both our minds that we could be really good friends so long as we did not have to see each other.

CHAPTER TWELVE

On Sunday morning, whilst I was still getting dressed, I glanced out of my bedroom window and, in the spaces between the quivering leaves, saw Mrs Benyon going down the front path on her way to her day off. Despite the fact that the sun was already blazing out of a cloudless sky, the housekeeper wore a coat and a hat with a wintry look to them, perhaps to advertise that there was nothing in the universe she did not view with deep distrust, not even the sun. She carried, besides her black handbag and an umbrella, a large straw bag whose braided handles she could barely hold together, so crammed was it with – what? Gifts for the friends with whom she proposed to spend the day? What kind of people could possibly be friends with a woman like Mrs Benyon?

It was a mystery, one I lightheartedly engaged myself to solve, so soon as I could get round to it; just as, sooner or later, no hurry, I would solve all the mysteries of Chandos House. It had taken yesterday – my trip into town and my return for the first time to a completely empty house, mine to come to terms with without interruption – to bring home to me how content I was to be Miss Gosse's lodger, even if I didn't get enough to eat. On tiptoe at the mirror I put my tongue out at Mrs Crail, who had intended me to be miserable.

From the moment yesterday when, fagged with the uphill drag from the tram terminus, I had, as instructed, up-ended the flower pot hidden behind the trunk of the quivering tree to get at the front-door key concealed there, I had sensed a heightened awareness on the part of both of us – the house, that is to say, and me. The others out of the way, now we could really get to know each other.

Not that, once inside, and with all its closed doors vulnerable to my curiosity, I rushed to take advantage of my opportunity. The ambivalence of Chandos House was its most powerful attraction, one that I was in no hurry to construe. In St Giles – until, that is, my father, for once keeping himself outrageously to himself, had upped and died – there had been no secrets of any kind; an agreeable existence but, as I was now coming to see, bland: a criminal waste of the excitement with which the world was filled, only waiting for me to key into it.

Miss Gosse and Miss Locke were already having breakfast when I got downstairs. At the dining-room door I almost collided with Miss Locke as she emerged from the kitchen with the tray bearing the teapot, milk jug and hot-water jug.

'Make way for the skivvy!' she cried merrily.

She was wearing a skimpy vest and shorts, and I could tell, by the shine in her eyes and the way the straight line from her forehead to the tip of her nose looked less forbidding than usual, that she was pleased with her appearance – which, to tell the truth, I did not think all that much of. Her legs were too thin, for one thing, too all of a piece, not at all like the legs of the chorus girls in *The Broadway Melody* photographs. There weren't enough curves and, at the top, they were narrow where they should have broadened out, so that it was quite a relief when your eyes got to the shorts, which were made of red-and-white checked gingham, and there wasn't any more leg for you to have to see.

Miss Gosse, for once, was also showing more than I could wish to have revealed for my embarrassed inspection. She was wearing a sleeveless frock that showed the tops of her arms which were veined and lumpy in a peculiar way as if somebody had secreted little pouches of fat here and there underneath the skin. Her left arm was pocked with absolutely enormous vaccination marks, which were no help to her beauty either. The white cotton material of her dress, though, was pretty, with a pattern of green leaves.

I blushed the way I always tended to when confronted with something in any degree troubling. Miss Locke, who had put the tray down on the table for Miss Gosse to do the pouring out, exclaimed delightedly: 'I've shocked her, Lydia! Our little puritan is shocked! Perhaps she thinks schoolmistresses should wear their gowns even for a day at the sea.'

Miss Gosse smiled happily, first at Miss Locke, then at me. 'You know what a tease Miss Locke is,' she observed indulgently, using her favourite phrase. Handing me my tea: 'Especially on holiday. Then there's no holding her!'

She informed me that Miss Malahide and her niece would be calling for them shortly, any minute now, in their Austin Seven. They were all going to drive down to Ormesby for a picnic on the beach, and weren't they lucky to have such a glorious day? 'Do get yourself into the garden for a time,' the kind woman finished, her pleasant, puggy face bright with concern. 'Don't spend the whole day poring over your books.'

Miss Gosse was in the middle of telling me that I would find my midday meal inside the meat safe in the larder when a honking from the road, loud enough for a Rolls let alone an Austin Seven, signalled the arrival of their transport. Immediately Miss Gosse and Miss Locke both got very busy and excited, running about collecting towels and bathing costumes and a canvas windbreak; a basket of strawberries from the kitchen, spoons and fruit bowls and a crock of cream which, as an old hand at picnics from St Giles days, I offered to swathe in several sheets of newspaper so that it wouldn't go sour in the heat.

At last, the honking going non-stop, the two were away down the garden path, trailing towels and full of admonitions, one to the other, about not tilting the strawberries and not spilling the cream. I stood at the front door waving goodbye, feeling like a mother seeing off her children to a party or a scout jamboree. The honking ceased and I shut the door intending – with the same maternal relief, I fancy – a retreat to the dining-room for a second cup of tea to be savoured in blessed peace. Sliced bread being still uninvented, I decided first to run up to my room for the loaf I had hidden in my book box; to bring it down to the kitchen for slicing with Mrs Benyon's bread knife. I would never have a better chance. I might even, greatly daring, light the grill on the gas stove and make myself an extra slice of toast.

I was coming down the stairs with my loaf cradled tenderly in my arms when the front door opened and Miss Locke came into the hall.

'What on earth are you doing with that?' she asked, looking up at me; and then, as if my answer were of no consequence, commanded, 'Put it down, anyway. I came back for the sugar sifter. And you.'

I followed Miss Locke down the path to the front gate unwillingly, my bathing costume under one arm and not knowing what to think – or, rather, concentrating all my strength on not thinking at all for dread of the possibilities thought might suggest to me. The moment we came out into the road I could tell by the faces of the three people waiting in the Austin Seven that I had been right to have qualms. Miss Locke had lied when she told me, as she had, that they had one and all decided that I simply must come too, they wouldn't take no for an answer. They had expected her to come back with the sugar sifter and nothing beside. Apart from anything else, the Austin Seven, open to the elements, was more like an outsize baby carriage than a real car. There was barely room for the four of them, let alone anybody extra, especially the way it was cluttered up with all the things they were taking with them.

I would have run back, cheeks burning, to the sanctuary of Chandos House, only Miss Locke put her arm round my waist, squeezed me so tightly I couldn't possibly have got away without making an exhibition of myself.

'There she was,' Miss Locke announced. 'A waif. Pathetic. I couldn't, in Christian charity, see how we could possibly enjoy our own day, knowing we had left her behind, all alone.'

Miss Malahide, who was at the driving-wheel and wore a straw sunbonnet out of which she peered like a whiskery milkmaid, nodded warmly. 'Quite right, Helen! Poor little thing. Pa kicked the bucket – did she tell you?' Twisting round in her seat: 'Move over, Noreen love – make room! You're only a little one!'

Miss Malahide's niece, who was a small young person with a neat face and body and a neat way of wearing her clothes that made other people (well, me) feel untidy just to look at her, moved over as far as she was able, which was not far. Her face showed neither pleasure nor annoyance, just neatness. In the front passenger's seat Miss Gosse, holding the crock of cream carefully between her knees, looked, not angry, as I had feared, either with Miss Locke or with me, but fussed, as if finding it difficult to rearrange her vision of the day ahead into one that could include me. I wanted to say to her that it wasn't my fault, that I understood perfectly how schoolmistresses, who had to put up with schoolgirls all week long, wouldn't want them tagging along in the weekend. But of course I just stood there looking down at my plimsolls like a half-wit, waiting to be disposed of.

Miss Malahide had a strange way of driving. Like a falcon or a hawk that hovers until it has pinpointed its prey, then drops down upon it in one deadly swoop, she targeted each successive bend in the road: a momentary pause before pressing down the accelerator in a mad rush to round it before any other predator got there first. For the better part of our journey to the coast I had the sensation that whilst the major portion of my anatomy might be a passenger in the Austin Seven, my stomach certainly was not; was far back down the road, struggling in a forlorn attempt to keep up with the rest of me.

Silently, intensely, I prayed to my father to put in a word with God *at once*, to interrupt Him no matter what He was doing, to stop me being sick. In the same moment, so muddled was my reaction to the way the day was turning out, a nasty little demon tucked away in some obscure corner of my being contemplated with glee the havoc I had it in my power to wreak on people who bossed one about so that one didn't know where one was, if anywhere at all. With a perverse pleasure it conjured up visions of green bile and yellow vomit descending impartially on strawberries, towels, Miss Malahide's picnic hamper, neat Noreen's neat frock and most of all, most of all, Miss Locke's bare legs and gingham shorts. If my stomach, despairing, had not by then been left abandoned by the roadside a good mile back, I could easily have made it happen out of my own imagining.

Fortunately, apart from Miss Malahide's occasional shouts at some passing motorist and Miss Gosse's involuntary gasps when, as happened every now and again, disaster threatened to overwhelm us, there was no conversation. One was not, thank God, in addition to everything else, expected to shine. The wind we created with our passing filled the little vehicle, possessed it, and us along with it. Fields and farmhouses swished past, yielding place to marshes and windmills, all equally unreal. As we neared the coast the wind blew even stronger and louder, joining airs already waiting there. The trees alongside the roadside verges no longer spread their shade impartially. They all leaned one way, away from the east wind.

Miss Malahide screamed, 'I smell salt!' and slammed her foot down on the accelerator to celebrate it. We all – even Noreen What's-her-name – smiled at each other and took deep breaths as if we had accomplished something. Miss Locke who, throughout the journey, had kept her right arm extended behind my neck along the folded car hood, squeezed my shoulder, heaven knew why. Miss Gosse exclaimed with heartfelt gratitude: 'The sea!'

CHAPTER THIRTEEN

We came to the sea by a narrow lane which ended at a cliff edge topped with a few wooden huts which could have done with a lick of paint. Three or four brick cottages on the other side of the lane, a way down to the beach that was more a ladder than a stair, and that was it: not a soul to be seen on the wide expanse of sand, only a mongrel dog barking at the waves. When Miss Locke, stretching her long legs thankfully, came up to me as I stood looking down at the view and asked, 'Well? Wasn't it clever of me? Aren't you glad you came?' I hardly knew what to say.

The truth was that I didn't like the sea at all, as such. Hated it, in fact. It was a desert, worse than the Sahara which at least had oases: no flowers, no trees, only a killing wetness hammering at the shore with a manic persistence that must one day achieve its object – and then goodbye, lovely land! On the other hand, I adored what went with the sea – any sea, even the sea at Yarmouth edged with piers and cockle-stalls and weighing machines: an access of surprise and freedom, of certainty that beyond the seeming finality of the horizon there was another one waiting, and another, and so on ad infinitum.

'Yes,' I answered her at last. 'Very glad.'

I approved of the way Miss Locke helped Miss Gosse down the ladder, going ahead and, with hands on the ankles, guiding the stunted legs towards the next hold. Miss Gosse went down backwards, her body to the cliff face, so that I couldn't see her expression, if she was enjoying it or not; only the top of her black hair which, seen from an unusual perspective, had more white in it than I had realized. Miss Malahide, also watching, remarked to her niece, 'Let that be a lesson to you, dearie!' but immediately, disdaining assistance, lowering herself with ponderous assurance from rung to rung. Pausing in her progress, she tilted her head back to shout: 'You two young 'uns can bring the stuff down – and make it snappy, will you? I want a swim before we eat and I'm famished!'

Noreen and I quite enjoyed getting everything out of the Austin Seven and down to the beach – at least I did, and I believe she did too, because she began to giggle, which I had never heard her do up to that moment; to act younger, to be the girl she looked under all the neatness. She stopped looking down her nose at me. We almost became friends.

Partly, I'm afraid that our pleasure in our task was not very nice, based as it was on a kind of showing-off, a celebration of our youth for those old fuddy-duddies down below to eye and envy. How easy it was for *us*, we demonstrated, to run up and down like the angels of God on Jacob's ladder ascending and descending, and *they* hadn't had to carry picnic hampers and crocks of cream into the bargain.

Down on the sands Miss Gosse said that she would stay and guard our possessions.

'Who were you expecting?' boomed Miss Malahide, looking meaningfully to right and left along the deserted beach. 'Man Friday?'

'We don't want that dog nosing round our food.' But I thought that perhaps the real reason was that, with her legs, Miss Gosse did not want me to see her in a bathing costume. At Chandos House, even in a dressing-gown, she always took care, going to or from the bathroom, that we did not meet on the landing. Out of the corner of my eye I would see her door opening a fraction as she waited for me to pass.

When Noreen announced that she wasn't going swimming either; in fact, couldn't – 'You know –' she said, casting down her eyes – nobody made any comment, and I decided it must be because she did not want to risk messing up her hair which waved and curled in a fancy way I did not think could possibly be natural. Miss Malahide removed her sunbonnet and the long loose garment she was dressed in. Underneath she already had on her bathing costume which was grey with a full skirt and a string round the neck which she hauled on like a fisherman pulling in his nets and knotted, winching her large breasts into a solid mass without any division showing in the middle. Miss Locke's bathing costume was scarlet, very chic, with a diving girl embroidered on one corner of its half-skirt. She laid it out on the sand whilst she undid the button at the waistband of her shorts.

'Helen!' cried Miss Gosse. But it was too late. Miss Locke slipped off her shorts and panties and stood there with absolutely nothing on down below, before nonchalantly, without haste, poking her feet through the leg holes of the bathing costume and pulling it up as far as her belly button, where she desisted for as long as it took her to take off her vest. Her breasts were so small they hardly seemed to belong to a grown woman. It was difficult to believe they belonged to the same category of anatomy as the big bump on the front of Miss Malahide.

With your eyes screwed up against the strong light Miss Locke looked very beautiful – slender body, curly cropped head, the small ears showing; one of those dancing figures made of some kind of silvery bronze that you sometimes saw in the windows of posh jewellers. Only if you made the effort, kept your eyes open sun or no sun, could you see that it wasn't true, an optical illusion. Whatever she might have been in the past, she wasn't young, she wasn't beautiful any more.

I didn't know where to look when she stood there, naked from the waist down. It wasn't behaviour I was used to. Except that of course I did look and was amazed. Miss Locke's hair – the hair on her head, that is to say – was light brown, the colour that hair which has been blond when you were a child often turns when you grow up: but the hair between her legs was black, and besides, there was so much of it! My face must have been at least as red as her red bathing costume.

'Look at Sylvia!' Miss Locke pointed mockingly. 'I've shocked her again. Have you ever known anyone shock so easily?'

The sea was very calm except at the edges where it had worked itself up into its usual pointless lather. Past the froth but still safely in my depth, I swam sedately to and fro doing the breast stroke, the only stroke I knew: not very far in each direction either, for I was not a good swimmer. I was quite unable to understand the ecstasy with which some swimmers launched themselves into the briny, as if suddenly they had found everything in life they had been looking for.

Miss Locke was one of those. What is more, she could do the crawl, which in those days not a lot of females knew how to do. She positively burrowed through the water, her flashing arms and legs diminishing in the distance. She made for the open sea as if she meant never to come back.

Miss Malahide remarked calmly, 'Hope she's got enough petrol for the return journey.' The art mistress herself did no swimming at all; stood in water up to her chest and dipped herself in and out of it, submerging completely, head and all. As she rose from each immersion, the sea cascading off her grey costume, her grey hair and her grey-whiskery face, she looked very like one of the seals which, at Blakeney Point, further up the coast, often bobbed up out of curiosity to look at the people in the boats going out to the bird sanctuary.

Having proved to my own satisfaction, as well as to that of anybody who might be watching, that I knew how to swim – (every time I went into the water after an interval I found myself assailed by a little demon of doubt asking, *had I remembered since last time how it was done?*) – I rearranged myself and floated on my back, the only thing about bathing I actually enjoyed. Floating on a sunny day, the water warm, the light intense, always made me feel sleepy, made me wonder whether, if I let myself fall asleep, would I go on floating until I woke up again, or would the sea, taking advantage of my innocent trust in its good intentions, pour itself into my mouth and up my nose and drown me dreaming, in which case, would the dream go on for ever?

I was pondering the possibilities when I found myself suddenly lifted from the water, almost completely out of it, by sinewy arms and thin fingers that dug hard into my skinny flesh before setting me down on my feet.

'Call that swimming?' Miss Locke inquired laughingly.

With none of the splashy bravura of her departure, she had come back from the far reaches of the ocean to play a silly trick on me and disturb, as so often, my composure. 'Lydia's waving like mad,' she said. 'She's terrified the cream will go off.'

I was too taken aback to reply, and followed silently out of the water. Miss Malahide was already trudging up the beach to the picnic.

At the water's edge Miss Locke cried: 'Race you to the dunes!' and set off as she spoke, her long legs going like pistons.

It was so beastly unfair, so cheating not even to have said 'One – two – three – *off*!' so that we could at least have started on equal terms that, powered by my burning sense of injustice, I actually overtook her, even holding my lead above the high-tide mark where the lovely firm wet sand gave way to powdery stuff that dragged you down and took away your strength. As I reached the nearest dune, the undisputed victor exulting in her victory, Miss Locke at my heels reached forward, grabbed at my bathing suit; sent me sprawling, herself landing on top of me.

The spiky marram grass that grew on the dunes scratching my chest, her panting body enveloping me – I was mortified! I could feel the sand plastering my wet bathing suit and the front of my legs and sifting through my hair. I had felt so peaceful out there floating in the sea, and so clean. The Chandos House geyser was so chugging and threatening that I had never enjoyed what one could call a proper bath since going there – only a frenzied soaping and rinsing before flinging myself out again, thankful to have escaped once more from the jaws of death. And now this ghastly woman – what a weight she was, a ton of bricks pressing down on me – had messed me up all over again.

'Get off me!' I shouted, before realizing the enormity of what I had said, and modulating to a tone more nearly proper when addressing one of your schoolmistresses. 'Please get off, Miss Locke. You're hurting.'

She sent me back to the sea to wash off the sand, which I did, more or less. I hadn't the courage to do as I had seen Miss Malahide do – put my head completely under water. Although the sun was shining with undiminished ardour the sea seemed to have become colder. I came out of it shivering, glad to outpace the last salt dribble that pursued me up the beach before returning sulkily to the rest of its kind. As I trailed back up the sands to rejoin my companions – not the right word: how could *teachers* ever be companions? – I wished that Miss Locke had given me time, back at Chandos House, to collect a towel before setting out. Thanks to her, I would have to sit in my school bathing suit, baggy old cotton with an edging of faded yellow – the colour of my house, Sewell – round the neck and armholes, until I was dry enough to put on my clothes again. True, I was only a child and it didn't matter that I hadn't a lovely red costume with an embroidered diving girl on it. It didn't matter how I looked.

But it did.

Miss Malahide, I could see as I neared the little party, was already back in her long sack or whatever it was, the grey bathing suit spread out on a towel nearby. Had she got nothing on underneath? I don't know why the thought of Miss Malahide knickerless should have bothered me, but it did. I hoped, for her sake as much as mine, that she had brought spare knickers with her even though, as anyone could see, she had not thought to bring along a brassiere to keep her big bosom where it belonged. I was surprised that Noreen, so neat, had not packed extra undies for her aunt. She could have put them in the picnic hamper where they could have helped to keep the crockery from rattling.

At my approach Miss Gosse pulled out from underneath her the towel she had been sitting on. It was still warm from her bottom as she handed it to me with a very nice smile. 'We don't want you coming down with a cold,' she said.

I took the towel, feeling rather weepy: not just, or even mainly, on account of her kindness, but because I had caught sight of the picnic. Noreen, I guessed it was, from the neat way it was done, had set out the food and the plates and cutlery on a pretty cloth patterned with daisies which had napkins to match. After a week of Chandos House fare, the sheer generosity of the spread on offer made me feel emotional.

There were thick slices of roast beef, any single one of which would have made three good Chandos House portions; bowls of assorted salads, rolls with poppy seeds on top, hunks of cheese, a bottle of wine wrapped round with a white cloth. Even Miss Gosse and Miss Locke, their normal appetites presumably augmented by the sea air, put away as much as anyone. I ate and ate and wished passionately that Mrs Crail had thought to suggest that I lodge with Miss Malahide instead of with Miss Gosse and Miss Locke. The art mistress watched benevolently, heaped second and third helpings on to my plate. Said to the others: 'Don't you love to see youngsters enjoying their grub?'

I had something of everything – even, at Miss Malahide's insistence – the wine. 'She has to start some time,' she countered when Miss Gosse looked anxious. Miss Gosse steadfastly refused to drink any wine herself, her father, as she explained, having signed the pledge on her behalf when she was seven years old.

'That's a pa for you,' was Miss Malahide's comment. 'Mine never let me have a drop either, but that was only so there'd be more for him, the old sot!'

When, with a certain hauteur, I announced that I had already tasted wine; that at home on special occasions I was often given a little port and some sponge fingers to dip into it, the art mistress snorted: 'What way is that to develop a palate!'

Miss Malahide's wine was not sweet at all, and although I pretended it was lovely, actually I did not care for it one bit, although I drank a glass and a half because I was thirsty. After the strawberries and cream I fell fast asleep until Miss Locke woke me up saying it was time to start for home. I discovered to my surprise that I had been sleeping with my head in her lap.

I was also surprised to find that I had been asleep at all, something that had never happened to me in the daytime since I was a baby. Miss Locke said: 'It must have been the cream. It was definitely off.' At which everybody laughed, including Miss Gosse who was looking a little peaky, as if she had had too much sun.

CHAPTER FOURTEEN

That night I woke up angry, which puzzled me because, all in all, it had been a lovely day – more importantly, a lively one: *I had lived*. I awoke to find the bedroom bright with the risen moon. Instead of silhouetting themselves against its shining, as you might have expected, the quivering leaves had become semi-transparent, their veins a delicate tracery on a background of gauze.

I awoke in no mood to appreciate the artistry of silvery greenery. Discomfort, not moonshine, was what had brought me awake. My hair was full of sand. I put my hand in the hollow of the pillow where my head had rested and, with a shudder of repulsion, touched a little deposit of grit diversified with some sharp-edged fragments which – having turned my torch on them – I was able to identify as bits of cockleshell.

I absolutely couldn't stand it! I hated Miss Locke for having pushed me over on the dunes, for filling my hair with the sea's rubbish. All week, even without her silly tricks, my hair had been becoming a problem, one of those things to which, when I came to live at Chandos House, nobody whose business it was to think about such things had given a thought. How was I to get my hair washed? At home, Maud had washed it twice a week, to the invariable accompaniment of my non-stop threnody that the water was too hot, too cold, too wet, too dry; that the lather was in my eyes, my ears, my nose, my socks – a thoroughly enjoyable performance made the more explicit by the loveliness of clean, light-floating hair which was the end product. But who was to wash my hair at Chandos House? Mrs Benyon? My scalp crawled at the very thought of those masterful fingers kneading my poor little skull. I could not possibly ask the mistresses; and Mr Johnson, the hairdresser in Dove Street who, so long as I lived in St Giles, had cut my hair once a month, charged one-and-sixpence for a shampoo – I had seen it on his list of prices. I had, in fact, toyed with the idea of doing it myself; had even, once, for a pregnant moment, stood poised on the brink in the bathroom with my cake of soap in one hand and my daily can of hot water in the other, only to be deterred by the certainty that one can wasn't nearly enough to get all the soap out, especially making due allowance for what I should undoubtedly slosh on to the bathroom floor.

I ran my hand through my hair and found sand deposited between my fingers. Outside the window the moon and the leaves quivered with the utter awfulness of it. I picked up my torch and my matches and crept along the landing, past the closed doors, to the bathroom. It had to be done. I was going to wash my hair in the Chandos House bath.

What made this a desperate and illicit undertaking was that I still had not been initiated into the mysteries of lighting the bathroom geyser, and had been in no hurry to press for enlightenment. Even when Mrs Benyon lit the thing on my behalf there was always a lancing of flame and a gurgling bang that sent me cowering against the woodwork. Now I encouraged myself with the thought that the housekeeper probably made the geyser act that way on purpose, to pay me out for having made her climb the stairs. I wasn't a child. In the chemistry lab I used a Bunsen burner to heat up dangerous substances without turning a hair. If I couldn't light a simple thing like a geyser, I didn't know who could.

Having brought my torch with me, I decided not to light the gas mantle, though that at least was a manoeuvre in which I had become well practised. The geyser was another thing. Brooding and metallic, it even had a look of Mrs Benyon. I found it perfectly possible to envisage that the housekeeper too, inside her, carried hidden fire and would go off with a bang if you knew which tap to turn. I took a deep breath, did – as I thought – all the things Mrs Benyon did when lighting the contraption, and gingerly, as one proffering a bone to a doubtfully friendly dog, applied a lighted match.

There was a gentle *plop!* and then the match went out.

I struck another and tried again. Again the *plop!*, this time sounding distinctly apologetic as if the apparatus truly regretted having to disoblige, before the match was once more extinguished. Five matches on, the geyser still not doing its stuff, I began to feel puzzled, not to say woozy. It came to me without any particular feeling of alarm that the bathroom was full of gas and here was I, so good at chemistry, cheerfully striking match after match in the miasma, not the cleverest thing in the world to do.

I bent over the geyser to turn it off. I could not do it. Any bits that moved, I turned them to the left, I turned them to the right. It made no difference. The gas continued to flow into the room.

Vaguely aware that something needed to be done fast, I went towards the window. I never made it. Half-way there, I fell over Miss Gosse's mahogany and brass towel rail which, in turn, fell over Miss Locke's weighing machine. As for myself, having once fallen it seemed altogether too much of a fag to get to my feet again: but the resultant noise must have been sufficient to penetrate those closed doors on the landing because the next thing I remember was my head, the terminal of my stomach, stuck out of the bathroom window being sick on to the marigolds down below. All that lovely picnic!

I heard Miss Gosse's voice: 'I've damped a towel. Let me wipe her face.' How kind she sounded, and how unkind Miss Locke when she exclaimed: 'The little fool, she must have been completely blotto! What did she think she was doing? She could have blown us all up.'

'My hair's full of sand!' I shouted, called rudely back to the cares of the world. Tears ran down my face at such a rate that, for a moment, I thought Miss Gosse must have soaked her towel instead of wringing it out, as she had said. Adding, to myself only, of course: 'And I'm only sorry I didn't!'

Miss Locke washed my hair. Washed it with some shampoo that smelled of lemons. Her long, strong fingers whipped up such a lather I felt like a lemon meringue pie. Heavenly. Miss Gosse stood fussing somewhere in the background wondering whether she ought not to get dressed and go and wake up the doctor down the road despite the lateness of the hour. 'After all, we are responsible for the child –'

'Nonsense!' was the robust rejoinder. 'The child's old enough to be responsible for herself – and if she isn't, it's her funeral. If you want to be of help, bring me water for the rinsing.'

Whilst Miss Locke rinsed the shampoo out of my hair and Miss Gosse trotted obediently to and from a geyser now acting docile as a lamb, I could not help feeling important, having two mistresses dancing attendance on me as if they were mere serving wenches and I a princess. It was a pity there was nobody I could tell about it. I knew, in some obscure way, that it wasn't something to talk about in school, however avidly the girls of IIIa would have gobbled up such juicy gossip. If I wrote to my mother, all she would do was get herself in a state about the gas. People she had known in the Great War had got themselves gassed and never been the same again, so she said, though probably not from a bathroom geyser.

'Clean as a whistle!' Miss Locke pronounced at last. She told Miss Gosse to turn off the geyser and go to bed. She herself took a towel and rubbed my head until I felt my head coming off, but it was lovely just the same. Miss Gosse observed in a plaintive voice that it was very late, whereupon Miss Locke announced her intention of seeing me safely into bed – 'and then we can all get some sleep, thank heaven!'

In my bedroom Miss Locke sat me down on the bed and, kneeling beside me, combed my hair for me, parting it in the middle with a good deal more regard for accuracy than I ever bothered with myself, and teasing out the tangles with unexpected gentleness. Probably because there were still some vestigial whiffs of gas floating about inside me looking for the way out, I felt floppy and foolish, close to sleep and yet not close. I could see the aspen leaves goggling in at the window as if wondering what on earth was up, and I mouthed silently, so that Miss Locke shouldn't hear, 'I'll tell you all about it in the morning.'

When my hair was done, Miss Locke pulled back the covers and helped me into bed, which I didn't need, but there! It was pure luxury. I had a feeling she might easily have curtseyed before withdrawing if Miss Gosse had not called out from the landing just then to repeat that it was really very late indeed.

'Just finished getting our invalid to beddy-byes!' Miss Locke called back. 'Just coming!' Having tucked me in, she bent over and asked, in a different kind of voice, 'How would you like me to wash your hair for you every week?'

A picture of Mr Johnson's price list with 1s 6d on it for a shampoo flashing instantly through my mind, I would surely have answered an eager 'Yes please!' if her face hadn't been so close. It made me feel uncomfortable, her face so close; so instead of saying anything I shut my eyes and pretended I had just that moment fallen asleep. One-and-six or no one-and-six, it was something that needed thinking over.

Miss Locke kissed me, whispered 'Good-night!' and went out of the room, shutting the door softly behind her. I could hear her voice and Miss Gosse's retreating down the landing: the sound, not what was said. I settled down to sleep clean-haired and cosy, not thinking of anything much except that Miss Locke ought to know better than to kiss people full on the lips the way she had kissed me. It not only made you feel uncomfortable. That way you could catch germs.

But not thinking much about that either.

CHAPTER FIFTEEN

I came down to breakfast next morning to discover that I was
not to go to school that day. Since my mirror, a bare minute
earlier, had given back the reflection of a face tanned by sun
and sea and looking healthier than it had for months, I took the
decision as a schoolteacher's weird idea of punishment for my
contretemps with the geyser. What could be worse, ho, ho, than a
day deprived of lovely school?

I did Miss Gosse an injustice. Her little pug face creased with
earnestness, she told me that, her conscience troubling her, early
in the day as it was she had already been down to the telephone
box at the crossroads to let Dr Parfitt – whose number my
mother had left with her against emergencies – into the details
of what she delicately termed my little mishap. Did he think
he ought to pay a call if only to satisfy all concerned that no
permanent damage had been done?

Had I known beforehand what she intended I could have
saved my landlady the trouble. Knowing Dr Parfitt for the lazy
old booby he was, and greedy with it, I could have told her in
advance what his reply would be to the suggestion that he get
himself all the way from St Giles to the Wroxham Road solely to

examine one uneconomic child, sole remnant of a family which, one way and another, had removed itself from his sheltering wings, never to be billed by him again. So far from harm, the good doctor had asserted, the gas, so long as it had stopped short of actually killing me, could have done nothing but good. 'Flushes out the tubes,' were his words apparently, followed by a request to be told the make of the geyser. Dear Dr Parfitt, just the same! As was his wont he had concluded the consultation with the suggestion that I be kept at home for the day just in case. Perhaps he was not such a booby after all, a day away from school curing many infant disorders.

Miss Gosse said consolingly: 'You'll be able to catch up with the work you weren't able to do yesterday.'

'So long as you don't get under my feet,' warned Mrs Benyon, after the two schoolmistresses had departed. 'Monday's my cleaning day. I've got my work to do.'

I replied that I was going to go for a little walk to get a breath of fresh air, after which I would happily settle down to my studies in whatever part of the house best suited her convenience.

The housekeeper looked at me with somewhat more interest than usual.

'Nearly did for yourself last night, from what I hear.'

I said that it wasn't nearly as bad as all that.

'Hubby of a friend of mine,' Mrs Benyon said, in the nearest we had ever come to conversation, 'put his head in the gas oven, and it was a funny thing. Never been much to look at, pasty-faced, constipation was his trouble, but in his coffin, blow me if he wasn't rosy as an apple. Could've gone on the stage looking like that.

His lips were that red!' Scanning my face with one of her marble stares, in a vain search for some sign of rose-tipped beauty: 'Tha's what gas does to you. First turns you blue an' then rosy.'

'I don't think I even got to the blue stage,' I said apologetically. 'Doesn't look like it.' Mrs Benyon stumped off to the kitchen with the breakfast things, leaving me unsurprised to learn that the hubbies of her friends put their heads into gas ovens. It was only to be expected.

I went upstairs to my room to get my loaf of bread and the buns out from under the bed, covering them up with my blazer, draped with careful negligence over one arm. What with the heat and not being eaten after all because of the picnic, they had turned out to be an unwise purchase. Even with the window open I could smell a fermented smell hanging about the room, not unpleasant exactly but one that would be bound to lead Mrs Benyon to the book box like a bloodhound to blood.

So as to be sure of not running into her whilst thus burdened, I went the long way round to the field at the rear of the house; out of the front door, down to the crossroads, turn right into the Catton Road until I came to the back path. To my surprise, the rusty old white van was again parked in the opening, but this time sufficiently to one side for there to be plenty of room to squeeze by. Of the driver there was no sign, except that I could hear something going on at the back of the van. I edged through the space and there he was, smiling like last time, even more unshaven, but with all his teeth in place! Knowing I possessed an exceptionally good memory, this last so took me aback that I said – rudely, I'm afraid – 'What happened to your teeth? You had two missing last time.'

Fortunately the man took no offence; smiled even wider. 'That were on account of I didn't know I was goin' to run into a little lady, did I? Today I weren't taking no chances.' Having said which, he put some fingers into his mouth and prised out two false teeth, which he held out on the palm of his hand for my inspection. 'Beauties, aren't they?'

Little prig that I was, I observed severely: 'I suppose you ate too many sweets as a child.'

'No such luck,' returned the man, still taking no offence, thank goodness. He seemed really nice. He put his teeth back again and wiped his slimy fingers on the front of the khaki shirt he was wearing. 'Bit of an argy-bargy arter closing time, tha's all it were.'

When I said that I was sorry to hear it, he assured me that I had no reason to be: the new teeth were in every way an improvement upon the old. We parted with mutual goodwill, he finishing off the job he had been doing when I arrived, which was to tie up the back doors of the van with string, there being no handles; I continuing on my way to Bagshaw, seeing no reason for letting on that I had seen what was inside.

Bagshaw was not in a good mood. (I had begun to wonder if he ever was.) He ate the buns and the bread more with the air of one doing a favour than being done one. He seemed particularly out of sorts. I didn't blame him. It must be hard, I felt, on a gorgeous summer day to find yourself a donkey mooching about a field when the world outside was overflowing with so many more interesting things to do and to be.

I decided not to try the gate into the garden, but returned to Chandos House by the way I had come. The white van had gone. In the front hall Mrs Benyon, folded in half like an airing mattress, was poking a long-handled brush about under the hallstand. It was always a surprise to find that she could bend at all. You would never have guessed from the look of her.

She straightened up and told me to take my books into the drawing-room because that was the only room in the house which was 'done', something I was glad to do as I had not seen the drawing-room until then. When I went inside I saw that it was not only 'done' but done for. Dark despite the bright day, it was more like a mortuary chapel than a salon for polite conversation, the brown walls, the mantelpiece and every available ledge covered with paintings and photographs of a man who had to be Miss Gosse's father. In some of the pictures he was a young man, with moustaches which had been twiddled at the ends: in others he was white-haired with a beard that looked like a dishcloth, one it was time to throw away and get a new one. Only the eyes told you that the young man and the old man were the same person – boot-button eyes like Miss Gosse's, but whereas Miss Gosse's eyes were limpid and trustful, her father's looked like boot buttons and nothing beside. There were no pictures of anybody else, nor of Mr Gosse with anybody, not even with a funny little girl with short legs who would have been Miss Gosse when she was a child. No woman who might have been Miss Gosse's mother.

It was quite a disappointment that, despite all the pictures, Miss Gosse's father did not look anything special. His clothes, dark and heavy, were more interesting than the face which peeped out from the top of his stiff white collar for all the world like one of those big Easter eggs on which, for no extra money, confectioners write in white icing the name of your choice. I pulled up one of the horsehair-covered dining-chairs to the big mahogany table and spread out my work in a businesslike way, but it was hard to concentrate with those Easter eggs popping up all over the place. They reminded me that, as usual, I was hungry, so I ran upstairs and fished one of my two whipped cream walnuts out of my book box. I wrapped it in a handkerchief because the heat had melted it a little and also because I did not want to risk running into Mrs Benyon on the way down.

On second thoughts, I fished out the second whipped cream walnut as well, and went out into the garden to give it to Mr Betts.

Mr Betts was picking peas. His knobby face crinkled in a smile at the sight of me, even though his first words were: 'That there Grecian Vase of yours, gal, it must have had a crack in it. Last heard of, she were still running.'

All the same, and despite my renewed protestations that I really did not think I possessed any particular gift as a tipster, he stopped picking and led me over to the seat, where I could see the pink sports paper sticking out of his jacket pocket. I presented him with the whipped cream walnut, which he sat comfortably licking, as if it had been an ice-cream, whilst at his behest I ran my eye over the lists of runners. I had never seen anybody eat a whipped cream walnut like that before, and I found it difficult to keep my mind on my task. It had, I could see, the advantage of making the whipped cream walnut last twice as long as usual, assuming one had the patience or the self-control to restrain one's greed, the unbridled loosing of which was itself part of the pleasure. But how on earth was one expected to deal with the cream filling once the restraining chocolate walls had dissolved into gooey oblivion?

Mr Betts, who was making a right mess of himself, urged: 'Get on with it! I haven't got all day!'

In the end I chose a horse called Clair de Lune, the mere sight of whose name in print was enough to set up resonances in my fingertips, but did not affect Mr Betts in the same way. He wiped his hands on his trousers and took the paper back from me, frowning.

'Debussy,' I explained helpfully.

'Never heard o' him. Who else he train? Thought you didn't know nothing about horses.'

'I don't. Debussy's a composer. "Clair de Lune" is a piece of music.'

'What you on about?' The gardener studied the list again before commenting disparagingly, 'Frenchies.'

'Where you reckon I got that lot; then?'

Mr Betts was certainly very bow-legged, a condition he seemed less inclined to assign to heredity than to the circumstances of his former employment. It appeared that, before becoming a gardener, he had been – grudgingly, because he couldn't abide horses – a stable lad at Newmarket, like his ma's pa and grandpa before him. The day after his grandpa, who had lived with them, kicked the bucket, so he declared, he had bunged his old ma into an old-age home and caught the next bus to Norwich, shaking the dust of his native town from his feet for ever.

'Couldn't you have stayed and become a gardener in Newmarket?' I asked, shaken by the thought of his bunged old ma. But Mr Betts dismissed the suggestion out of hand.

'Newmarket!' he echoed. 'The village idiot could be a gardener in Newmarket!'

The town, I gathered, thanks to all those bloody horses, laboured under the dire handicap of too much muck. It was drowning in it: you could smell it down the road ten miles off. For a gardener worthy of the name there was no challenge: anything grew there, from begonias to banyan trees. 'One o' them four-legged shitters let fly, you go for a brush an' pan to sweep it up, an' by the time you get back blow me if there in't a dozen half-hardy annuals growing out of it, ready for transplanting.'

Having subtler ends in view, I offered, since it was a French horse, to forgo my commission if Clair de Lune won, but Mr Betts said absolutely no. Business was business, he warned me, and don't you ever go forgetting it. Living as I did with two schoolteachers, ladies of education, I could be expected to pick up a lot in the way of learning, one way and another, but – he would lay a fiver on it – nothing so helpful to me in later life as those three words.

He hoped I had taken notice.

'Business is business,' I repeated happily, my conscience appeased. I could have hugged him.

On Tuesday afternoon I wheeled my bicycle out of the school drive to find my brother Alfred waiting by the gate. It seemed a long time since I had seen him last, longer than it actually was, and I think he must have felt the same because we embraced with the mixture of pleasure and embarrassment common to people who have not set eyes on each other for ages and think they ought to have. He even looked different – but no: it was the perspective which had altered. From being central to my existence he had moved to the periphery where outlines tended to merge with the surrounding scenery. He said that he had decided to come on the spur of the moment, leaving the telephone ringing and his work undone, out of a sudden need to see with his own eyes that I was all right. I was very touched even as, unbidden, there flickered through my subconscious the hope that he wouldn't stay too long. I wanted my tea.

Alfred had driven to the school in the tub of a car which belonged to his future father-in-law. The Morris Oxford, I was told, was sold – gone to a good home, I was assured. But as to the sports car which was to have replaced it – the frown mark between my brother's blue eyes deepened. He began to speak, rapidly, like one who has a lot to say and little time to say it in. As he spoke, the distance between us began to diminish, my heart to throb with the old affection, augmented with a new pride in my own worth. My father was dead, the rest of the family in London. In all Norwich there was no one else to talk to, really talk to: and so my grown-up brother had come to confide in me.

He had bought a plot of land in Cecil Road on the edge of the city and the builders were going to build on it the house he and Phyllis would live in when they were married. It was, he didn't mind telling me, going to cost a packet. 'I don't suppose I'll see much change out of £1,000,' my brother said, as much appalled as exhilarated by the prospect. Unlike me, who had been living for more than a week at Chandos House, it was the first time he had had to think seriously about money. I knew exactly how he felt. It was, after all, only a case of Mr Johnson and his 1s 6d shampoos writ large.

'What do you think, Sylvia? Do you think I'm biting off more than I can chew?'

The metaphor was unfortunate. Reminded of the yawning abyss inside me, I longed to be home at Chandos House chewing my bread and butter. Today might just be one of those glorious days when Mrs Benyon unaccountably lost count and piled the serving dish with more slices than it could comfortably hold. If I hadn't been so hungry I might possibly, looking all the time as if butter wouldn't melt in my mouth, have convinced Alfred that as between a wife and a thousand-pound house on the one hand and a snazzy sports car on the other, the car was infinitely the better buy. But no: I had outgrown such childish jealousies.

Instead, I overflowed with enthusiasm; asked all about the house, how many bedrooms would it have, would there be a garage, what kind of flowers would they grow in the garden, until the frown between my brother's eyes erased itself. Being good at drawing, he found an old envelope in his jacket pocket on which to sketch the front elevation and the back; a sundial and a lily pool and a summerhouse with a roof like a pagoda –

'And a steeple and weathercock!' I added.

How we laughed! Just like the old days.

'How are you off for money?' Alfred wanted to know. I observed with a truly maternal satisfaction that he was feeling much better for our conversation, his old generous self once more.

'Fine!' I answered nevertheless. How could I possibly ask someone committed to the outlay of £1,000 for the wherewithal to buy shampoos and whipped cream walnuts? 'I've got plenty!'

We parted fondly, our intimacy not only re-established, but deepened; and I cycled home famished but full of beans, confirmed in the absolute rightness of my plan to blackmail Mr Betts.

When, on Wednesday, straight after tea and before I weakened, I went down the garden, red-faced, heart beating faster than was comfortable, to let Mr Betts know that, going by the back way to feed Bagshaw, I had caught sight of lettuces and strawberries and goodness only knew what else in the back of the white van, and that as a consequence I was very sorry but I was going to have to blackmail him, his answer was not what I had expected.

'Crikey!' he exclaimed. 'Not the two of you!' And when I stood stupid, not understanding: 'The Bunion – the Lady of Shallotts, who else? The Greta Garbo of the servants' hall. First her, now you!'

'I didn't know she –'

'Nothing goes on in this house she don't know about and takes her cut out of. You ought to know that by now! If I got ter pay all me profit out in hush-money, I might as well turn it in, call it a day. Not worth the blooming candle!' Despite the emphasis with which he spoke, Mr Betts did not sound really angry. He looked at me with a humorous disbelief. 'Too shy to speak up fer a second helping, but not too shy to put the screws on me like a ruddy pro! An' looking such a little lady, too!'

That put my back up.

'And you don't look like a thief, but you are!'

'Name callin's never goin' to get us nowhere.' The gardener, who had been tying up some lupins which had flopped over, stopped doing it; went over to the bench where his jacket was lying, fished his pipe out of the pocket and sat sucking it, empty and unlit, like a baby. He remarked mildly, as if we were in the middle of a perfectly ordinary conversation: 'That French horse you picked came in second. Didn't back her both ways, but tha's my funeral. You're still entitled to yer commission.'

I burst out that I didn't want his commission; that I didn't want to go on picking out horses when I knew nothing whatever about them and couldn't be sure if they'd win or if they'd lose. What I wanted, if I wasn't to die of starvation and get nits in my hair into the bargain, was a regular source of income I could rely on.

Mr Betts thereupon offered to lend me some money, but I replied that I would be grown up before I could pay it back, if then, and besides, my father had taught me that I must never on any account allow myself to get into debt. The gardener sucked at his pipe, then gave it as his opinion that it was a mistake to let dead people go on telling you what to do. Enough was enough. They had had their turn and now ought to lie quietly in their graves, letting people get on with things in their own way.

This upset me, because he seemed to be getting at my father, who wasn't, properly speaking, in his grave at all, but in heaven. It made me cruel.

'You're an old man,' I pointed out. 'If I borrow some money from you, by the time I can pay it back you'll be dead yourself.'

'More fool me, then,' said Mr Betts.

The conversation was not going at all according to the scenario I had rehearsed so often beforehand. Planning it in my mind, everything falling out the way I intended it to fall, I had been entranced to discover how easy crime was. No wonder so many people went in for it.

'The trouble wi' you is –' Mr Betts took his pipe out of his mouth and waggled it at me – 'you don't think things through. As I understand it – right? – if I don't pay up on demand you'll up an' tell Miss Gosse I bin on the fiddle?'

'Right!' I agreed between clenched teeth, feeling terrible to hear my threat put into words.

'But where'll that get you? How'll you be better off? I'll get the push sure enough, but you won't be any nearer a steady income. New bloke gets taken on, stands to reason Miss G.'ll be watching him like a hawk arter what's happened. Ten to one she'll decide it's time to ferget how the garden was in her pa's day and have the whole vegetable plot put down to grass. Get herself a goat, maybe, to keep it down. An' that'll make two of 'em on the premises!'

Aggrieved by the insult, I stopped having qualms. The gardener was simply not playing the part I had allotted to him in the drama. It had never occurred to me that a blackmailer's victim might refuse to be blackmailed. It did not seem fair.

I played the trump card Mr Betts himself had put into my hand. 'You said yourself you're paying Mrs Benyon not to say anything.

Why her and not me?'

'Because *she* scares the living daylights out of me,' Mr Betts explained. 'And you're such a dear little gal, I don't think.'

'Oh!'

I knew that I wasn't a dear little gal. I knew that I wasn't a child and I wasn't a grown-up either, something between the two that there wasn't a word for. I knew I was too old to cry like a child, but like a child I did, wailing that I couldn't possibly manage on a shilling a week with biscuits alone costing sixpence for half a pound and that was only the plain sorts, goodness only knew how much you had to pay for Bourbons or Milk 'n Honey. It wasn't good for growing girls to go hungry. It stunted their growth. Perhaps that was why Miss Gosse had legs like she had, and I would grow up with them too if I didn't get enough to eat. I couldn't ask my mother to send me more pocket money. Since my father died she didn't have nearly as much money as she had had when he was alive, and it cost a lot more to live in London than it had in St Giles. What on earth was I to do? My brother was building a house from which he didn't expect to get any change out of a thousand pounds and Mr Johnson in Dove Street charged 1s 6d for a shampoo: 1s 6d! – it was unbelievable. When I had tried to wash my hair myself the geyser had refused to light and I could easily have blown Chandos House to smithereens, to say nothing of myself. My ululation petered out with the information that whilst it was true Miss Locke had volunteered to wash my hair for me once a week for nothing, somehow I didn't think much of the idea –

Mr Betts waited for me to finish. Then: 'You look a picture, I must say!' When I had achieved a semblance of equanimity he inquired, in a tone of mild interest: 'How much were you figuring on touching me for?'

Having done my sums over and over in preparation for just such a question, I was ready with the answer. I told him that, taking my own shilling pocket money into account, I reckoned I could just about get by on 4s 6d – that was to say, 3s 6d weekly was what I had looked forward to receiving from him as the price of silence.

The gardener regarded me with disgust.

'That all? All that tarradiddle over 3s 6d?' Shaking his head: 'You got t' learn to set yer sights higher 'n that, gal, if you want to get anywhere in the world! You should've asked five bob at the lowest.'

I pointed out forlornly that since he had refused to let me blackmail him at all, the size of my demand was now of academic interest only.

'I wouldn't say that,' Mr Betts said. He got up from the bench and told me to follow him, rolling along with his bowlegged gait to a small building which stood against the garden wall a little distance from the greenhouse and was called the bothy. It was built of bricks, with a high-pitched roof, the whole covered with Virginia creeper so that it looked quite romantic, but inside the dim interior there was nothing but an old pot-bellied stove at the further end, some stored deckchairs, and Mr Betts's garden tools and horticultural supplies. There was also a queer old-fashioned nest of drawers on a stand which was where Mr Betts kept his packets of seeds, and it was towards this that he now led me. Selecting one of the drawers in the lowest tier, he levered it out, emptied it of the few seed packets that happened to be there and turned it upside down to get rid of some shrivelled-up bits and pieces that clung to its sides. A spider fell out on to my shoe and scampered away, its eight legs pumping indignantly.

Mr Betts replaced the drawer, leaving it open a mere inch or so. He dug into his trouser pocket and produced a handful of change from which he selected a two-shilling piece, a shilling, and four sixpences which he dropped through the slit; shut the drawer smartly. He informed me that so long as he was at Chandos House or I was – whichever way it turned out – there would be five bob in the drawer, at my service. I could rely on it. 'If I see it's gone, I'll fill it up again, and tha's how we'll go on.' He must have seen the expression on my face for he added sharply: 'An' don't let me hear no more about blackmail, nor about borrowing neither. You're a little lady an' one o' the things I reckon a lady's got t' learn is how to accept a present from a pal in the spirit it's given, no strings attached an' no thanks necessary. An' no more water-works neither –' he ordered, as my chin began to quiver uncontrollably – 'or Mrs Benyon the Bunion'll be chargin' down here wanting to know what I done to you. An' *then* the fur'll fly!'

CHAPTER SIXTEEN

One Saturday morning, when we were having breakfast, Miss Locke leaned across the table and said to me: 'Don't make any arrangements to be out today, Sylvia, unless you want to miss Miss Gosse's sweetheart. He's coming to lunch.'

'Helen!' Miss Gosse cried, and then, to me, with that mixture of dismay and indulgent affection which I had come to recognize as her usual reaction to one of Miss Locke's enormities: 'Pay no attention, Sylvia. Mr Denver's an old friend of my father's. He lives in a hotel at Cromer and he's coming to see us. It's only Miss Locke's idea of a joke.'

'No joking matter.' Miss Locke shook her head and her short curls jumped about engagingly. She always looked her best in the morning, tending to grow progressively more severe and Ancient Greek as the day wore on. This particular morning she looked particularly good, having herself visited Mr Johnson in Dove Street after school the day before to have her hair cut.

It was a relief to me that he had done it so well. There could not be many customers in Norwich who wanted their hair cut in Miss Locke's style, and I had been anxious lest he make a botch of it and I be held responsible. 'Since he washes your hair so superbly that you turn down all my offers to do it for you for nothing,' Miss Locke had said in her mocking way, 'he must be the best hairdresser in town.'

Thank heaven, he had cut it beautifully. Thank heaven and my father, that is, whom I had asked to put in a private word with God to endow Mr Johnson with the special skills needed to do a good job; Miss Locke, as I was only too well aware, having that disconcerting tendency to put people off their stride. She looked young and mischievous, as if having her hair cut had somehow, at the same time, improved her complexion, which was what usually made her look not exactly secondhand but a bit shopsoiled.

'His name is Mr Maurice Denver,' she announced. 'He is handsome, clever, immensely rich, and he has been dying to lay his fortune at Miss Gosse's feet ever since she was a child, as young as you, if not younger. But always – can you credit it? – the foolish woman has spurned his honourable advances, can you possibly think why?'

'Helen!' Red-faced, Miss Gosse cried out again, her boot-button eyes shining. I was blushing as well, it was something Miss Locke was always making me do, but not out of embarrassment this time, not really: more out of pleasure at being invited in on a family joke. Well fed at last, thanks to Mr Betts's darling generosity, I had settled down at Chandos House. I had got used to Miss Gosse's and Miss Locke's little ways, as I hoped they had got used to mine. After the strains and stresses of school, the prick of ambition, the minefield of play-ground friendships, I rode home each afternoon savouring in advance the gentleness that was left of my day: tea with a favourite book propped against the tea cosy; the garden to wander about in, the piano to play, homework which I enjoyed – being, except for arithmetic, good at school; the quivering leaves, their round faces innocent of guile, welcoming me to my bedroom. It was a peace to which even Mrs Benyon, in her odd way, contributed: an ogress as in the fairy stories, to be kept sweet with frequent poultices of 'Pale Hands I Loved' her strange, scented breath puffing over my shoulder.

I could not tell how clever Mr Denver was just by looking at him, nor how rich, though certainly, with his malacca walking-stick, his shantung suit and his panama hat which had a ridge, very precise, running from front to back across its top, he looked prosperous enough. He did not look at all as if he had just come from Cromer, but rather from much further away – from planting tea in Burma or rubber in Malaya or whatever else they planted in the stories of Somerset Maugham. One thing, however, was beyond question: handsome he was not. Miss Locke must have got him mixed up with someone else, unless, of course, being her, she was jealous that Miss Gosse had a suitor when she had none. On second thoughts, I doubted that she was jealous over Mr Denver who was an old man whose cheeks hung down and whose stomach stuck out, egg-shaped. He moved along the hall polished by Mrs Benyon to an extra degree of slipperiness with careful slowness, shuffling one foot after the other as if he feared to crack the precious shell.

He relinquished his hat to Miss Locke with some reluctance, I thought, looking quite sad to see it hung up, abandoned, on one of the knobs of the hallstand. I could sympathize with his feelings, for it had given him a certain consequence. Without it he was a king without his crown, his head, for the most part, bald and splodged with large freckles out of each of which a few white hairs sprouted irresolutely, like house plants it was time to harden your heart against and consign to the dustbin since they were beyond help.

Miss Gosse, who greeted him affectionately and seemed genuinely glad to see him, suggested that I be sent outside to let his chauffeur know that a meal awaited him in the kitchen; but luckily for the chauffeur Mr Denver replied that that would not be necessary. The chauffeur already had his orders, which were to drive the Rolls into the city and procure his lunch there, returning to Chandos House by 2.30 p.m. on the chance that the ladies – 'and this little lady as well,' he added, including me with an old-world courtesy which made me quite warm towards him – felt like taking a drive. I was sorry to hear Miss Gosse say it was so hot, they would be better off after luncheon resting in the garden under the shade of the apple trees and having a nice chat about old times, than driving about for the sake of driving. I should have enjoyed telling Alfred that I had been for a drive in a Rolls-Royce.

Mrs Benyon had outdone herself. The new potatoes, the creamed spinach and the baby carrots that went with the roast lamb tasted so deliciously fresh she must have gone down to the vegetable garden earlier that morning and picked them herself, since Mr Betts did not – officially, at any rate – come in on Saturdays. This surprised me, as I had never before known her to venture further into the garden than the paved area outside the scullery where she hung out her tea-towels and her dusters:

but even she, apparently, subscribed to what I had grown up accepting as a Law of the Medes and the Persians – namely, that one went to special trouble for men.

There was summer pudding to follow – gorgeous, except that I could have done with three times as much as I was offered. However, thanks to Mr Betts I no longer got neurotic about being hungry. More than money was now kept stashed away in the funny little nest of drawers in the bothy. With the gardener's permission I had cleared the seed packets out of some more drawers to accommodate my stores, and there, I was now comfortably aware, they always awaited me in a moment of need, give or take an occasional bun or biscuit pre-empted by the ingenious mice who knew how to get into drawers that were shut tight and who also called the bothy home. I did not begrudge them their commission. It was heavenly to feel that from now on my lovely victuals were safe, no longer hidden in the book box where Mrs Benyon might come upon them at any time.

Mr Denver enjoyed his food and did not hesitate to say so. He asked for a second and a third helping of the roast lamb and expressed astonishment at ladies' bird-like appetites. Heartened by his example I almost opened my mouth to say that I too would like some more, please; but then I saw Miss Gosse and Miss Locke exchanging glances, and my courage failed me.

After dessert, and as a great treat, coffee was served, though not to me; poured into dear little cups which, it appeared, had been a gift from Mr Denver to the Gosses centuries ago. The sight of them made Mr Denver's eyes water. 'How Agnes loved those cups,' he said, making me wonder if Agnes was the name of Miss Gosse's mother. Of course I did not dare to ask.

Whilst they sipped their second cups Miss Gosse suggested that I entertain the company with something on the piano. As both she and Mr Denver seemed in a rather goofy mood of reminiscence and even Miss Locke was smiling at me for once with an expression of unsoured encouragement, I got 'Clair de Lune' out of my music case and played that – not very well, often missing a note or two out of chords that have to be played whole or it isn't moonlight at all but drizzly day. With no more music lessons to keep me up to the mark, since coming to live at Chandos House I practised much less than I had done in St Giles. As I played I felt sad to hear myself slipping away from a standard I had worked hard to achieve: sad for me, sad for Debussy, sad for the clapped-out sound of Miss Gosse's piano, even sad for Mr Betts who had omitted to back 'Clair de Lune' for a place and lost his money. The odd thing was that all my little sadnesses were somehow so caught up and enmeshed in Debussy's heavenly notes that, although I played badly, I also played well – something which happens occasionally, especially when you are young, and is one of the mysteries of piano-playing.

When I had finished Mr Denver clapped his elderly hands together and exclaimed first 'Bravo!' and secondly, 'Encore!' He was still saying the second when Mrs Benyon came back into the room to ask whether any more coffee was wanted. Feeling bold the way music always emboldened me, I interposed, before Miss Gosse had a chance to answer if they wanted more coffee or not, to say that Mrs Benyon was awfully good at singing 'Pale Hands I Loved Beside the Shalimar'. Though she had told me she never sang anywhere, perhaps she would do it today, just for once, as it was a party.

'"Pale Hands I Loved!"' Mr Denver echoed. He took out his handkerchief and blew his nose. 'How many years is it since I heard anyone sing that!'

To avoid having to field one of Mrs Benyon's looks, I concentrated all my attention on fishing 'Indian Love Lyrics' out of the piano stool and settling it, open at 'Pale Hands I Loved', on the music rack. My back to the room, I began the introduction with no idea of what was going to happen. Not until the last possible moment did I feel the housekeeper's hands bearing down on my shoulders, making my own hands tremble and my fingers reach for the notes desperately, a charm to deliver me from evil. Her strange scented breath blew lustily past my ear, my nose, before, for once, passing through the mauve-lined fretwork on the front of the instrument, to be absorbed for ever by the felt that coated the tiny hammers within. I was certain that Miss Gosse's piano would never sound the same again.

'Pale hands, pink-tipped, like lotus-buds that float
On those cool waters where we used to dwell,
I would have rather felt you round my throat
Crushing out life than waving me farewell.'

Mrs Benyon came to the end of her strange song, her strange, unflinching tones vacating the air with the abruptness of a crocodile snapping its jaws shut. Mr Denver blew his nose again and said 'Splendid!' Miss Locke exclaimed in her jolly voice, 'Mrs Benyon has been hiding her light under a bushel!' I busied myself with putting the music away, not daring to look round in case the corners of Miss Locke's mouth were turned down, ironical. If they were, and the housekeeper saw it, I knew that, one way or the other, I would be the one to suffer for it. Miss Gosse said with unaffected enjoyment: 'That was lovely, Mrs Benyon, and I think we've all the coffee we want, thank you.'

After lunch, Mr Denver went to sleep in the garden. At his request I had brought him his panama hat and his beautiful walking-stick from the hallstand, and he had nervously lowered himself into one of the deckchairs which Miss Gosse, that morning, had set out under the apple trees. Miss Gosse and Miss Locke had accompanied him outside. I stood at the open french window watching, not out of nosiness but because I was, as usual, unsure of what was the right thing to do. Would they think it cheek if I joined them? Would they think me rude if I didn't? Behind me I could hear Mrs Benyon clearing the table. One thing I was quite sure about not doing, and that was turning round and risking having her speak to me.

The talk that was going on under the trees seemed desultory and languorous – it was that kind of day, the summer air sparked with insects swerving from here to there and back again as if testing out in a practical way that the square on the hypotenuse really was equal to the sum of the squares on the other two sides. It wasn't long before Mr Denver, his hands clasping his stomach like a child's clasping its teddy bear, was gently snoring. Miss Gosse and Miss Locke conferred together, their foreheads almost touching. They seemed in very good spirits in their flowered dresses, Miss Gosse's with a lot of frills and fullness, Miss Locke's straight-skirted with a narrow belt. Then Miss Locke got up from her deckchair and, in exaggerated mime, came tiptoeing over to where I stood looking out.

'Miss Gosse and I are going for a little walk round the garden. If Mr Denver wakes up, call out "Yoohoo" in your most ladylike voice and we'll come tearing back.' She put her hand under my chin and brought my face close to hers – not as close as hers had been to Miss Gosse's, but closer than I cared for. But then, I knew she was short-sighted and had gold-rimmed spectacles which she seldom wore, as I could well understand and sympathize with. They did not go at all well with her Ancient Greek look.

'You little imp!' Miss Locke said. 'All these years and we never knew Mrs B sang! How on earth did *you* find out?' And when I had explained how the housekeeper had come into the room whilst I was playing and launched into singing without any help from me, 'You little imp!' she said again; bent forward and kissed me lightly on the lips before I could find any tactful way of turning my head away. 'What do you think of Miss Gosse's sweetheart? Isn't he yummy? Why on earth doesn't the woman say yes and put him out of his misery? Don't forget to yoohoo!' And she was off, to where Miss Gosse stood waiting for her on the grass, eager, bouncy, like a puppy waiting to be taken walkies.

I went upstairs to my room and brought down a book to read: *Barnaby Rudge*, which I had won as a prize at Eldon House the term before I changed schools. It did nothing to stop my being bored and lonely, which was my own fault because it was a book I did not much care for, and I had only picked it out to impress Mr Denver in case he inquired what I was reading and then I could say, looking sweetly demure, '*Barnaby Rudge*, by Charles Dickens.' I soon put the boring old book down and went outside, walking on the grass as far as I could get from

Mr Denver. I did not want to be held responsible for waking him up. I would have popped down the garden and got myself a whipped cream walnut out of the nest of drawers in the bothy, if I hadn't been afraid of running into the two mistresses. Well, not afraid exactly, but I had, after all, been left on guard. Miss Locke would be sure to say something in her inimitable way about deserting my post.

There were a lot of windfalls under the trees, and for want of anything better to do I began to kick an apple about very quietly, until it broke open and there were maggots inside. I had squatted down with moderate interest to get a better look at them when Mr Denver called out in his pleasant, old-fashioned voice: 'Have I stopped you from going out to play with your little friends?'

'Oh no!' I answered, springing up and bringing out one of my winsome smiles. I would have gone to the edge of the lawn to yoohoo if the old man had not called me back. I explained: 'Miss Gosse and Miss Locke have gone for a walk in the garden.'

'Capital!' Mr Denver said. 'Don't disturb them on any account. They need the exercise after being cooped up in school all week. In the mean time –' patting the grass by his side – 'you and I can have a little conversation. First of all, though –' With some difficulty and at some risk to the stability of his deckchair he succeeded in getting a hand into his trouser pocket and withdrawing four half-crowns, which he held out to me. 'Two of these are for you, for playing me such a nice piece so nicely, and two are for Mrs Benyon, for singing and also for cooking such a delicious luncheon. Please give them to her after I have left, with my compliments.'

A moment earlier I had been wondering what on earth

Mr Denver and I were to talk about. But five shillings! Not for the first time I discovered that there was nothing like money to lubricate conversations. We got along like a house on fire.

Unlike most grown-ups who seemed to think they were showing a praiseworthy interest in children by peppering them with a fusillade of personal questions which they would have accounted a great impertinence if directed at themselves, Mr Denver, it quickly became obvious, proceeded on the assumption that confidences, even those of the most trivial nature, were gifts to be proffered, not forfeits to be demanded willy-nilly. Thus, although he must have known all about the death of my father – it was, after all, the *raison d'être* for my being at Chandos House in the first place – he made no reference to it, sparing me that display of compassion which grown-ups seemed to consider mandatory; one that demanded in return that I feel instantly guilty for smiling, for laughing, for being alive.

It hardly seemed possible that such a nice old man could ever have been a great friend of Miss Gosse's father, that dire image which haunted the drawing-room, a feeling confirmed when Mr Denver mentioned that although he had, of course, been acquainted with the late Mr Gosse – 'a remarkable man,' he said, with, it seemed to me, a certain ambiguity – he had known Miss Gosse's mother better. Having first blown his nose, he said: 'I knew Miss Gosse's mother before she was married. We were children together.'

How romantic! What a darling old man he was!

Mr Denver continued that he had known Lydia – Miss Gosse – since she was a baby. 'She is a fine woman.'

'Oh yes!' I agreed enthusiastically. I really did like Miss Gosse, even if not quite as enthusiastically as I made out. But when Mr Denver, though with somewhat less passion, went on to say that Miss Locke also was a fine woman, an awkwardness entered our discourse. In the half-understanding way of children faced with the decoding of adult signals, I became aware that what Mr Denver really wanted was to say something about Miss Gosse in particular relation to myself; something he was having difficulty putting into words.

To help him over a bad patch I agreed that Miss Locke was a fine woman also.

'She and Miss Gosse have been together for several years now.

Miss Gosse is very fond of her.'

'I'm very fond of her too.'

Too late I saw that this was not the right thing to have said, quite apart from the fact that it was not even true. The best I could have said about Miss Locke, truthfully, was that she was all right. I was, however, too shy to make a correction. Besides, it would have made me look such a fool.

Mr Denver went on, in a rather stumbling way, to say something about Miss Locke being so jolly, he could understand anyone enjoying her company; but she and Miss Gosse led such busy lives, there were so few hours left at the end of the school day in which to enjoy each other's companionship, and as a consequence – an astonishing note of appeal had come into his voice – if I could see my way to taking up a little less of Miss Locke's time –

'But I don't!' I broke in: I could not help it. 'I don't take up *any* of her time!' I nearly said, but choked it back as being too impolite, that, if anything, the boot was on the other foot: it was Miss Locke who took up mine – interrupting my music practice, for example, by insisting we play some of the awful duets in the piano stool, all mill wheels and cradle songs and stupid things like that; on top of which, more often than not, I was commanded to take the bass part whilst she made a hash of the treble. Me take up Miss Locke's time! The very thought made me go red.

I think, with hindsight, Mr Denver may have read my blush differently because, going red in the face himself, he muttered something about not wanting Miss Gosse to be hurt. I stared at him uncomprehendingly. Whatever was the man on about? It was quite a relief when, after one or two abortive attempts, he located the watch hanging from a chain draped across his abdomen, pressed the little knob at the side of the watch case which made the golden lid pop up, and announced that it was time for him to be going.

I got to my feet and went down the garden to find Miss Gosse and Miss Locke.

I didn't feel like yoohoo-ing, so I didn't. Mr Denver had confused me, but I looked down at the four half-crowns still clasped in my palm, and felt better. Providing the two schoolmistresses were not anywhere in the vicinity I would take the opportunity to slip into the bothy and pop my share of the loot into the nest of drawers.

What a lovely surprise for Mr Betts, when he next looked there, to find for once my funds did not need topping up!

Miss Gosse and Miss Locke weren't among the herbaceous borders, nor in the shrubbery, nor the vegetable garden. I wondered if they hadn't gone out of the back gate to say hello to Bagshaw. The greenhouse, though, was so full up with tomato-plant leaves that I thought they might be in there: a few of the tomatoes were almost ripe and, fresh from the vine, they tasted delicious, as I had reason to know. But they were not there.

The greenhouse being close to the bothy, I decided to put away Mr Denver's largesse whilst I was about it. The tiny building's creeper-covered roof was dazzling in the sun. The interior looked dark and cool. As I came up the narrow path which led to its half-open door, my crêpe-soled sandals making no sound, I heard a noise coming from inside, an animal noise but too loud for the mice who lived there. I was wondering what animal it might be when I heard Miss Locke laughing.

Annoyed that now I should not be able to hide away my half-crowns after all, I went back a little distance from the bothy and called out: 'Yoohoo, Miss Gosse! Miss Locke! Mr Denver wants to go!'

In a little while the two came out of the bothy door, Miss Gosse with her hair half-down and looking rumpled, Miss Locke holding a spring onion, earth still clinging to its little roots.

Miss Locke said: 'You see in front of you, Sylvia, a very naughty woman. She won't eat her spring onion. I tell her how good they are for the blood but she will not eat it.' Holding out to me the thin green shaft with its white bulb like a large pearl at its base: 'Would *you* like to have a go at persuading her?'

'Helen!' Miss Gosse was pinning up her hair, not making a very good job of it. Down and unplaited, the white hairs among the shiny black seemed to have multiplied. 'Really!'

'It's dirty,' I pointed out. 'It's got earth on it.'

'Just what *she* said! How horribly hygienic everybody is round here!'

After Mr Denver had gone, driving off like royalty in his Rolls-Royce whilst the three of us stood in the road waving, I went into the kitchen to give Mrs Benyon her money. She was standing at the table opening the little green net umbrella she fixed over the remains of a roast to keep the flies off. As much as her face ever registered a change of expression she looked annoyed to see me; but then, as she said often enough, she did not like anyone coming into her kitchen. Even Miss Gosse, whose house it was, got a 'what-do-you-want' look.

I put the two half-crowns down next to the dish with the roast lamb on it and relayed Mr Denver's compliments and thanks, all of which she received with no apparent gratification. She was half-way to the larder, the covered dish in her hands, before she said over her shoulder, in her usual flat voice, heavy as lead: 'You can keep that. On account.'

I goggled. I positively goggled. It seemed impossible that I had heard her aright. 'You mean – my pound, you mean? You mean that will leave fifteen shillings you still owe me?'

'The day I owe you, miss, that'll be the day,' said Mrs Benyon, pulling open the larder door.

'But –'

'Leave it if you want. It's all one to me.'

After a further stupefied moment I took it, scooping the lovely half-crowns into my palm, back with the other two before she changed her mind. I was unsure whether it was the done thing to say thank you to someone returning the proceeds of theft, but in the end I did say it – I suppose out of habit. I always seemed to be saying thank you to grownups for no particular reason except that that was what they were, the people with power it was only good sense to stay on the right side of.

'Thank you very much,' I gushed, overdoing it.

Arranging the dish of lamb on the slate shelf reserved for things liable to go bad, the housekeeper said in that marbled voice of hers: 'Put it away somewhere safe next time.'

CHAPTER SEVENTEEN

Not long after Mr Denver's visit, the mistresses arranged to go to Ipswich for a weekend, to a seminar or conference. I was not sure what it was exactly: they never told me the details, but they seemed quite excited at the prospect. Miss Gosse, Miss Locke, Miss Malahide and Miss Barton, my house-mistress, were going to travel there together in Miss Malahide's Austin Seven. I was to be left with Mrs Benyon, who was to forgo her usual weekend time off in order to guard Chandos House in their absence and – Miss Locke's phrase – see that I didn't get into mischief.

On the Friday afternoon before they were due to leave – the plan was to make an early start on Saturday morning – Miss Malahide collared hold of me in the north quad to let me know that there had been a slight change of arrangements. Noreen, her niece, was so nervous at the thought of being left alone in the house overnight that Miss Gosse had agreed for me to go over there on Saturday evening and stay the night to keep the silly baby company. In that airy, grown-up way which took it for granted I could have no possible objection to being moved about like a piece on a chess board, the art mistress hoped that it was all right with me.

It wasn't, actually. I had been looking forward to a luxuriously sluttish weekend on my own, fortified with bought biscuits, whipped cream walnuts and lashings of good, swashbuckling literature. In preparation I had been to the library and got out *Scaramouche* by Rafael Sabatini and *Black Bartlemy's Treasure* by Jeffery Farnol, both writers I knew I could rely on in the swashbuckling line. I would never have taken Noreen for the nervous type. But what could I do? One day I would be free to arrange my own life instead of having it arranged for me. I couldn't wait.

'Noreen's looking forward to seeing you again,' said Miss Malahide, which I took leave to doubt. She was miles too old for me: I was miles too young for her. I supposed it was just that none of her own friends was available.

I put on my winsome smile and told Miss Malahide that would be lovely.

It was the first time I had been to the art mistress's home – unless it was Noreen's. I never knew the truth of their domestic arrangements, never even knew which of the two actually owned the Austin Seven – which turned out to be one of a row of cottages in a rather slummy part of Norwich. I parked my bike against the dividing hedge, undid my attaché case with my toothbrush and pyjamas in it from the carrier, and banged on the brass knocker which was much too splendid for the mean little door. It was in the shape of a woman, obviously Medusa because she had serpents instead of hair. What made her unusual and a bit disconcerting was that the knocker came down as far as her bare breasts, and each breast had a serpent coming out of the nipple, which I certainly didn't remember from the myth of Perseus and Andromeda, though I was very fond of Greek and

Roman myths and read a lot of them. But then, although I had a very good memory, one couldn't remember everything.

Noreen opened the door, looking neat and pretty and smelling very nice as I followed her into the narrow hall, too narrow even for a hallstand. I was a little surprised that she had dressed herself up the way she had, just for me – quite the reverse of myself in an old frock which, being made of Irish linen, creased when you so much as looked at it, and I had been wearing it all day. I was even more surprised when she turned, looked straight at me, and said: 'Wuff, wuff! The watchdog's come!'

I must have looked as stupid as I felt, because Noreen went on: 'Don't tell me you swallowed all that piffle about my being afraid to be left on my own in the dark? You're bright enough to know you're here to keep an eye on me, to make sure I don't get up to anything I shouldn't.'

At some cost to my self-esteem I assured her that I wasn't bright enough at all; adding, because I was quite fond of Miss Malahide really, that I had four aunties myself and they were just the same. They loved to fuss.

'Aunties!' Noreen laughed, louder than she did as a rule. 'Old Mallie's as much my auntie as I am yours!' Before I could settle on the right expression with which to receive this astonishing intelligence, she went on: 'Will you promise to keep a secret?'

I promised, eagerly. It was a question I loved being asked. It brought you so close to the person who asked it, made you a friend, if not for life, then for twenty-four hours at least. Perhaps Noreen wasn't all that many miles too old for me after all.

The secret was that Noreen had a boyfriend called Graham, whom Miss Malahide knew nothing about and of whose very existence – for some reason not clear to me – it was important that she not be made aware. I wondered, but was too shy to ask, if the trouble was that Graham was common – which was to say that he had left school at fourteen and spoke with a Norfolk accent; because, otherwise, Noreen was quite of an age to have boyfriends. In fact, it would have been something to worry about if she hadn't any.

It appeared that, any minute now, I was to have the opportunity to pass my own personal judgement on Graham, because he was coming to supper, bringing with him his friend Geoffrey, with whom, so Noreen assured me, I was bound to get on like billy-o because he liked little girls.

When I protested vigorously that I was not a little girl, she merely remarked in an offhand manner: 'Well, he'll have to make do, won't he?'

Noreen had prepared a lovely supper. There were salads, so beautifully arranged it was almost a pity to disturb them, and little pastry boats filled with delicious savoury messes, to say nothing of a chocolate cake and a sherry trifle for afters. Noreen had it all set out on the table at what I took to be the dining end of the living-room, which was a cheerfully shabby place with a large, lumpy sofa covered in what looked like sacking taking up most of the space, and splashy flower paintings on the walls, the canvases not even framed. Over the fireplace was a big painting of Noreen with no clothes on, which I told myself was no different, really, from having a print of *The Birth of Venus* or *The Judgement of Paris* – except that it *was* different, somehow, since it was someone you knew. When we sat down to eat I was glad to have my back to it.

We sat down as soon as Graham and Geoffrey arrived, which I was also glad of because, apart from being hungry, it gave us something to do and filled up the long silences. The minute I set eyes on the visitors I saw at once that, by my usual yardstick for measuring young men, they were not the kind my brother Alfred would have made friends with. They had, both of them, in my opinion, a cloddish look, and they had no conversation. I should have thought that Noreen could have done much better for herself, but then I had been briefed sufficiently by books and movies – it was one of the few chilling minuses that balanced the otherwise glorious plus of being grown-up – that people tended, as a general rule, to fall in love with the most unsuitable people.

By the time we came to the sherry trifle Noreen and Graham were conversing a lot, but only among themselves – whispering rather, giggling, and feeding each other titbits. It was deeply embarrassing. How I wished myself back at Chandos House with *Scaramouche* or *Black Bartlemy's Treasure*, the leaves rustling against the window the only sound! From the look of him, Geoffrey wasn't having all that good a time either. Less than me, in fact, because I had eaten hugely whereas he had hardly touched anything, just sat there looking brooding, which was easy for him because his eyebrows were joined together over the bridge of his nose without any space between. About the only thing he said was when I helped myself to a third slice of chocolate cake. 'Have you in the house,' he observed coldly, 'and you don't need a dustbin' – a remark which confirmed my estimate of his lack of breeding.

Somehow – it was skilfully done – whilst Noreen and Graham drifted entwined down the room to wind up the gramophone, the two of us were lumbered with the washing up; which, however, funnily enough, turned out to be the best part of the evening. It did us both good to be busy. Though the kitchen was tiny, Geoffrey contrived to stack plates, dry china and cutlery without knocking into me at the sink and with a calm efficiency of movement which surprised and pleased me. I began to wonder if he might not be less cloddish than I had at first thought.

From the living room came the sound of my favourite 'Birth of the Blues' and a voice singing:

'They heard the breeze
In the trees
Singing weird melodies
And they made that
The start of the blues –'

I waited until Geoffrey had hung the damp dish towels tidily on the string stretched above the gas stove and then suggested, shyly, that we too might join the dance. As if something more than dish towels had been hung up, I watched the animation die out of his face.

'If you want,' he said.

Noreen and Graham were not exactly dancing. They stood swaying in front of the fireplace under the painting of Noreen with no clothes on, their arms round each other's necks. Grim-faced, in sharp contrast, Geoffrey and I took the floor, only to find, to our mutual astonishment and satisfaction, that the other could dance well; that despite the difference in our heights, our steps meshed perfectly. When the record ended Geoffrey asked:

'Where did you learn to dance like that?' and when I replied that when I lived in St Giles I had gone to Mrs Barwell's, he inquired further, 'And who's Mrs Barwell when she's at home?' Which, all over again, made him seem a stranger – more, a visitor from an alien planet – because everybody who was anybody in Norwich knew that Mrs Barwell was positively the best dancing teacher in the city.

Next, Noreen put on 'Jealousy', and she and Graham began to dance the tango, trying to look fierce and Hispanic as they swooped up and down the room and only, to my way of thinking, making themselves ridiculous. I loved the grave, ritualistic movements of the dance and their melodramatic exaggerations offended my sense of rightness. Geoffrey said that he didn't know how to do the tango, and, when I offered to teach him, relapsed into surliness and refused, maintaining it was a dance for lounge lizards. Half-way through their travesty Noreen and Graham stopped dancing and announced that they were going upstairs for a bit. There was something they needed to talk over in private. Their footsteps sounded up the narrow stairs and then in the room overhead, but only for a little.

When 'Jealousy' came to an end, neither Geoffrey nor I put on another record. We sat in glum silence until the lure of Chandos House, that distant oasis where *Scaramouche* and *Black Bartlemy* wandered among the whipped cream walnut trees overwhelmed me with a desire too intense to be denied. I got up and said, 'Excuse me,' coyly, as if I needed to go to the lav. Instead I went out into the little hall, picked up my attaché case which I had left there, opened the front door softly and went outside, shutting it after me with equal care. The night was warm, which was just as well since I had, on arrival, handed my cardigan to Noreen and what she had done with it I had no idea. Anyway, I thought, she would be pleased to have it as proof of my presence overnight in case Miss Malahide got suspicious.

I had turned on my bicycle lamp and was strapping the attaché case back on to the carrier when the front door opened softly and Geoffrey came out, making no noise. At first he seemed taken aback to see me, but then he actually laughed, something I had never heard him do so far, and probably never would again.

'I'm off to the pub,' he announced. 'If you want, I could fetch you a shandy outside.'

I declined the offer gracefully and we parted good friends, Geoffrey even going so far as to declare that one day, maybe, he would get me and Mrs What's-her-name to teach him the tango. As I mounted my bicycle and drew away from the kerb he waved me on my way with a gesture, I felt, worthy of Rafael Sabatini at his swashbuckling best.

CHAPTER EIGHTEEN

By the time I got home it was dark, Chandos House shining silver under a star-salted sky. They were the only lights in evidence. As I wheeled my bike up the front path I could see no sign of life. For the first time it occurred to me that Mrs Benyon might well have turned in for the night. As I tugged at the bell pull and heard the resultant carillon distantly clanging, I began to rehearse phrases of explanation and apology.

I might as well have saved myself the trouble. No answer came to my summons, neither there nor round at the back where, having put away my bicycle, I tried my luck at the scullery door, banging on it with the handle of a mop which I found propped outside. Desperate, I took the mop round to the side of the house, to Mrs Benyon's bedroom window, and swished it against the glass, at first diffidently, then with a reckless abandon that took no heed of the consequences.

Nothing. Doubly opaque with net curtains and drawn blind, the window stayed blank, no frame for an enraged housekeeper awakened from her beauty sleep. The thought struck me: could it be that Noreen was not the only mouse to be out playing that night whilst the cat was away? – that Mrs Benyon had deserted her post, was living it up in town until the small hours, even, it was conceivable, not planning to return until morning?

I went round the house again, hopelessly seeking an open window. All that offered was a ventilator over the sink in the scullery, too narrow for me to squeeze through at the best of times, let alone after having supped on savoury pasties, trifle and chocolate cake. Tiredness possessed me. Taking my bicycle lamp by the way of better illumination than was offered by Perseus, Andromeda *et al.*, up there in the sky, I went down the garden to the bothy, reflecting that Noreen, at least, would be pleased: no chance of Mrs Benyon finding out the true state of things and giving the game away.

I could have done with my cardigan. It was chilly and damp inside the little house, not even the thought of my money in the nest of drawers sufficient to warm me. The squeaks and scuffles which I had heard coming up the path ceased abruptly as I crossed the threshold, carrying my lamp. The mice knew when they were not wanted.

I set up one of the folded deckchairs, found two spider-webbed sacks with which to cover myself. I left the lamp on to keep the mice away, only to find besotted moths blundering in from outside, and an amazingly varied proliferation of creeping things moving across the floor to the light source like pilgrims processing to a shrine. I knew that in such horrifying conditions I would not be able to sleep a wink, an error persisted in until the moment a familiar voice awoke me with the waggish inquiry: 'Chucked you out at last, then, have they?'

Mr Betts lost no time in restoring me to the interior of Chandos House. Having, the two of us, rung bells and banged on doors to no purpose, the gardener went back down the garden to the bothy, returning with a step-ladder and a tattered umbrella that might well have been lying there since old Mr Gosse's day. He placed the steps under the scullery ventilator, climbed up and inserted the umbrella, crook handle down, jiggling it about until, more by good luck than judgement, it engaged with the catch on the window beneath. A jerk and the casement was open, as simple as that.

'You're younger 'n I am,' announced Mr Betts. 'You hop in an' get the door open.' Which, excited with the adventure of it all, I did, sliding on my bottom down the draining-board before jumping down to the red-tiled floor. I looked a mess, I knew, spiders' webs in my hair and my linen dress a honeycomb of creases, but I felt gloriously swashbuckling just for that moment when I stood in Chandos House scullery on my own, guilty of breaking and entering.

I withdrew the bolts on the back door and let Mr Betts in. For a moment we stood smiling at each other, congratulating ourselves on our joint cleverness. Only then did we become conscious of the noise.

It was not so much a snore as a bubbling, like the sound Saracens in films about the Crusades made smoking hookahs, or the kind of noise you get when, seeking out the site of a puncture, you slowly rotate an inner tube in a basin of water. *Bubba-lubble* it goes, once you have found the hole.

'Hold on!' Mr Betts ordered.

He pushed open the door into Mrs Benyon's bedroom, myself at his heels. Whatever he said, it was no time to be holding on. The room was too dark for anything much to be seen, but the *bubba-lubble* went on unremittingly. The gardener made his way to the window and tugged the cord at the bottom of the blind. Full of energy and as if waiting for that moment, the blind sprang up, wound itself round its roller and only then desisted, the acorn bobble at the end of the cord swinging against the window pane and away again until it finally calmed down. The room was suddenly full of light and a bad smell and the massy landscape of Mrs Benyon on her back on the bed, legs apart, nightgown rucked up to her armpits, her mottled stomach rising and falling in time with the *bubba-lubbling*.

I cried out: 'Fetch the doctor! She's dying!'

'She's dead,' Mr Betts corrected calmly. 'Dead drunk.'

I don't know what I would have done without Mr Betts. Assaulted by the smell of vomit in Mrs Benyon's bedroom, it was all I could do, after the rich fare of the night before, not to throw up myself. In the nick of time the gardener opened the window as far as it would go, and the lovely fresh air poured in, saving me from humiliation. As for attending to the housekeeper's personal needs, as one woman to another in her predicament, that was something which, sick or well, I simply wasn't up to.

I never knew whether Mr Betts had a wife or not, drunken or sober, but either way he evidently knew all about what went on a woman between being naked and being properly dressed, because when he eventually emerged with Mrs Benyon into the kitchen – she leaning heavily on his arm – she was in her usual get-up of flowered overall over a grey skirt, her stockings unwrinkled, which must have meant that she had on her corset and suspenders as well. The only thing that was out of place was her hair, which was sopping wet, with her perm turned into wiggly corkscrews which reminded me of the serpents on Miss Malahide's brass knocker; the gardener's first step in her rehabilitation having been to drag her to the sink and force her head under the tap.

I had been told to put on the kettle and make some good strong coffee. With Mrs Benyon screaming like a stuck pig as the cold water cascaded over her head and down the front of her nightgown it did not seem the best moment to inquire how many spoons. I had never made coffee before and had no idea how much to put in the pot. In the event, I found a pound packet in the larder and put in half – the gardener, after all, had stipulated strong. Later, as the three of us sat drinking at the table, Mr Betts said it was the first cup of coffee for which he could have done with a knife and fork; but he was ready to admit that it did wonders for Mrs Benyon. After three cups of it she looked almost normal – normal for her, that is; which was to say, as awful as usual.

She turned on me that familiar glazed look of hers as if, in the course of her cooking, she had set her eyes in aspic.

'What've you been up to? You look as if you'd been dragged through a hedge backward.'

You're a fine one to talk! I thought angrily, but I didn't say anything. To have told about sleeping in the bothy would have meant giving Noreen away, and I had promised.

Her ill temper with the gardener was more specific. No gratitude for his services rendered: quite the contrary. He had, she alleged, been the root cause of what she called her little accident. She had suspected it at the time and now she knew for a certainty. That last bottle he had brought her had been definitely 'off'.

'Any more like that,' she finished balefully, 'and you know what.' Mr Betts's habitual expression of knobby good humour did not waver. 'An' what,' he asked, with the air of one launching a paper dart into the wind for the sheer interest of seeing how far it would go, 'if, when she gets back, I give the missus a blow by blow account of how I found you this morning?'

'Tell her what you like,' the housekeeper returned with a shrug. 'I got too much on her. She'll never give me the push, no matter what.' And to me: 'And that goes for you too, little Miss Know-all.'

Never had my room seemed such a haven. I sat down on the bed with my head in a whirl. I knew now that Mr Betts paid his blackmail to Mrs Benyon in gin, which I had been brought up to believe a very bad thing, making people go blind, or worse. I knew it was gin apart from what had been said because there had been several empty bottles labelled 'Gin' lying about her bedroom. But what was it that the housekeeper had on Miss Gosse?

Part of the whirligig in my head was due to pleasant excitement that so much was happening to me. Not all, though. After an unsuccessful attempt to block off all thought of it, I gave in and thought about the horribleness of Mrs Benyon's body, the mountainous stomach, the triangle of grizzled hair that looked like a fur the moths had had the best part of.

I needed to change anyway, so I took off all my clothes, stood on my chair to get a good look, and, for the first time in my life, consciously examined my own body in the looking-glass. It seemed OK, if a bit on the skinny side. I could see my ribs. I felt better for seeing them because it came to me that even if, by a stroke of ill fortune, I grew up to have a horrible body like Mrs Benyon's, once I had been dead long enough I would end up a skeleton as elegant as any film star or mannequin. Dead, we would all be elegant together.

The quivering leaves at the window seemed especially agitated. It may have been that they had never before seen me standing naked on a chair and it bothered them. Or perhaps they had been worried to discover that my bed had not been slept in.

'Where were you?' they seemed to be saying, pressing against the pane in their anxiety. 'Are you all right?'

I got down from the chair, went over to the window, put my face against the glass, cool, calming. Whispered, reassuring the leaves and myself: 'I'm all right. All right!'

In the afternoon, Alfred called by to ask if I would like to come with him to see how the house was getting along. I answered that I would have loved to, only I had homework to do, which was both true and untrue, as I think we both understood. I came out with him to the car and we parted very lovingly, waving to each other across the unbridgeable abyss which had again opened up between us and was getting wider by the minute.

CHAPTER NINETEEN

Oddly enough, once her secret was out, Mrs Benyon became, if not exactly friendly, at least a good deal less overtly hostile to my presence in Chandos House. It was almost as if she took it for granted that by the very act of uncovering a weakness in herself, I had laid bare a corresponding one in me. By staying quiet about her alcoholism – and what else could I have done, anyway? – I had assumed my own burden of guilt – one, in my case, not to be lightened by a tumbler of mother's ruin. For one thing, tea became a much less unpredictable meal than hitherto. Often, without being asked, she provided me with stale bread for Bagshaw.

On one occasion she gave me the best part of a loaf which seemed quite fresh, and I hurried off with it down the garden to the back gate in case she changed her mind. Bagshaw and I shared the windfall together, the donkey staring dourly when he finished up his allotment long before I had come to the end of mine. I got back to the house to find Mrs Benyon in a state. She must have taken more drink that day than she had thought, because what in fact she had done was give me all the bread in stock, and Miss Gosse and Miss Locke had not yet come in for their tea, to say nothing of breakfast next morning.

Armed with fourpence three-farthings, the price of a large white, I sprang gallantly to the rescue, whizzing down the Sprowston Road on my bike as if the Red Indians were after me; down to the baker's, only to find, as at that time of day I should have anticipated, that the shelves were bare except for a lopsided cottage loaf that nobody, for good reason, had wanted. In fact, the baker knocked a penny off the price which I purloined without shame.

Whatever else it had achieved, living at Chandos House had not improved my moral tone.

The housekeeper, as I should also have anticipated, was not best pleased with my acquisition. I guessed that, awaiting my return, fearful that the schoolmistresses might arrive first, she had fortified herself with additional potions of Mr Betts's blackmail. I was unable to convince her that I had purchased the loaf *faute de mieux* and that I had not – repeat, had not – lopsided it on the way home.

'You'll get me sacked,' she growled, snatching up the bread knife as if she would be at least as pleased to use it on me as the bread. Privately, I thought her remark quite amusing in the circumstances, but of course I said nothing to show what I was thinking.

One afternoon, as she was clearing away my tea, she asked, out of the blue: 'How would you like to have a little chat with your pa?'

My face went red, my heart pounded against my ribs. My father still had not been long enough dead for me to be able to talk about him or to hear him referred to by others without those tiresome physical reactions being instantly in evidence. And anyway, what did the woman mean?

The woman explained that what she meant was that a good friend of hers, whom she said was called Madame Sadie, possessed a wonderful gift for getting in touch with people who had, as she put it, passed over. Twice a month people who had been bereaved gathered at her home, where she was able to be a great comfort to them, passing on messages from their loved ones. Since I was looking peaky, the thought had occurred to Mrs Benyon that a visit to Madame Sadie might cheer me up something wonderful.

In St Giles we had taken several newspapers so that I knew quite a bit about séances, which were always fakes or they would never have got into the papers in the first place. Whilst recognizing that mine might be a prejudiced view, nevertheless, so soon as the pounding stopped and the red ebbed out of my cheeks, my first impulse was to say no thank you, restraining myself with difficulty from adding that if I were indeed looking peaky, which I took leave to doubt, it was more likely because I didn't get enough to eat than because of anything to do with my father. My second impulse also was to say no, for a different reason. Over the weeks the two of us, my father up in heaven and I down below in Chandos House, had, slowly and painfully, come to an accommodation, evolved a relationship I felt it dangerous to disturb. Might I not, if I unilaterally changed the terms of engagement, risk losing him altogether? Apart from anything else, what would he be likely to think of a Madame Sadie getting in on the act? She didn't sound my father's type at all.

Moreover, it transpired that Mrs Benyon's words about my having a chat with him were overstating the case. The dead people (the housekeeper called them 'the people on the other side') did not actually converse with their grieving relatives. Perhaps they were too far off to make themselves heard without shouting. Instead, they spoke via Madame Sadie, who had this amazing ability to hear across the endless reaches of eternity.

What if you wished to say something back, I wanted to know. Mrs Benyon brushed the question aside: no problem. Madame Sadie would convey the gist of it, if it was something that needed to be said, which she doubted. *They* already knew all there was to know about *us*.

Obstinately, because I was reluctant to reach the point where I would have to make a final decision one way or the other, to go or not to go, I persisted: 'Suppose you couldn't find the key to a certain cupboard and only the dead person knew where it was?'

'Get in a locksmith!' snapped the housekeeper. She was clearly coming to the end of her patience, always on a short leash. 'Do you want to go or don't you? I thought I was doing you a favour.'

Mrs Benyon said that naturally people paid Madame Sadie for her services. She had to pay the butcher's bills like everyone else. She didn't normally take children, but she would make an exception of me as a favour to a friend. Her charge was half a guinea a sitting which – cutting across my expression of horrified surprise – could easily be met by deducting it from the fifteen shillings still outstanding between us, leaving a mere 4s 6d to close the account.

Evidently prepared for my compliance, Mrs Benyon took two florins and a sixpenny piece out of her overall pocket, plunked them down on the table in front of me and declared, 'Now we're quits!'

One didn't need to be clever to know one was being had. I wouldn't have minded betting that no half-guinea would change hands as the price of my admittance to Madame Sadie's next get-together. She would be bound to let me in for nothing to oblige an old acquaintance. But it was no good. Deep down, from the moment that the possibility of going to the séance had been broached I had recognized that there was no alternative.

'OK,' I said. 'I'll go.'

The séance took place the following Saturday afternoon. Mrs Benyon and I travelled into town on the bus, the housekeeper being unreceptive of my suggestion that we walk down to the tram terminus so that I could use one of my Scholars' Tickets and save myself the bus fare. I did not protest too much at this, as I saw it, unnecessary expense as we were rather loaded down with packages. Mrs Benyon carried one bag and I another. My bag, when she handed it to me, felt strangely warm, and once we were on the bus I dared to open it a little, not enough actually to see inside, which Mrs Benyon would have been sure to have spotted, but enough to be able to identify an unmistakable aroma of the casserole we had had for lunch. At last I had the answer to something which had puzzled me from my first days at Chandos House – the reason why though, thanks to Miss Gosse's frugal carving, the joint was customarily removed from the table barely dented, it never reappeared cold or in any other guise. Now I knew where it went– into the mouths of Mrs Benyon's cronies. The housekeeper had already informed me that after the séance I would have to make my own way home: she herself would be staying behind for a meal with Madame Sadie and her husband Bert. Surely, over the years, Miss Gosse must have noticed the unaccountable disappearance of the ribs of beef or the legs of lamb. Why had she never said anything?

The smell from the casserole was somewhat overlaid by the strange sweet smell that came from Mrs Benyon. Another small mystery was resolved when she opened her handbag and took out a pretty little tin, small as a snuffbox, with a design on it, so far as I could see, of an Eastern maiden complete with a veil, baggy trousers and shoes that turned up at the toes. The printing on the box said Shem-el-Nessim, whatever that was. The housekeeper prised the lid off the tin and offered me one of the minuscule greyish tablets with which it was filled. 'Don't swallow it, don't chew,' she admonished. 'Let it melt slowly.'

I put the tablet on my tongue out of curiosity, but was immediately aware that if I followed instructions I would soon smell like Mrs Benyon, something which did not appeal; so I swallowed it despite having been warned, trusting that my father – whose fault it was after all, in a way, that I found myself in such a situation in the first place – would fix it with God so that the awful pong I had just generated inside me did not turn my liver forever against my lights or vice versa. Mrs Benyon settled back on the bus seat and informed me that there also existed other tablets called Phul-Nana which were equally available in reputable sweetshops for the convenience of people who had been smoking or eating onions or garlic – (or drinking,

I added mentally, when she didn't) – but for her money there was nothing like Shem-el-Nessims for sweetening the breath.

In Madame Sadie's home in Trinity Street, Arabian Nights influences were also evident – no veiled houris, but bead curtains, a good deal of beaten brasswork and a hookah perched among the family photographs on the mantelpiece. Three other customers – clients, petitioners – were already present, sitting round the table which took up most of the room. Two of them were obviously husband and wife, young and pale and looking terribly bereaved. From the look of their clothes, they couldn't have found it easy to come up with the 10s 6d admission money. Out of sheer nervousness, because I did not want to think about why I was there myself, I worked myself into one of my familiar worries wondering if Madame Sadie allowed them both in for the same half-guinea, or did they have to pay 10s 6d each? At the very least, she should, in justice, have made a reduction for quantity, the way they did with oranges on the Market Place.

The third seeker after comfort looked as if she had already found it – materially, anyhow. She had on a fashionable coat-frock, a powdered face, and, although it was much too warm for furs, a narrow scarf made up of two stone martens, the two tails dangling down the middle of her back, and in front, two little animal heads glaring bad-temperedly at each other across a short length of silver chain. Her black hat had a red rose on it.

Madame Sadie would have looked very Arabian Nights herself in her long loose gown of some shimmering green stuff sewn with diamanté and at least six bangles on each wrist, if the body underneath and the face above had not been so comfortably Norfolk, padded out, at a guess, with a good few years of Norfolk dumplings. She appeared a friendly soul, dispensing tea and strips of toast smeared with Salancho* with a generous hand, solicitous of the young couple who were looking as if they were sorry they had come. Madame Sadie was nice to me too, in her way, saying that she hoped I would go away comforted. I wanted to say that I didn't need comforting; that comforting was not what you needed when you lost a father. What you needed was – but as I could not possibly have put into words what it was you needed, I said nothing.

Being me, I would probably have said nothing anyway.

Once the tea things were cleared away, Madame Sadie drew dark-blue curtains over the bay window. The daylight was not entirely cut off because the curtains, though heavy, were unlined; but the room took on a mysterious, underwater aspect. Here and there a muted reflection from a brass tray or vase hinted at pirate treasure wrecked on the floor of some shallow sea.

Madame Sadie ordered us all to join hands round the table. 'Gloves off!' she commanded sharply to the customer with the fur scarf. She warned us that the completion of the circle would set up an area of force sufficiently powerful to wrench our dear ones out of the celestial orbit they now inhabited and bring them back to the world they had left behind. Only one thing could make them feel that their journey was worthwhile, and that was our love; so that we must concentrate all our thoughts on the dear departed, willing them to sense how much we missed them, how much we grieved that they had passed over to the other

* A popular brand of fish-paste.

186

side: how much, just the same, we unselfishly hoped that they were happy in their new existence beyond the stars.

'Don't go upsetting them just because you're upset yourself,' Madame Sadie instructed severely. 'Making them discontented won't do anybody any good.'

Madame Sadie went on to explain that it was not actually herself who would be making contact with the dear departed, but her spirit guide, a wonderful person called Zalbaran who in the flesh, long ago, had been a Red Indian, but one who had never scalped a paleface in his whole life. If the day were propitious – and here Madame Sadie made it plain that she could promise nothing: though nothing specific was said on the subject it was made clear that in the event of the spirit guide drawing a blank no half-guineas would be refunded under any circumstances – the dear departed would speak to Zalbaran and Zalbaran in turn would speak to her, so that she could then pass their words on in language the listeners could understand.

'They still speak English, don't they?' Fur Scarf wanted to know. 'Why can't we hear ourselves what they have to say?'

The answer was that we could not – the dear departed, as was only to be expected once we thought about it, having left their vocal apparatus in the grave along with all their other physical bits and pieces. They had become all spirit, which was why they could now only communicate with others of their kind.

'So, now – all join hands. Hold tightly and, whatever you do, don't let go till I say so, not even to blow your nose.' Madame Sadie did not say what would happen to us if we broke the circle, but we could tell by the expression on her face that it would be something serious.

I sat between Mrs Benyon and the young wife, whose hand trembled so much that I squeezed it with mine, in what I hoped felt like reassurance. On the other side, Mrs Benyon's solid flesh anchored mine as in a vice. I wondered fleetingly what she was doing round the table at all. Was she there just because she had brought me, and that earned her a place, or was there a Mr Benyon out there among those who had passed over? If there was a dead Mr Benyon and he had any sense he would know that today was not the day for hobnobbing with Red Indians.

We sat. We sat in a silence which was only deepened, not fractured, by Madame Sadie's increasingly heavy breathing: a silence which pressed down on us as if tangible until, to a general gasp of astonishment and relief, it was broken by the voice of a young girl issuing from the plump middle-aged throat of Madame Sadie.

'Zalbaran, where are you, my lovely? Are you there, my darling?'

There was no response, and no further sound save an imploring 'Zalbaran! Zalbaran!' It was unsettling to be forced to witness what could only be interpreted as a rejection of love. Zalbaran might be Madame Sadie's darling, but was she his? Who could say the Red Indian might not, at that very moment, be promenading the fields of heaven with some Minnehaha on his arm, paying no attention whatsoever to the circle of force concentrating like mad in Trinity Street, Norwich, Norfolk, England, the British Isles, the British Empire, the World?

'Zalbaran!' Madame Sadie cried aloud, this time in greeting, the joyful young voice soaring through the ceiling. And now there began a curious humming, as of a distant swarm of bees. The humming did not seem to come from Madame Sadie or from any particular quarter of the room. It simply grew louder and louder, closer and closer, until it filled every inch of space there was, even insinuating itself – or so it seemed to me – into the tiny pockets of air enclosed in our clasped hands. With it all, and though the noise grew and grew – this is the hardest part to convey without exciting incredulity if not derision – the silence remained unbroken.

Madame Sadie, who had been leaning forward in an attitude of listening, straightened up and announced in her normal voice: 'A message from little Clara to her mum and dad to say they mustn't cry for her any longer because she is very happy among all the flowers. They have such lovely colours, all the colours of the rainbow. She never saw such lovely colours. She wishes she could pick a bunch to give them, so they could see for themselves how lovely they are.'

Some of the tears which were running down the face of the young woman fell on to the back of my hand. After what Madame Sadie had said about not breaking the circle neither of us could take out a handkerchief to wipe them away. The young woman said with a kind of groan: 'I hope they don't bring on her hay fever.'

Madame Sadie spoke with confidence. 'There is no hay fever across the divide.'

The young woman's husband ventured apologetically: 'I hope she's got some other kids to play with. I wouldn't like to think of her out there all on her own.'

The strange humming noise recommenced. Madame Sadie listened, then began to sing in a child's voice, younger than the girl's voice which had come out of her before.

'Ring-a-ring o' rosies,
A pocket full o' posies –'

When the humming faded away with the song's end, she reported in her normal voice: 'Dozens of children. Hundreds! As many as there are flowers. Your little Clara is *so* happy!'

The husband and the wife looked at each other as if there were nobody else in the room but themselves.

'She is *so* happy!' they said, speaking together. The young wife's hand that was joined with mine did not tremble any longer. On my other side, Mrs Benyon's hand still felt like a slab of solidified lard.

'Zalbaran ducky –' Madame Sadie was the young girl again. 'Have you got Henry there with you?' The woman with the fur scarf frowned. 'Last time you couldn't find him for us. He did not come. And here is his heartbroken Muriel longing to know if he has settled down comfortably on the other side.'

'Ask him about –' the woman with the fur scarf began.

'I know what to ask him!' Madame Sadie cut her off tartly. 'You've told me often enough. Let's make sure he's there to ask first, shall we?' She listened to what the humming had to say, then looked up, pleased. 'He's here. Henry is here. He says he's feeling fine. He says look after yourself, old girl.' Shaking her head to discourage a further interruption from the disconsolate widow: 'He also says to say there aren't any more share certificates, that's why you haven't come across any. He turned them in years ago for cash and gave the money to you know who. He says you've no cause to grumble, you're well provided for.'

'Oh!' The woman with the fur scarf let out a cry and would have broken the circle then and there if Madame Sadie had not called out in alarm, 'Don't let go!' A grunt came from my left side. I turned my head and there was Mrs Benyon smiling as I had never seen her smiling before. I couldn't help hoping that if there was a dead Mr Benyon wandering about on the other side who had owned share certificates, he too had given them away to you know who, just like Henry.

At last it was my – or rather, my father's – turn. When the humming had once more dwindled away, Madame Sadie said: 'There's a daddy here who hopes his darling Sylvia is being a good girl.'

My skin crawled. If I hadn't been too shy I would have cried out in protest, stood up and ruined the circle once and for all. I had never in my life called my father daddy, any more than he had ever called me darling. It simply wasn't the way we communicated. As for being a good girl, it was only my mother who invariably, whenever I came home from having been out somewhere, would ask, sweetly but in a way that drove me up the wall, 'Have you been a good girl?' Often I said 'No,' even though I had in fact been as good as gold, just to register what I thought of such a demeaning question; one that, alive or dead, my father, who knew my feelings on the subject, would never have dreamed of asking of me.

'Many a time these last few weeks,' Madame Sadie went on, 'your daddy has peeped in at the window to watch over you sleeping peacefully in your new little room.'

Certain now that the whole thing was a fake, that Madame Sadie had been primed by her pal Mrs Benyon with what to say, I demanded, laying on all the sarcasm I could muster: 'Please ask my *daddy* what kind of tree it is growing outside the window.'

The humming went on for a long time before Madame Sadie reported back. 'He says the kind of tree isn't important.'

'But he always said trees were *very* important! That we'd have deserts if we didn't have trees. We had a tree book and he knew all their names –'

I stopped because Madame Sadie had begun to breathe heavily again and because Mrs Benyon was bearing down on my hand so that it really hurt. The humming had died away completely. Madame Sadie said in her girlish voice: 'Are you very tired, Zalbaran, lovey? Are you being called away? Do you really have to go, taking our loved ones with you? See that they take our love back with them, do you hear? – Our fondest love, to cherish across the great divide and to the end of time. And come again, come again, darlings all, when those who love you call –'

I sat on my bed listening to the leaves quivering against the window, my lips curled at the very suggestion that my father could not recognize an aspen tree when he saw one; worried sick all the same that perhaps it was true after all, and that after you were dead there were things you no longer remembered, like the name of a tree and whether you did or did not call your daughter darling. After all, with all the changes to your way of life (though that didn't sound right) you must have a lot on your mind. Assuming you still had one, that was. And what did you remember *with*, anyway, your brain being left behind in your coffin, decaying to dust along with the rest of your body? What if it was only the living who remembered, the dead who forgot, or – worse – couldn't be bothered?

Suddenly, I wanted desperately for the séance to be genuine. Madame Sadie had said that the dead were all spirit. What did that mean exactly? I tried hard to puzzle it out and only came up with my father, looking the same as he always had looked – dark hair, blue eyes, moustache a little yellow at the edges from too much smoking – except transparent. You could see clear through him, which would, if you thought about it, have made it impossible to be sure how he looked, what with beds and chests of drawers and goodness only knew what else getting in the way all the time. Perhaps it meant invisible, which was even worse. With transparent you might at least catch a glimpse.

Only hunger saved me from utter despair, conjuring up a picture of Mrs Benyon – nothing transparent about her! – sitting down to tea with Madame Sadie and her husband Bert, a meat tea with warmed-up casserole, probably accompanied by the rest of the redcurrant jelly we had had at lunch. Chandos House was empty. Miss Gosse and Miss Locke were out somewhere and I wouldn't have minded betting that nothing whatever had been done about my tea. I ran downstairs to the dining-room. Sure enough, the plush cloth was in place on the table. Nothing in the kitchen either. There was a lovely new loaf in the bread crock in the larder, but I didn't dare to cut into it. If it had been started, that would have been another matter.

I went out into the garden, down to my store in the bothy, and there was Mr Betts sitting on the wooden bench reading his sports paper and eating one of my whipped cream walnuts. Even though it could be said he had a perfect right, since it was his money which had paid for it, it was too much. Everything and everybody was against me. I began to bawl in a childish way I hadn't used for years.

Mr Betts popped the last of the whipped cream walnut into his mouth, folded his paper and put it away in his jacket pocket.

'I jest lost meself thirty bob on the gee-gees,' he informed me, not sounding too put out about it. 'Wha's your excuse?'

As ever, the knobby little man made me feel instantly better, an improvement compounded by the whipped cream walnut I fetched from the nest of drawers in the bothy. Sitting close to him on the bench, the smell of chocolate blending amicably with the sweaty earthiness of his clothes, I told him what I and the housekeeper had been doing since lunchtime: whereupon he turned his eyes up comically to the heavens and exclaimed 'Women! Ain't they got nothing better to do of an arternoon?'

When I corrected him to the extent of pointing out that a man had been among the company forming a circle in Trinity Street, to say nothing of Madame Sadie's husband Bert, who was presumably somewhere on the premises although I personally had not laid eyes on him, the gardener commented offhandedly, but in a tone that carried absolute conviction: 'Well, you wouldn't, would you? He was the one doing the humming.'

I gaped at Mr Betts in wide-eyed admiration. *Of course!*

'Comin' up the road,' Mr Betts said, 'I saw you an' the Bunion waiting fer the bus. I'd 'a known where you was off to, wild horses wouldn't have stopped me comin' along.'

I inquired delicately, since except for what he had told me about his parents, I had no idea of his family circumstances, whether there was anybody on the other side he would have wanted to get in touch with.

'On the other side o' the fence, you mean! All them horses what refused once they heard it were my money they was carrying on their bloody noses! Your Madame What's-her-name call *them* up fer me, I'd've had a few choice words to say!'

Somehow I found myself leaning against the man's sleeve, feeling strangely tired. Close by, on a tin tray on the ground, were two bunches of asparagus neatly tied with strands of raffia. They explained why the gardener was in on a Saturday afternoon. If I hadn't been so tired I might have asked how his mate with the white van was getting on.

I liked the taste of asparagus and would ordinarily have been quite interested to know if we were going to have it with Sunday dinner, or had Mr Betts other plans for its disposal? Unfortunately, in the mood I was in, I took against the inoffensive vegetable. The waxen stalks, faintly flushed with purple and green, looked so very dead.

Mr Betts was going on, something about it not being important whether the séance was a fraud or whether it wasn't. Being dead or being alive was what mattered – being alive, anyhow. 'When you come down to it, all you're on about is how your pa in't around any more fer you to drive him potty with your takin' ways, ain't I right?'

If Mr Betts said more, I did not take it in. Not exactly asleep, I was not exactly awake either. One thing he said that did get through. Commenting on what I had reported about dead people being 'all spirit' he pointed out that you didn't have to be dead to be that. Look at the Bunion – weren't she all spirit, bless her? He ought to know, what it cost him in best London gin!

When I woke up, under my head a couple of sacks neatly folded, the gardener had gone. In the distance, somewhere among the apple trees, Miss Locke was calling out something – I couldn't make out the words – and Miss Gosse exclaiming 'Helen!' in that voice of hers which showed she would be very upset indeed if Miss Locke were to kick the bucket. If that happened, I bet Miss Gosse would be round at Madame Sadie's before you could say knife.

I picked up the two bundles of asparagus and went back to the house carrying them; hoping against hope that there might, after all, be some tea going.

CHAPTER TWENTY

One Saturday morning as I was in the hall on my way to the kitchen to pick up some stale bread for Bagshaw, the front door opened and Miss Locke breezed in, in high spirits; Miss Gosse, button eyes bright, button nose wrinkled in laughter, frisking like a puppy at her heels.

Catching sight of me, the history mistress called out: 'Sylvia, you naughty thing, you've been holding out on us! So Miss Gosse isn't the only one at Chandos House to own a sweetheart! Yours is outside waiting, face like a mashed potato, his broken heart bleeding all over his bicycle.'

'Helen!' Miss Gosse's face was as red as my own. 'Just a boy, Sylvia, wanting to know if this was where you lived.' She added, kind as ever: 'Not like a mashed potato at all.'

'Quite right!' Miss Locke conceded. 'More like soggy chips.' She looked at me critically, at Mr Johnson's latest trim, which I had ordered extra short for economy's sake. 'You'll have to let it grow,' she pronounced. Then you'll be able to let it down from your window like Rapunzel, for the young lover to clamber up to your bower. But oh dear!' – the corners of her mouth turning down in familiar derision – 'Do you think he'll wait that long?'

Miss Gosse said that she had invited him in but he had said no thank you. 'A nice, mannerly boy, I thought, whatever Miss Locke says.'

I went into the kitchen, collected Bagshaw's bread, and came back into the hall carrying it.

'How romantic!' Miss Locke trilled. 'They're going on a picnic!'

I muttered something about feeding the donkey, and went out of the front door, hating her.

Underneath it all, I was not displeased. Thanks to the egregious Sybil, Robert Kett's cousin, I had definitely benefited from the myth that I had a boyfriend. Whatever was the case at Chandos House, in Form IIIa a boyfriend gave you status. We recognized the importance of boys without in the least knowing why. Like the weather, they were there and had to be taken into account. Close to, on the whole, we did not even like them, their smell, their dreary clothes, their lumpish inability to carry on anything approaching a civilized conversation. Even the 'common' clique that went in for hanging about street corners conceded that there was nothing to beat girls when it came to having a good time together: yet unaware, unquestioning, we played out our evolutionary role. If you couldn't boast a boyfriend by the time you were twelve, the outlook was bleak. You could easily end up like that gaggle of old maids, our mistresses.

Seen down the tunnel of time, our innocence seems incredible. Even the street-corner brigade partook of it, every last one of them convinced that it was kissing – so long as you were married, that was – which produced babies. A classroom symposium on the subject of beds one morning when it was too wet to go out to play had produced a consensus to the effect that though (heaven only knew why) married people were expected to share the same one, this need not necessarily be an insuperable obstacle to marriage. One could probably get used to it.

'Even if it was Stanley Osborne in there with you?' someone objected, naming a drip of some local fame. Or Brian Willis? Or Ivor Perse? The names came thick and fast. There were any number of boys IIIa did not fancy getting into the same bed with.

Would you do it for £10, was the next question. For £100? £1,000? After an animated discussion, the sum of £50 was agreed as the minimum making it worthwhile to get into the same bed as a boy you couldn't stand. Always assuming, that is, that it was a good wide one where there was plenty of room for two to lie without touching, in which case you could hug the edge and more or less pretend there was nobody else there at all.

I was grateful that, so far at least, nobody had classed Robert Kett as a drip, which would have lost me public esteem, though that was what I myself thought him. The only thing about him, apart from his name, which was in any way memorable, was his utter lack of memorability. Every time I saw him approaching there was always a second of doubt as to whether it was Robert Kett or somebody else with mousy hair and a minus personality. It would have been so embarrassing to make a mistake.

Robert Kett was hanging about a little way down the road from Chandos House, pretending to be doing something to his bike. If I had not recognized him I would have recognized his bicycle anywhere, a birthday present from parents whose perception of their son clearly differed from my own. It was blue and white with turned-down handlebars and the lines of a cheetah poised to spring upon an unsuspecting gazelle. Not that I had ever seen – nor ever expected to see – Robert Kett riding it with the panache it deserved. He seemed happiest quietly pushing it along, himself padding alongside in a submissive way that did not make entirely clear which of the two was in charge.

We said hello to each other and were, as usual, immediately at a loss for words. I think I said something about liking his pullover, which was a dazzling new white, hand-knitted in cable stitch. Going bright red – when it came to blushing there was not much to choose between us – he told me his Auntie Mabel had knitted it for him. To break the painful silence which followed this intelligence I mentioned that I was on my way to feed a donkey. I was not conscious of framing this information in the form of an invitation, but so he took it, and I did not contradict, such a relief it was to discover a purpose for our being together. Bagshaw might have something to say: that was up to him. I decided privately that the boy was even drippier than I had thought: also that I would have to be very hard up indeed for whipped cream walnuts to contemplate getting into the same bed with him for £100, let alone £50, even with the bicycle plumped down the middle between us.

We walked in a depressive quiet down to the crossroads, turned into the road to Catton, and so to the back path. I had long ago resigned myself to the sad recognition that – in the circles I frequented, at any rate – people did not converse with either the wit or the high seriousness they invariably exhibited in books. Even so, with nothing but Auntie Mabel's pullover between us and silence, I could not help feeling that we had touched rock bottom.

Once we got into the back path things got even worse. Robert Kett grew fussy and I could never abide fussiness. With the exception of the Chandos House boundary, which Mr Betts kept trimmed to a boring neatness, nobody, it seemed – neither the other householders on the one side nor the owner of Bagshaw's field on the other – cared a fig for the state of the hedges which flanked the path. With spring passing into summer, the wild roses had grown prodigiously, the brambles arching over what might laughingly be termed the carriageway or snaking thornily along the ground with the express aim, surely, of tripping up the unsuspecting or myopic passer-by. Even Mr Betts's partner in crime must be thinking twice about backing his mouldy old van off the road into such a jungle.

As a place for picking up scratches on the beautiful blue and white enamel of a brand-new bike, it took a lot of beating. Much as I hated fuss, I felt sufficient sympathy for my companion in his obvious distress to suggest that he and his bicycle change their minds about accompanying me further and retreat to the safety of metalled roads. Robert Kett's refusal to withdraw might have demonstrated a gratifying desire for my company despite all danger, if only he had not said: 'It's ages since I saw a donkey.'

Robert Kett and Bagshaw liked each other instantly. It was love at first sight. His bicycle parked against the back gate at Chandos House, his worries for its wellbeing assuaged, my titular boyfriend took to the donkey in a way I had never seen him take to me. Undaunted by the large yellow teeth that made me prefer to throw the bread down on the ground rather than risk my fingers in a friendlier proffering of largesse, Robert Kett – showing, possibly, for the first time in our acquaintance, the heroic stock from which he was descended – fearlessly held out lumps of bread for the animal to snuffle up with its slobbery lips. He patted Bagshaw on the muzzle like an old friend, shooed the flies away from his eyes; even snagged his new pullover on the barbed wire and didn't seem to care.

If I was, to be honest, a little put out by this access of a vivacity never triggered off by my presence, it was as nothing to my annoyance at Bagshaw's response. Here was I who had been feeding the wretched beast day after day without receiving so much as a hee-haw of thanks in return, and here was a complete stranger – a drip of the deepest water – moving in effortlessly to take over the heart which should, if there were any justice in the world, belong to me. Bagshaw purred, Bagshaw simpered, Bagshaw fluttered his long eyelashes at Robert Kett in a way that was quite disgusting. I might as well not have been there at all. *It takes one donkey to recognize another*, I thought ferociously, but remained uncomforted. I suddenly felt lonelier than I had ever felt since coming to Chandos House; and when my faithless lover turned to me and demanded (though the answer must have been plain to see – where, for heaven's sake, did he think I kept extra bread? Up my knickers?), 'Is that all there is?' I burst into tears.

I don't know which of the three of us was most embarrassed – me, Robert Kett or Bagshaw; but only the donkey had the sense to do something about it. Pushing his head even further than usual between the strands of barbed wire, he first rubbed his nose affectionately against Robert Kett's new pullover, then, opening his mouth wide, clamped his teeth with an audible *clack!* down on to Auntie Mabel's handiwork and bit a large piece out of it.

It was masterly done. The shock of it dried my tears instanter, the destruction so utter as to preclude pettifogging worries about whether or not the damage could be repaired. Even as the boy stood staring down unbelievingly at the vacancy spread over his front, the nothingness enlarged itself. It seemed that breathing was enough to send more stitches dropping into oblivion, more wool unravelling, more cables untwisting themselves. It was a sight to see.

Bagshaw stood with the piece of pullover in his mouth, moving his head from side to side and looking insufferably pleased with his own cleverness. He seemed uncertain, however, as to what to do with his trophy now that he had it, and finally settled for swallowing it, all except a few strands which caught in his teeth, after which he did not look quite so pleased. It was probably giving him indigestion.

Robert Kett went pale, his freckles standing out dark on his milky skin. Even his hands went pale, making me think of pale hands I loved beside the Shalimar, except that I doubted whether those particular hands had freckles on them the way Robert Kett's had. The reason that I noticed his hands was because I was afraid to look directly in his face in case I burst out laughing, something I was aching to do, and then where would be my boyfriend, my burgeoning love affair? Gone like the wind. When Robert Kett demanded in a high-pitched voice, 'What am I going to tell Auntie? What's she going to say?' I took charge, the way, it seemed to me, girls often had to when faced with boys' inability to cope.

'Tell her you lost it. Tell her you took if off because it was so hot and you strapped it on your bike carrier only it must have fallen off without your knowing. She'll knit you another. Women always buy more wool than they need. She'll be glad of a reason to use it up.' Red with the effort of stifling my laughter I helped Robert Kett divest himself of the mangled remains of the pullover – not easy because some of the loose bits of wool had wound themselves round the buttons of the sports shirt he wore underneath.

'Hang on a jiff.' Pressed close against his chest I worked at getting the buttons free. If our faces touched, I have no recollection of it. Only of a dull thump as the blue-and-white bicycle propped against the gate heeled over on to its handlebars, the gate opening, and Miss Locke's voice inquiring icily: 'What on earth is going on?'

Obeying orders, I walked with Miss Locke up the garden towards the house. Well, not exactly with. As befitted a mere child, a lesser mortal, and one out of favour what was more, I walked a little behind, projecting my spleen against the slender back where the shoulder-blades could be seen sticking out under the white blouse. What business was it of hers to come spying on us?

It would have been too much to expect that Robert Kett would stand up to the woman, show himself worthy of his ancestors. Instead, acting true to form, he had blushed and mumbled, picked up his bike and stumbled away down the track without venturing a word in his own defence – or in mine: though why we should, either of us, be called upon to defend ourselves was beyond understanding. Not that I blamed him. He was only a child like myself in a world where, it seemed, for some grown-ups at least, it was always open season for humiliating children under the guise of doing what was good for them. It wasn't fair, I shouted silently at the shoulder-blades. It jolly well wasn't fair!

When we came to the open space by the greenhouse and the bench and the bothy, Miss Locke stopped and waited for me to catch up with her, which I did reluctantly, knowing what was in store, knowing what was always in store when grown-ups felt the urge to show off their power. She was going to tell me off.

She was going to do nothing of the kind. What she did, before I could make any movement to fend off the attack, was grab hold of me, pinion me against the bothy wall, among the dusty trails of Virginia creeper. Her cropped head with its small ears was between me and the sun, so that I could not distinguish the expression on her face, nor even the features, save for the small mouth grown suddenly large which she clamped over mine like a sink plunger over a recalcitrant plug hole.

Unpleasant as it was, worse was to come. Something forced itself between my lips, something thick and wet and exploratory. Slugs, lampreys, giant worms were the images which flashed through my mind before I realized that, incredible as it seemed, the something was Miss Locke's tongue.

My mouth was anchored, but my stomach was free, despatching the taste of bile and the remains of my breakfast to coat my throat. I was quite sure that I was about to die when Miss Locke took her tongue back, stepped away a little and stood contemplating my crimson face with her familiar expression of amused derision. Only the fact that she was breathing more heavily than usual advertised that anything out of the ordinary had occurred.

'You and your silly little pecks!' declared Miss Locke. With a deep sigh of what I suppose was satisfaction: '*That's* how you kiss when you love somebody.'

Confused and tired to death, I protested: 'I wasn't kissing anybody. I don't know what you're talking about!'

'Oh, you little fool!'

CHAPTER TWENTY-ONE

That Sunday, Mrs Crail came to tea. As soon as I heard, earlier in the week, that there was to be a tea-party, I went down to the telephone box at the crossroads and telephoned Alfred to ask if I could spend the day with him. From the way he stammered before saying, 'Yes, of course. That would be lovely,' I knew he must have made prior arrangements for himself and Phyllis, only he didn't want to hurt my feelings. Providentially, I suddenly remembered that I had got the wrong Sunday, that the one I had really meant was the Sunday after. That, for this Sunday, I already had an unbreakable commitment to play tennis. The court was booked and you know how difficult it was to get a court on Sundays. And even for the Sunday after, now that I came to think about it, there were plans brewing –

We exchanged words of unaffected affection before I rang off. Walking back to Chandos House, I steeled myself to further lying. I would say that, much as I should have loved to be present I could not be in to tea on Sunday because I had a long-standing engagement to meet my brother and his fiancée. By the time I came up the front path I had tried out various forms of words only, as I reached the front door, to abandon them all as impractical. Even in rehearsal, my reddening face – I could tell by the way it felt hot and then hotter – gave me away.

'It's quite an honour!' said Miss Gosse, her button eyes shining. 'Mrs Crail is in such demand at weekends.'

Mrs Crail in demand! I wanted to ask by whom – a couple of prize saddlebacks? But of course I did no such thing. More likely, I decided uncharitably, the headmistress spent her weekends lying low. Weekdays, in term time at least, she had her billowing gown to protect her: anyone could see that she was a person of some authority. But outside working hours it was quite easy to imagine how Mr Martin the butcher, having left his glasses at home, might mistake her for a pig with ideas above its station, and there she would be, too late to do anything about it, hanging by her trotters in his shop in St Benedict's, only the snout, the piggy eyes and the balefully smiling curve of the lips still recognizable to those in the know as belonging to the Scourge of the Secondary; and they wouldn't say a word, not if they had the sense they were born with.

There were other guests – Miss Barton, my house-mistress, and Miss Malahide and Noreen, the latter looking sweet and compliant and so much a one for the Syllabus that I was sure Mrs Crail would take to her on the spot – that was, if they hadn't met already. Swagged in draperies, the headmistress was the last to arrive, by hired car. When she saw Miss Malahide she said, dripping honeyed poison, that had she known the art mistress was to be among the company she would have begged a lift in the Austin Seven. In reply Miss Malahide could not, of course, point out that Mrs Crail was much too fat to fit into an Austin Seven, so she shook her whiskery head sadly and said if only she had known. Miss Gosse's little doggy face wrinkled in distress since the breakdown in communication was obviously due to her own poor organization, but Miss Malahide did not seem bothered. It was possible that being an artist had armoured her against the Crails of this world. Unfortunately, she now went on, deciding I suppose to get the matter settled at the outset, the Austin Seven would not be available for the headmistress's homeward conveyance either. When the party broke up, she and Noreen were engaged to drive post-haste to Wroxham in order to spend time with a sick friend whose supper they had promised to prepare and serve, and goodness only knew at what hour they would be free to return to the city. To Mrs Crail, I think, as to everybody else, it sounded altogether too much of an excuse – as with her oil paintings, Miss Malahide had a tendency to lay the colours on too thick. At any rate, the headmistress didn't say anything more to Miss Malahide all afternoon but devoted herself to being absolutely charming to Noreen, who fluttered her eyelashes and was absolutely charming back.

Tea was one of Mrs Benyon's specials – tissue-thin sandwiches, scones with home-made jam and clotted cream, three kinds of cake as well as raspberries I myself had picked earlier in the day, moving from cane to cane with a certain reluctance which came from wondering how much profit I was doing Mr Betts out of by so doing. The conversation was less scintillating. Miss Gosse had installed Mrs Crail in the one chair in the dining-room which had arms, and there she sat like the Holy Roman Emperor, flanked by underlings who knew better than to speak before they were spoken to.

Miss Barton, a sad-featured woman reputed to have an invalid mother given to wailing like a banshee, seemed the only one untroubled by any sense of constraint. As the senior maths mistress, with an impressive record of getting her pupils into university, often with scholarships or bursaries to boot, she may have felt her position unassailable; unless living with a wailing banshee had taught her the value of good teas and dullness.

'A dainty meal is such a joy,' she said, reaching for her umpteenth scone.

Miss Barton would not be teaching me until I got into the Vth, the form where you took the Cambridge Senior, that dire exam which for matriculation demanded, even if you were a genius at everything else, passes in English and Mathematics if you were not to be cast into the outer darkness of shorthand and typing, an academic reject. Would a year be enough for Miss Barton to teach me the arithmetic which Miss Gosse had so signally failed to do? There were times when I felt that not even God Himself could teach me arithmetic, though I wished He would at least have a try. Pending divine intervention, I was always as nice as I could possibly be to Miss Barton.

For something to say, I suppose, Miss Malahide looked at me and announced that 'Noreen says you are very intelligent,' at which Mrs Crail laughed prettily and asked the girl, 'Did you really say that?'

Noreen fluttered her eyelashes and murmured, 'I really did,' at which the two of them laughed prettily together, as at some secret joke too exquisite to be shared with the lesser orders below the salt.

'Aren't you glad, Sylvia –' recovering her composure, and daring me to say different, Mrs Crail wanted to know – 'that I arranged for you to stay here at Chandos House?'

Naturally I answered that I was very glad. Miss Locke who, as the youngest teacher present, perhaps, or the one with the least seniority, had been unusually subdued all afternoon, put in: 'We're delighted to have her, aren't we, Lydia?' To which Miss Gosse, looking a little wan, I thought, added: 'We can hardly remember what it was like without her.'

'I hope,' the headmistress went on, re-addressing herself to me, 'that you are taking full advantage of your opportunities here – and that you are doing all you can to show your appreciation of Miss Gosse's kindness in taking you?' You would never have thought, from the way she went on, that my mother was paying 30s a week for the privilege of having me 'taken'. Miss Gosse, obviously suspecting a trap, fell over herself to assure the monster that neither she nor Miss Locke had given me so much as a minute's extra coaching, and had no intention of ever doing so. 'It wouldn't be fair.'

'Very proper,' Mrs Crail commented, inclining her head on its short neck and beaming all over her piggy face.

Whilst the others were drinking their positively final cups of tea, eating their final slices of cake – I shouldn't have minded another slice myself but nobody asked me – I was commanded to play something on the piano. I chose one of Brahms' Hungarian Dances, the one everybody knows: *da* di-*da* – di-*da* – diddy-*da*, and so on; played it with a wholly synthetic verve and a lot of pedalling which I vainly hoped would blur the many mistakes. It was a deeply depressing experience. Not even my losing struggle with arithmetic had dispelled the illusion that life was something you became progressively better at, instead of, as it now appeared, an accumulating inventory of wrong notes.

When I had finished, Mrs Crail tapped her beringed fingers together, very, very softly. No half-crowns were going to be forthcoming from that quarter, that much was certain. Not so much as a threepenny bit.

After tea was cleared, Mrs Crail slumped in her armchair like a beached whale and Noreen swept me off for a walk in the garden.

'Sylvia is determined to teach me the names of all the flowers,' she apologized to the others in her old-fashioned way, gently making it appear that the idea for our desertion of them was mine, not hers, which it wasn't, yet speaking with such an air of regret as almost to convince even me that such was indeed the case. Once we had got as far as the shrubbery, however, well out of sight and sound of the house, 'Whew!' she exclaimed, stretching her arms outwards and backwards, bringing her shoulder-blades together and her usually diffident breasts into unwonted prominence beneath the pale yellow crêpe de Chine of her dress. 'What a lot they are!'

'Do you or don't you want to know about the flowers?' I demanded with childish crossness. Mr Betts had taught me all the names and since she was the one who had brought up the subject I was quite keen to show off my erudition.

'All I know about flowers,' was the reply, 'all I want to know, is that nettles sting and dandelions make you wet the bed.' Looking at me with a hard critical eye that did not exactly go with the rest of her get-up: 'What a baby you are! Geoffrey was quite taken with you.'

'I shouldn't have thought so.'

'He was,' the girl insisted. 'When I said we were coming here this afternoon he said to be sure and give you his love.'

After what had happened the day before with Robert Kett I couldn't help feeling pleased. Being completely absentee, I thought, Geoffrey would make the ideal boyfriend. He certainly wasn't one to come hanging about Chandos House on any pretext, whereas at school it wouldn't do me the slightest harm to be able to boast the ownership of a boyfriend who was actually grown up.

Just the same, and as usual pleased with the dream but rejecting the substance, I said crudely, 'Don't give him my love back.'

I began to reel off the names of the flowers even though Noreen appeared not even to be listening. When we came to the soft fruit she went along the rows of canes helping herself to more of what I had come to think of as Mr Betts's raspberries.

To make her stop, as much as anything, I asked her if she was intending to marry Graham.

'Marry him! You must be mad! Do you know what he does for a living? He works in the post office in Davey Place, handing out stamps and things over the counter.'

'One day he may be the Postmaster-General.'

'And me the Queen of Sheba!' Noreen laughed her tinkling ladylike laugh. 'You don't happen to know any rich old men, I suppose? They're the kind to marry, just you make a note of it. The richer and the older the better.'

When I mentioned Mr Denver she seemed quite interested, especially when I said about the Rolls and the uniformed chauffeur.

'Except that he belongs to Miss Gosse,' I finished.

Noreen laughed again and hooked her arm through mine. 'One day you'll grow up,' she said. 'Now, tell me the names of these stinking flowers.'

I don't think, really, she cared a brass farthing about them. I had hardly pointed out the lupins and the delphiniums, the peonies and the aquilegia, before she was off again, talking of this and that so pleasantly and as to an equal that I began to feel a bit above myself. I inquired if, as Miss Malahide had asserted, she had really said that about my being intelligent.

'I really did,' was the reply. 'And I do think it. That's why I got you out here – to say thanks for not giving the show away.'

I put on a suitably shocked look and said of course I would never do that.

'I should have known.' Adding blithely: 'But then, as I'm not to be trusted myself I tend to tar everybody else with the same brush. At first, let me tell you, when I came downstairs and discovered you'd done a bunk I was livid. What would that old bag of a housekeeper say when you came ringing to be let in last thing at night? She'd be bound to say something to Miss Gosse and then the fat would be in the fire. There'd be no way to stop it getting back to Auntie. You ask Graham – I was in a right old tizz. I only calmed down after I found that you'd left your cardigan behind, obviously for Auntie's benefit. And then I thought, she's not a fool, she'll find some way not to blow the gaff. And I was right, wasn't I? Though I have to admit I had a bad day or two after they came back from Ipswich, waiting for the axe to fall.'

Basking in Noreen's praise, however undeserved, I served up a shamelessly inflated version of how I had in fact passed the rest of that fateful night. Nothing about Mrs Benyon's drunken stupor which had made it impossible for me to get back into the house anyway: only horrific hours of darkness spent in the bothy fending off rats as big as fox terriers – well, as chihuahuas, anyway – an ordeal unflinchingly undertaken rather than risk betraying a friend.

Noreen, less impressed with my heroism than I could have wished, laughed and said, 'What a lark!' and that she was glad it had all turned out so well. She said Miss Malahide was not such a bad old thing if only she wasn't such a randy old dyke. Not liking to ask what a randy old dyke might be, I made a mental note to ask Mr Betts.

When, comfortably gossiping, we got round to Mrs Crail, I said that I thought she was very ugly.

'*She* doesn't think so, that's all that matters. She thinks she's the cat's whiskers. She's headmistress. She's made it.' Noreen continued: 'She'll do anything to make mischief. Did you see how she made a beeline for me?'

'You encouraged her.'

'Mustn't let Auntie take me for granted.' Noreen looked demure. 'And why d'you suppose Her Imperial Majesty wanted you to board here at Chandos House in the first place?'

I explained – haltingly: it was still a matter for recurrent regret – that it was because, for some reason, she hadn't thought Mrs Curwen suitable.

'Don't you believe it! She did it to make trouble between Gossy and Cocky Locky.'

Now I was completely at sea. 'How could my coming here to stay do that?'

'God give me strength!' Noreen exclaimed, casting her eyes skyward. We walked about for a little in silence, each of us baffled in our differing ways, until Noreen began again, her manner carefully casual: 'Of course you know Miss Locke is soft on you. You can't be that daft. Handle it right and you can have her eating out of your hand.'

'Soft!' I exclaimed. It was my turn to laugh, albeit with some bitterness. On the contrary, I pointed out, Miss Locke was hard on me, very hard, always jeering and poking fun. As clinching proof I nearly told Noreen about the unspeakable kiss and the tongue pushed wetly into my mouth, only that was what it was, unspeakable. I could hardly bear to think about it, let alone put it into words. As it was, Noreen merely repeated that, no matter what I said, Miss Locke *was* soft on me, it was plain as the nose on your face, and if I played my cards right I could do all right for myself.

'Be nice to her,' she urged, as one friend to another. 'At least she's the only one of the bunch that hasn't got one foot in the grave. Play with her, why don't you? You must know what I mean. Let her do things –'

'I *do* play with her!' I countered heatedly. 'And I do let her do things. She's always hiking those boring old duets out of the piano stool *and* making me play *secondo* all the time, which isn't fair, but I never say anything –'

After that, somehow, talk petered out and I went back, a little distractedly, to naming the flowers. I couldn't remember achillea for the life of me, and I probably got centaurea wrong as well. Ignorant I might be, like most of my contemporaries in IIIa, but I was not a complete fool. My body, if not my brain, alerted me to the fact that in some way I didn't understand my conversation with Noreen had consisted of more than the words actually spoken.

'Trollius,' I instructed, pointing to something yellow. It was almost certainly not trollius at all, but I didn't suppose Noreen would notice. Her mind seemed to be on other things.

CHAPTER TWENTY-TWO

After they had gone, Mrs Crail in her hired car, Miss Malahide and Noreen resolutely driving off in the direction of Wroxham and, in all likelihood, looking for the first place where there was room to turn round once they were safely out of sight, Miss Barton – who had not been offered a lift by the headmistress – stepping out with sturdy resignation for the tram terminus, I sat alone in the front room doing my homework. I had been at Chandos House long enough now for the photographs of Mr Gosse which covered its walls no longer to trouble me. I was not even conscious that they were there. The room, the whole house, seemed blessedly tranquil and at ease after all the socializing.

I had an essay to write for Mrs Crail – 'Family Pets'. She went in for soppy subjects like that, probably in order to provide herself with the opportunity to tell us off for writing soppy essays. So far as pets were concerned, St Giles did not have a happy history. Apart from the puppy who had been run over, there was only Pillow the toad, whose violent end still haunted my dreams.* Otherwise there had only been a couple of cats who

* See *Opposite the Cross Keys*

had disdainfully accepted our proffered board and lodging on the understanding (or rather, our misunderstanding) that in return they would keep down the mice. Anyone calling that pair pets to their faces would, I am pretty sure, have felt the unsheathed edge of their claws. The truth was that, at St Giles, the family pet had been me, so much the youngest of the family, the spoilt darling.

As I had no confidence that this reading of her title would be acceptable to Mrs Crail, I invented a mynah bird named Joey, formerly the property of a sea captain in the China trade, and consequently arriving in our home with a vocabulary calculated to make spinster ladies go into shock. Fortunately for his avian soul, the Salvation Army hall was situated a few doors further up St Giles. Thanks to their band which, every Sunday morning, passed the house in full flood, to say nothing of the prayer meetings held in the street outside, Joey became a reformed character, his rendition of 'Onward Christian Soldiers' in a clear and pure soprano enough to bring any sinner to the mercy seat. By the time I had finished with Joey – two sides were the minimum and I managed to cover four – I believed in him implicitly, even if Miss Crail, wielding her blue pencil (all the other teachers used red) and smiling her abominable crescent smile, was all too likely to make it clear that she did not believe a word of it.

The exhilaration engendered by the completion of this literary exercise did not last long. My other homework was arithmetic.

Arithmetic! The very word was like a knell. Geometry was fine, algebra an endlessly entrancing game. At both subjects I was the best in IIIa – but arithmetic! I simply could not understand how the three came to be lumped together under the heading of mathematics. *If a train travels 30 miles at an average speed of 65 miles per hour and a further 25 miles at an average speed of 70 miles per hour, how many eggs at a shilling a dozen will fit into the guards van?* – or words to that effect. Every time I sat down to do my arithmetic homework I was confronted with the unpalatable proof that whilst diagrams and codes might be right up my alley, at trains and eggs and miles per hour – at real life, in fact – I was a washout.

My trouble was not that I couldn't get the correct answer to arithmetical problems, but that I arrived at them by a forbidden route – *interdit! verboten!* – by algebra which, for some reason (the sacred Syllabus, I suppose, or the examining board at Cambridge having its bit of fun), was worse than getting the wrong answer altogether so long as you went wrong using the correct arithmetical method. Arithmetic homework was done on paper specially ruled with a wide margin on the right-hand side where you had to show your working, so that your maths mistress could check that you weren't committing the sin against the Holy Ghost – in other words, cheating by using algebra.

Yet what was wrong with that lovely science, if that was what it was: poetry would be a better word for it – with its dear little numbers that signified squares and cubes hovering over the x's and the y's like honey bees, as if about to rob them of their nectar: its plus signs that changed miraculously to minus when you transferred them to the other side of the equation; its brackets that opened out like gates into a magic garden?

I once looked up the word *algebra* in the dictionary and discovered that it came from the Arabic. Just imagine! If only I had had the luck to be born in Saudi Arabia or Morocco I might have lived out my life in those perpetually sunny climes with never the hateful shadow of arithmetic – that which must be passed – darkening my days. Let x equal the number of camels, of date palms, of belly-dancers. Allah was great! The Arabs, the lucky things, had x's everywhere, with no one to hiss the imprecation 'Arithmetic!' With x at my bidding, I felt reasonably sure, I could unravel the secret of the universe.

With arithmetic, so far from unravelling anything, every so-called explanation left me ever more entangled. Since I was obviously not constituted to understand what it was all about, I concentrated on acquiring not the why of it, but the how, which I figured ought to be enough for exam purposes at our humble level. Miss Gosse, having chalked some indecipherable mishmash up on the blackboard, was always pleading with me in class, her boot-button eyes bright with earnestness: 'You do see why we do this, Sylvia, don't you?' To which the honest answer, if I had only had the gumption to be honest, would have been, 'Yes, Miss Gosse. To get through Matric.'*

The front room, shaded by the trunk of my quivering tree, was always the first in the house to grow dark. Still I delayed lighting the gas, wallowing in the outward reflection of my inward gloom; yet, once lit, it only made more explicit the footling matters to which I was commanded to bend all my intellectual powers: the train travelling at an average speed of who cared; Farmers Smith and Brown and Jones who, each owning 75 head of cattle, had elected to share grazing land, the silly fools. Anyone but the crackpots who wrote arithmetic books would have known an arrangement like that was bound to cause trouble –

---

* Matriculation, the name commonly given to the School Certificate Examination taken at age 16

Half an hour's homework – ha! Time passed interminably, the soft summer evening giving way to night. From the bottom of the front garden, along the Wroxham Road, waxing and waning car headlights advertised people pursuing all kinds of pleasure whilst I sat on a prickly chair, slowly but surely sinking in a bog of arithmetic as into the Slough of Despond. Upstairs, either Miss Gosse or Miss Locke was having a bath. I coud hear the water bubbling in the geyser. Otherwise, not a sound . . . Nobody had thought to remark, *Oh dear! Sylvia hasn't come for her Bovril. I hope nothing is wrong.* Nobody cared whether I was alive or dead.

Not even my father.

Admittedly, of late, I had been thinking about him rather less than when I had first come to Chandos House; but he should have been glad about that. The last thing he would want was for me to go about moping all my life. Life had to go on, as people had kept saying to my mother after the funeral. I could not believe that my father could be so petty-minded as to feel resentment that I had been too occupied in recent days to give him all that much attention. Yet how, unless he was displeased with me, could he look down from heaven, see the state I was in, and do nothing about it? Not that he was all that good at arithmetic himself, which, when you came down to it, was probably why I wasn't either. A quick word to Galileo, say, or Sir Isaac Newton was all that was needed.

'Sylvia, what in the world – ?' Miss Locke stood in the doorway in her red-and-white striped pyjamas; barefoot, no dressing-gown, her curls damp about her beautifully shaped little ears. She came into the room and demanded: 'Do you know what time it is? I saw the light shining on the grass. I thought you must have forgotten to turn it off. I never dreamed you'd still be here –'

As if only awaiting the appearance of an audience, I burst into noisy crying, something I was conscious of doing altogether too much since coming to Chandos House. It was getting to be a habit. I felt that my relationship with the human race had reached an all-time low. I needed help, love, sympathy, and what had I got? Miss Locke!

Still, I had to give her credit, she knew the right form of words.

'My dear child,' she exclaimed, 'whatever is troubling you?' She came over to where I was sitting and put her thin, whippy arms round my shoulders. For a moment fear redoubled my sobs. I thought she might be positioning herself for another of those horrible kisses. But all she did was ask, in the tenderest of tones: 'Tell me, love. Whatever is the matter?'

Incapable of speech, I gestured at the open textbook and the sheets with the ruled margins for your working, still blank after goodness knew how many hours. I seemed to have been sitting on that beastly chair for centuries.

'Arithmetic!' Miss Locke pronounced the word with a distaste I could not but find endearing. 'I might have guessed. Leave it now, why don't you, and have another go before breakfast.'

I wailed that I wouldn't be able to do it before breakfast, before dinner or tea, before ever. Miss Locke gave my shoulders an affectionate squeeze and said that I should have asked her.

'But you're a history mistress!'

'I could have had a word with Miss Gosse, if you'd only asked.'

I whimpered that, as she knew, Miss Gosse didn't think it fair to give me extra coaching, and Mrs Crail wouldn't be pleased either. Miss Locke repeated smilingly that, just the same, had I asked her, she might have been able to persuade Miss Gosse to change her mind. 'Why didn't you ask, you silly little goose?'

Too miserable to be other than frank, I admitted that I was afraid of her, too afraid to ask her anything.

'Afraid!' Miss Locke repeated, as if genuinely surprised. With her straight nose and straight forehead, her short hair very curly after her bath, she would have looked beautiful if only her mouth, even smiling, had not been so small. From the look of it, you would never have guessed what a large wet tongue lurked inside. Miss Locke said: 'When are you going to wake up to the fact that nobody in the world loves you more than I do?'

Without waiting for an answer she straightened up and went swiftly out of the door and up the stairs, leaving me more than a little disbelieving. Miss Locke love me? All I could say was, she had a funny way of showing it.

Still, I wasn't sorry that the gaslight shining on the grass had given me away. Not that her discovery of me had solved anything – the ruled pages remained as blank as ever – but the crying had done me a power of good. Besides, I thought maliciously, with that residual resentment all children harbour against the adult world, let *them* know something of the misery they inflicted with their presumption and their power. What grown-ups ever had to do arithmetic when they didn't want to?

At that moment Miss Locke came back into the room, the arithmetic mistress dragging unwillingly behind her. Miss Gosse had her dressing-gown on over her nightdress, disguising her short legs. Her hair was in its overnight plait and her face was shiny with cold cream, this last surprising me as I had not thought her one who went in for such vanities. She was a kind woman, and I believe the thought of my seeing her in that condition was the prime reason she had responded with such obvious reluctance to Miss Locke's demand that she come to my aid. I could understand how she felt, and I looked away, as embarrassed as she herself was. Whilst I was ready to concede that the history mistress meant well, I wished she hadn't bothered.

And anyway, what for? It was speedily apparent that more than face cream was at issue. Swivelling her button eyes from Miss Locke to me and back again, Miss Gosse maintained stoutly that it would not be fair for me to take advantage of my uniquely privileged position to obtain the private coaching denied to all the other denizens of IIIa.

'Rubbish!' was Miss Locke's unsympathetic response. 'The others have got their mothers and fathers to help them. I've never heard you going on about unfairness on that score.'

Looking increasingly unhappy, Miss Gosse denied that this was an accurate statement of the matter. She appealed to me for confirmation that in class she was constantly exhorting girls to hand in their own unaided work. It wasn't her fault that there seemed to be no way of stopping parents from helping their children with their homework, whether the children wanted it or not. Whereas, so far as Sylvia was concerned –

'So far as Sylvia is concerned, you leave her to sit up all hours without a soul to turn to! It won't do, Lydia – it really won't do!'

It was awful, but also, in its awful way, magnificent. It was the first time in my life that I had been witness to a full-blown, stand-up-and-knock-down row, and I would have been a block of wood not to have derived enjoyment from the spectacle, not to have been myself vitalized by the rush of energy released into the adjacent air. St Giles had known its minor differences but generally speaking, even irked, we had remained courteous to one another; never anything to approach words that were like daggers, laughter that was sharper than a bacon slicer; noise that rose high as Everest and dropped to a silence deep in the earth's core. Appalled and fascinated, I made myself as small as possible, kept out of the way whenever the two contestants, as happened from time to time, swayed in my direction. But inside I was not in the least small. I was tall with the excitement of being important.

Because amazingly, in some way I was unable to account for, the fighting was all about me. Not about whether Miss Gosse should or should not show me how to do my arithmetic prep: that had been only the trigger. Now they were flinging love and hate at each other like cowpats, and it was all due to a girl called Sylvia, a girl who could only be me.

'Corruption of a minor!' Miss Gosse screeched, and burst into tears, just as if she was twelve years old like me. Confused as I was by this unexpected reversal of roles, the phrase lodged in my butterfly brain, something to hang on to gratefully. Miss Locke's pyjama jacket had come undone and gaped wide. Her breasts, actually seen, looked smaller and much less bumpy than they did under her clothes, but more than large enough to make me go crimson and concentrate like mad on thinking about something else. So – 'minor' as in a minor scale, I pondered, or 'miner' as in a coal mine? Unless it was Joey the mynah as in 'Family Pets'?

It was certainly no moment to ask; and anyway, thank goodness, during my interval of semantic excogitation Miss Gosse and Miss Locke seemed to have resolved their differences. The storm had subsided with the same suddenness as it had blown up. The two women were standing plastered together, and Miss Locke, her face blazing with triumph, was murmuring into Miss Gosse's hair: 'There– there. It's all right, girlie. All right –'

Miss Locke went into the kitchen to make us all a nice hot cup of tea whilst Miss Gosse gave me an arithmetic lesson. *A train travels 25 miles at an average speed of 65 miles per hour and a further 30 miles at 70 miles per hour. What is the average speed for the complete journey?*

I was never to know. Miss Gosse began to read out the problem in a shaky voice. She had barely got as far as the first 'average speed' when she broke down, put her hands up to her face and burst into tears all over again. Her crying made me cry too, I don't know why, except that, as I say, it was getting to be a habit; besides which, Miss Gosse did remind me so strongly of the puppy who had got run over, and thinking about him always made me feel sad. The only bad thing about that puppy had been the way it had of trying to lick you all over – ugh! As it happened, just as I was remembering that, Miss Gosse leaned across the table and kissed me, a perfectly acceptable kiss, luckily on the cheek and quite dry.

Miss Locke came back from the kitchen in high spirits, with cups of tea on a tray and also, wonder of wonders – a midnight feast, she called it – a plate piled high with custard creams.

'You two old miseries!' she hooted at the sight of our tear-stained faces. 'If that's what arithmetic does to you, I can quite understand why Sylvia can't stand it.'

Miss Gosse looked at Miss Locke with a smile that, without my being able to say why, made me want to cry some more. She said: 'I've decided to excuse her from this weekend's prep, Helen. I think we've all been a little under the weather.'

'Speak for yourself!' Miss Locke took one of the custard creams and lobbed it in my direction. 'Catch!'

I reached up and caught the biscuit perfectly, which made it taste twice as good. As a matter of fact, in the end I ate the whole plateful because, for some reason, neither Miss Gosse nor Miss Locke fancied any.

CHAPTER TWENTY-THREE

We had a quiet time after that. We acted as if nothing had happened. Exams were coming up and the school took on an anxious, delicate air, as if sickening for something; the swots steering clear of the lazy, the feckless and the thick who sought out their company as never before, in the hope, it might be, of absorbing knowledge by hanging about in its vicinity. At Chandos House Miss Gosse and Miss Locke were busy setting examination papers and I was busy with revision, which was no problem as I had a good memory. Every evening I had a coaching session with Miss Gosse, and though I grew no fonder of arithmetic I did at least learn how to fill up those loathsome margins with some semblance of working, so that I got some marks for trying even if I more often got the answer wrong than right.

The two mistresses needed the large table in the drawing-room for their papers, so I did my revision in the dining-room. From the kitchen came the intoxicating savours of strawberries, raspberries, gooseberries cooking as Mrs Benyon made more pots of jam, I felt sure, than the inhabitants of Chandos House could eat in a lifetime. Knowing her, it wouldn't have surprised me to learn that she was running a jam-making factory on the side. Once – one Sunday when I had been invited to have supper with my brother Alfred's future in-laws – I went into the kitchen in the morning and asked if I could buy a jar of raspberry jam to take along as a present, and the housekeeper snapped: 'Elevenpence the pound size; two pounds, one and seven-pence ha'penny,' just like that, without having to stop to think, just like the grocer.

It wouldn't have surprised me, either, to discover that she and Mr Betts were in the jam-making business together, except that I doubted it because the gardener was always complaining about all the fruit the Bunion's jammy demands were cheating him out of. On the other hand, I knew by then that Mr Betts, though in the nicest possible way, was a crafty man, who could have been covering up his tracks.

One afternoon I found him sitting on his bench by the bothy eating a whipped cream walnut. I wished he hadn't eaten that particular one, since I knew it was my last. What with one thing and another I hadn't been into the city for ages and my stocks were just about exhausted. I wouldn't have said no if he had offered me the bottom bit of chocolate, which he hadn't yet got to, but it didn't seem to occur to him. He scoffed the lot, the greedy so-and-so, and then took out his horrid pipe by way of dessert.

Feeling deprived – so far as tea was concerned, it had been one of Mrs Benyon's less generous days – I sat down beside him, contriving nevertheless to preserve a veneer of amiability. Mr Betts's friendship had become important to me.

In a conversational way I asked if he could please tell me what a randy old dyke was. The gardener took his pipe out of his mouth, regarded it for a little in silence, and then put it back again.

'You know what a dyke is. Can't be born in Norfolk and not know what a dyke is.'

'Not that kind!' I brushed the answer aside impatiently. 'The kind of dyke I mean is a person. What kind of person, though – that's the question. Do you know what kind of person it is?'

Mr Betts replied austerely that one thing he did know, which was that dyke meaning a person was not a word that ought to pass a young lady's lips. It was as bad a word as swearing and, if he might take the liberty, whoever I had picked it up from was not a fit person for a young lady to associate herself with.

I laughed and said that as a matter of fact it was a young lady I had picked it up from; to which Mr Betts returned a sardonic 'Oh ah? Some lady!'

'What about *randy*, then?' I persisted. 'Is that a bad word too?'

Mr Betts nodded and got up to go home. He seemed to consider the subject closed, which was intolerable.

'But what do they *mean*?' I cried. 'I promise not to use them. I just want to know.'

'Wha's the point o' bunging yer brains up wi' that garbage? Stuff enough of it in, it turns all the rest rotten.'

To this I responded by pointing out that although he, Mr Betts, evidently knew what both dyke and randy meant, *his* brains were still in working order. I walked with him a little way towards the back gate, piling on the winsomeness for all it was worth, and at last, when we were nearly there, I got my reward – distinctly disappointing when you came down to it. I couldn't understand what all the fuss had been about.

'A dyke,' Mr Betts explained, 'is a mannish woman' – which, all said and done, was only a factual description of Miss Malahide with her whiskers – 'and *randy* means –' the gardener searched about for an equivalent before coming up with 'vigorous'.

'On'y mind what I say,' he finished. 'Don't you go speakin' either of them to anybody – not even to the scrubber who spoke them to you.'

I would have gone on to ask him what a scrubber was, only by then he was through the gate. However, he came back to say: 'There's a pal o' yours outside in the lane, if you're interested. Don't look, though, as if he came to see you. He's feeding that blasted donkey.'

Robert Kett was feeding Bagshaw a Victoria sponge that looked as though someone had sat on it. He said that all his mother's Victoria sponges, so long as he could remember, came out like that, but that she never gave up trying. She had been about to throw her latest disaster into the dustbin when he had said that he knew a donkey who would be glad of it.

'A donkey!' she had exclaimed, but then she had burst out laughing and said it was something at least to know that all those eggs and the flour and sugar wouldn't be wasted.

I liked the sound of Robert Kett's mother. She sounded a nice woman. Bagshaw, judging by the way he went for the sponge cake, especially the jammy bits, had fallen for her in a big way, just as he had for her son. Whilst the two were busy smiling at each other I sneaked a small piece for myself and it wasn't all that bad, at any rate not on one of Mrs Benyon's meagre days: but I didn't try to get any more, both because I didn't want to deprive

Bagshaw, and because I had developed a kind of loyalty, not so much to Miss Gosse and Miss Locke and Mrs Benyon – certainly not to *her!* – as to Chandos House itself, its gaslight, the mauve lining in the piano front, my little room and the quivering tree outside my window. I didn't want to admit to an outsider that it was only too easy to be hungry there.

I was glad to see Robert Kett, even if he hadn't come primarily – if at all – to see me. Since our last meeting I had begun to think he wasn't as drippy as I had previously thought, and I was afraid his encounter with Miss Locke might have frightened him away for good and all, for which I wouldn't have blamed him one bit. For the first time I had found myself remembering what he actually looked like, and thinking that he was quite good-looking in a quiet way. His hair, I had decided, wasn't mousy at all, when looked at with an objective eye. It was ash blond.

Alas, when once more I saw him in the flesh, feeding his mother's cake to the donkey, I saw that my moony meditations had built up a picture beyond the reality. By the most generous standard, mousy was still the right adjective for his hair, and if he was good-looking in a quiet way, it was a quietness so profound as to be undetectable by any instrument known to man. A disappointing awakening, yet at the same time a relief at being let off some invisible hook.

Without waiting to be asked what he had done with it, Robert Kett told me that he had left his bike out of sight round the bend, a little further up the lane, where there was a gate into a field with no barbed wire nor brambles to threaten its beautiful paintwork.

'I know it,' I commented, not caring to admit that I did not know, that some childish superstitiousness prevented me from exploring where the path went after it had passed the back entrance to Chandos House. Actually, in moments of private horror, I knew exactly where it went – to nowhere, not a nowhere from which you were free to turn round and come back either: but of course I said nothing about that.

The boy jerked his head in the direction of the Chandos House gate and asked, 'How you getting on with *her?*'

'Not bad at all,' I answered; adding offhandedly, 'She just bought me a dress.'

I was glad to have someone to tell about the dress, because it both excited and troubled me. I would have brought the subject up with Mr Betts, only we had got bogged down in randy old dykes. It was a day when Miss Locke had come home on her own – I had no idea where Miss Gosse had got to – and she had come up to my room, barging in without knocking, in her arms an expensive-looking box with Chamberlain's on it. Chamberlain's was the poshest department store in Norwich.

'Well, go on! Open it,' she had ordered, tossing it on to the bed. 'Then come into my room to try it on. I've got a long glass you'll be able to see yourself in properly.'

Inside the box were sheets and sheets of tissue paper layered there with unthinking luxury, and, nestling amongst it, was a dress. But such a dress! The word is inadequate to describe its beauty and its mysteriousness. To begin with, it was red, and I had never possessed a red dress before, my mother believing clothes of that colour unsuitable for those of tender years; and then again, it was made of chiffon, a material equally out of my childish star, but one that moved about one's body as if propelled by built-in zephyrs over a lining of scarlet silk that whispered secrets when you so much as breathed.

Patterned with nebulous traceries of pale blue and pale yellow that made you think of lighted candles flickering in a draught, the dress was like a flame. Trying it on in front of Miss Locke's long mirror, embarrassed by being in her room for the first time and by her intent gaze watching as I stripped to my vest and knickers, I nevertheless felt myself transformed, made beautiful by its beauty. 'Something special for somebody special,' I heard Miss Locke say, from somewhere a long way off. The skirt, longer than any I had ever possessed, swirled like the skirts of a dancing dervish as I twisted and turned, trying to survey every aspect of the ravishing creature I had suddenly turned into. At the neck there was a kind of scarf thing which I flung over one shoulder with gypsy abandon. The sleeves, caught in tight to the wrist, were pleated and very full. I could feel the air trapped inside them.

'For heaven's sake, take off those stockings,' Miss Locke commanded, and I obediently stripped off my black school stockings and stood barefoot on the balls of my feet, heels off the floor, scarcely knowing what kept me anchored there and not rising to the ceiling and through it to the roof and beyond, up into the summer sky.

Miss Locke declared with a satisfied air: 'As soon as I set eyes on it, I knew it was made for you.' Then: 'Don't I get a kiss for thank you?'

Aflame in my flame-coloured dress, not even that could dowse my pleasure. I kissed her lightly on the cheek, and whirled away before she could make something yukky out of it. How I wished Alfred, Maud, my mother, were there to see how gorgeous I looked. How I wished my father could see me, until I remembered that he could, unless God had kept him busy with some special job, which wasn't likely with all those angels standing about waiting for orders.

I heard the front door open and shut and Miss Gosse's brisk little pitter-pat on the hall lino. Not knowing how I knew, I knew without question that she was not to be told about the dress. Miss Locke looked on in silent amusement as I hastily gathered up my clothes and ran across the landing, back to my room, where I showed off my dress to the leaves clustered against the window. They positively shook with joy and astonishment.

I wanted people to see me in my new dress. I craved to be admired.

I confided to Robert Kett: 'It's very unusual.' Seized by the sudden realization that here was an audience ready-made: 'Would you like me to go and put it on, so you can see it?' The boy looked bemused, positively thick.

'If you want to.'

I did want to. *Just you wait*, I thought to myself. *That'll take the silly look off your face!* I went through the gate into the garden, ran its length and round to the front of the house so as to be sure of not running into Mrs Benyon. A glance into the bicycle shed in passing reassured me that neither Miss Locke nor Miss Gosse had come home.

In my room I undressed quickly, remembering to take off my black stockings as well. The new dress slid over my head as smoothly as cream, the silk lining whispering a greeting. I put on my sandals and ran downstairs and out into the air again.

Robert Kett turned from feeding Bagshaw the last of the Victoria sponge and stared at me as I stood in front of him, panting a little from my run but otherwise quite still, the dress billowing gently in the soft breeze. Then he said: 'I'm going to buy you a red ribbon for your hair.'

'I was forced to stay still for fear the dress might catch on a protruding bramble or branch of wild rose, otherwise I would have executed a twirl of triumph then and there. In my exalted state I instructed the boy: 'See it's the right kind of red, then. Scarlet, not crimson.' And, with a sudden brain-wave: 'If you're going shopping, there's one or two things you can get for me at the same time.' No asking please, you notice. In my red dress I had only to command.

I told him that I needed half a pound of custard creams plus a dozen whipped cream walnuts, explaining away the size of the order by saying it was principally for Mr Betts the gardener, who was mad about them. I told him how I kept my money and my private store in a special place in the bothy, implying, without actually saying so, that I was conferring a great favour by entrusting him with my secret.

'Come in and I'll get you the money.'

He wanted to wait whilst I went and fetched it myself. Afraid of running into Miss Locke, of course. Invulnerable in my red dress, I made no attempt to hide my disdain: shamed him into following me through the gate before I said negligently, over my shoulder, the scarf ends floating wide: 'It's all right. Neither of them's in.'

It was the red dress he followed, not me. He followed it up the garden as far as the bothy, out of the sunlight into the fusty gloom within. At the sight of the nest of drawers he brightened up no end. Apparently, at school, woodwork was his favourite subject. It was, he asserted, a crying shame to keep a nest of drawers like that, so beautifully made, an antique, he shouldn't be surprised, in a shed open to the damp and with nobody to care what happened to it. He stroked the wood and said it was lovely. Miss What's-her-name must be barmy, leaving a nest of drawers like that out in the garden to go to the dogs.

Piqued that Robert Kett seemed to have quite forgotten me in my new red dress, I opened my money drawer wide, ostensibly to take out enough to pay for the biscuits and the whipped cream walnuts, but really to let him see how much silver still remained, that I was a woman of substance. All he did was push the drawer back in, a look of alarm on his face.

'Don't do that! You're putting too much strain on it.'

Robert Kett looked at the nest of drawers with a sigh of longing. 'I had a piece of furniture like that, I'd make it really look something.' 'Would you really?' I studied the nest of drawers in my turn, noting for the first time the neatness of its mitred corners, the elegant inlay, thin as string, which outlined each individual drawer. 'If you like, I'll ask Miss Gosse to let you come here and work on it in your spare time.'

For a moment the boy looked tempted, but then he shook his head. I guessed he was thinking about Miss Locke, though what he said was: 'Then she'll move it indoors and you won't have anywhere any more to hide your money in.'

'Or my biscuits,' I agreed. 'Or my whipped cream walnuts. And Mr Betts won't have anywhere to put his seeds.' I was content to leave it at that. He really was a nice boy. I was truly grateful to him for having taught me to see the nest of drawers with new eyes.

With exaggerated care I opened and shut the drawers where I kept my stores and, no more than an inch or two, some of the drawers full of packets of seeds, whilst Robert Kett marvelled aloud at the smoothness with which they slid along their runners. With that sudden transition from gravity to tomfoolery characteristic of our place in space and time – the narrow crack between childhood and puberty – we began to open and shut drawers at random, getting noisier as we went along.

'Here's where you keep your doughnuts,' Robert Kett sang out. 'And here's where I keep my glacier mints,' I countered. 'Here's where you keep your chocolate éclairs!'

'And here's where I keep my jam tarts!'

'Here's where you keep your rhubarb and custard!' 'And here's where I keep my summer pudding!'

'Here's where you keep your cornflakes – your poached eggs on toast – your liquorice shoe laces –'

We opened and shut the dear little drawers shrieking with laughter, forgetting what, as children, we should have remembered, that laughter was dangerous. But then, children never learn, they only grow up. We became so weak with laughing that we had to lean against each other for support. Gasping for breath, we never noticed that the gloom inside the funny little house had deepened, that a shadow blocked the door, until a stinging sensation of heat cut across my right cheek and a voice, as cold as the pain was hot, lanced across the bothy.

'You dirty little slut!'

CHAPTER TWENTY-FOUR

Miss Locke had a ring which she wore occasionally on the third finger of her right hand; wore it sometimes during the week though I don't think mistresses were supposed to wear jewellery at school, except for Mrs Curwen who wore her wedding ring and Mrs Crail who wore hers whether she was entitled to it or not, as well as a heavy gold chain and medallion that looked as if it might have belonged to a Lord Mayor. Miss Locke's ring – so she had once told me – had been made for her specially by a dear friend who wasn't alive any longer. She had gone out swimming one morning before breakfast and never come back.

I must say it seemed a fitting death because the ring, which was made of silver and a greenish enamel with bits of lapis lazuli stuck on here and there, was in the form of silver reeds bent, as it might be, under water. In the middle of them was the tiny figure of a girl with long waving hair who might have been asleep or a water nymph but who looked drowned to me in the brief time I was given to make up my mind about her. Miss Locke had taken the ring off her finger to let me have a better look at it, but then she had whipped it back brusquely, as if it was my fault she had ever let it out of her possession, even for a second.

It was a wide, bumpy kind of ring that could not have been very comfortable to wear, which was probably why Miss Locke did not wear it all that often. Unfortunately for me, she was wearing it that afternoon in the bothy when she struck me on the cheek and the bumpy bits opened up a jagged cut over my right cheekbone. There was a lot of blood which, in my state of appalled astonishment, I barely noticed. I had been hit! I, who had never known anything but loving-kindness and soft words all the years of my life, had been hit. Violence! I could not take it in.

Robert Kett was shouting – something about the blood dripping on my new dress, which, in my confusion, did not seem all that important. Red on red, it wouldn't show. He was also shouting something about going for the police and the Society for Cruelty to Children. I saw, as from a distance, that it was Miss Locke he was shouting at – shouting as if he had never been the least bit afraid of her. It was very brave, but too noisy. The noise gave me a headache. I was relieved when he stopped shouting and brought out a rather grubby handkerchief with which he tried to staunch the bleeding.

With her back to the light, Miss Locke's expression was indecipherable. Her voice was brisk and precise, the tone she used towards the end of lessons on a day when she thought IIIa had been particularly thick.

'Go to the police by all means, young man. Let me tell you, when I tell them what I saw, they will send you to a reformatory.'

'You never saw – we never did anything!'

'A liar into the bargain.' Miss Locke swivelled her body in my direction. Silhouetted as she was, I could not see, but I felt the unforgivingness of her.

Robert Kett was shouting again. I wished he would go home so that I could get some quiet. I put out my hand and tugged at his blazer sleeve, which made him turn and look at me. I was still bleeding.

'Haven't you got any iodine?' he demanded of Miss Locke, still shouting.

When the history mistress didn't answer; turned on her heel and went out of the bothy leaving us there, Robert Kett urged me not to stay at Chandos House a second longer. Never mind my luggage, never mind anything. He would take me home to his mother who would know how to stop the bleeding, and look after me. I would like his mother.

'Perhaps she's gone for the iodine,' I said, meaning Miss Locke; though I didn't think so for a moment.

The mention of iodine had brought me fully back to my senses. I hated the stuff, the way it stung, the crude yellow stain of it. Robert Kett's mother, I felt sure, kindly and with the best of intentions, would slosh on iodine by the bucketful, however much I protested that I would rather have the germs.

The important thing was to make the boy promise not to go either to the police or the Society for Cruelty to Children: nor to tell anybody about what had happened.

Reluctantly, he promised. I could have wished he had not added, on a note of disbelief: 'You aren't going to go on living here?'

How tired I was! Too tired even to think about decisions, let alone actually make them. I said that exams started the day after tomorrow and that was all I could think about at the moment; and he had better go, because I still had some revising to do.

I think Robert Kett must have been feeling tired himself after all the shouting, because he didn't make any more fuss. He gave me his handkerchief and told me to keep it pressed against my cheek and then the bleeding would stop. There was no need to give it back, he added, kind boy that he was.

We came out of the bothy together, the sunlight making us both screw our eyes up after the dark within. The two of us didn't look in the least alike ordinarily, but for some reason I was strongly aware that, just at that moment, despite the blood on my face and the freckles on his, we were as alike as two peas in a pod, two children screwing up their eyes against the sun and everything.

He said: 'I hope you haven't messed up your pretty dress.'

'Red on red,' I reassured him. 'It won't show.'

It was just my luck to run bang into Miss Gosse in the hall. She looked at the bloodstained handkerchief in horror, boot-button eyes protruding. I was a bit annoyed to find her there. I had been intending to take a quick look at my face in the hall mirror. Now that the shock of having been the victim of a violent assault was – not wearing off, but descending, as it were, to a deeper level of consciousness, I had begun to feel important again. I wanted to see if the damage was as gratifyingly awful as Robert Kett had seemed to imply.

I told Miss Gosse that I had slipped and fallen against something.

'Let me see.'

As soon as I took the handkerchief away she gave a little gasp and said we must go to the doctor's immediately. Dr Becket, thank heaven, lived only a few houses up the road and as it was surgery hours he was bound to be there.

Mindful of Dr Parfitt in St Giles who probably drank iodine where other men drank whisky, he was so fond of using it, I was on the point of insisting that I didn't think it worthwhile bothering a doctor for a little thing like that when a trickle of blood ran into the corner of my mouth. Robert Kett's handkerchief, pressed tightly against the cheek as per his instructions, had stuck to the wound, and pulling it away to show Miss Gosse had started up the bleeding again.

The blood, salty to the taste with an undertone of bitterness, ran over my teeth like something alive, and frightened me. I was afraid I would bleed to death and was irked no end to see Miss Gosse looking for her gloves, as if you couldn't go to see a doctor without them.

Whilst she was still looking, Miss Locke came down the stairs looking very spick and span as if she had just that moment washed her hands and face and run a comb through her curly hair. So far as I could see, she had taken off her ring.

Miss Gosse came away from the hallstand to meet her. 'I'm taking Sylvia to the doctor's. She's had an accident.'

'Dear me!' Miss Locke observed coolly. Without so much as looking at me she passed along the passage, towards the dining room. Miss Gosse looked after her in momentary perplexity before her little puppy-dog face cleared as she explained for my benefit: 'I don't think she even took it in, poor girl. Those exam papers! She's working herself to a frazzle.'

I need not have been afraid. Dr Becket, crisply clean-shaven, no soup stains on his white jacket, and hands that knew their business as he put two stitches into the gash on my cheek, proved as different as could be from Dr Parfitt. No iodine either, but something cold that stung hardly at all, followed by a powdering that was wonderfully soothing. He sponged away the dried blood that was making my face feel stiff with a gentleness that, judging from his severe appearance, I would not have guessed him capable of.

In fact, he looked amazingly like Miss Locke, except that his nose was not quite as straight as hers: it looked as if it might have been damaged in school boxing. Amid the large apprehensions and the small pains of the consultation I wondered vaguely whether he was married. If not, he and Miss Locke would make a well-matched pair, to say nothing of the advantage to a doctor, surely, of having a wife who could be relied on to bring in business whenever she took it into her head to hit people so that they needed stitches. Only four houses away from Chandos House, why hadn't Miss Gosse thought to introduce them?

Dr Becket pondered aloud whether he ought or ought not to give me an anti-tetanus injection, just, as he said, to be on the safe side. This upset me, because I couldn't remember whether it was for tetanus or rabies that they stuck needles into your stomach, too agonizing for words – or so I seemed to have read somewhere. His questioning – had I fallen on to bare earth? had I been in contact with any metal? – caused me further anxiety. Since I had not regained sufficient energy to concoct a credible story to account for my injury, I took the easy way out and began to cry. Somewhat to my surprise, considering the man's stern demeanour, it worked. He discontinued the cross-examination and produced a yellow pill which I was to go to bed and take as soon as I returned home. I would wake up in the morning, he said, feeling my old self (whatever that was, I added mentally). No more was said about anti-tetanus, that was something.

Back at Chandos House, on tiptoe at my awkwardly placed looking-glass, I at last had the opportunity of surveying the physical damage Miss Locke had done to me. Whilst I must have looked much better than I had before receiving Dr Becket's ministrations I still looked ghastly, the cheek swollen so that my right eye had the appearance of a sun about to set behind a hill which would shortly obliterate it altogether.

It occurred to me to wonder if I was scarred for life. No one would want to marry me looking like that, and I would live and die an old maid, probably a schoolmistress like Miss Locke, like Miss Gosse. My attempt to work up a good head of self-pity got nowhere. I simply could not be fagged. I swallowed the yellow pill.

One other thing the mirror had shown me. Red on red did show. The new dress was scarlet, my blood crimson. It was obvious that we were not, after all, made for each other. Untidy threads of blood showed all the way down the right side of the bodice from neck to waistline. Dr Becket hadn't done it any good either. Splashings of water darkened and patches of his therapeutic powder whitened a substantial area of the front. On the way to the doctor's, Miss Gosse had ventured nervously, as if afraid what the answer might be, 'I don't think I've seen you wearing that frock before, Sylvia.'

'Haven't you?' I said: and that was the sum of our conversation on the subject.

I pulled the dress over my head, not bothering to check that I had undone all the buttons, two of which promptly popped off and disappeared who cared where. The buttons were shaped like tiny acorns, covered with the same material as the dress. I could almost hear Mrs Benyon complaining that the dratted things had put paid to her carpet sweeper.

I bundled the dress up and thrust it into the drawstring bag which I used for soiled linen, lay down on the bed in my underwear. My mother was right in one thing, I told the leaves trembling at the window. Red was not a suitable colour for children.

Next day, though the swelling was worse and my cheek had turned a threatening shade of purple, I felt much better. Thanks to the yellow pill, I suppose, I had slept long and dreamlessly, awaking only when Mrs Benyon arrived at the door with my breakfast.

Breakfast in bed! And Mrs Benyon actually smiling! I could almost have fancied myself still dreaming and back in St Giles again.

I was not in St Giles. As the memory of where I was, of what had happened the day before took hold, my eyes filled with tears.

In a voice I scarcely recognized, so human was it, the house-keeper said: 'I didn't work my fingers to the bone making a slap-up breakfast for a cry-baby.'

Slap-up was the only word for it. I could never have imagined that Chandos House even harboured the makings of such a banquet – scrambled eggs, sausages and mushrooms with fluffy little potato cakes on the side, oodles of toast and marmalade;

two silver pots, one with coffee, one with hot milk, all disposed prettily on a pale blue tray with little legs that came down so that you didn't have to balance it on your knees.

The housekeeper, having plumped up my pillow and settled me comfortably (with no insistence that I get up first and go and wash), produced a silver bell which she placed among the dishes.

'Anything more you want, just ring.'

When, as she was leaving, I told her shyly that she was an angel, she turned in the doorway, her face arranged in that marble stare of hers I ordinarily detested.

'Make the most of it while it lasts, if I was you.'

'I will!' I promised, whereupon we both laughed. We actually laughed together!

The laughter seemed to have prompted second thoughts. Mrs Benyon came back into the room and informed me that the schoolmistresses had long ago gone off to school, Miss Gosse leaving instructions that I was to stay at home for the day and take things easy. Seating herself on the end of the bed, which made the bed tray teeter dangerously until mattress and spring had made the necessary adjustments, she inquired, with the ease of one settling down to a comfortable chat, 'So what really happened, then?'

Kicking myself mentally for still not having my story ready, and using a mouth full of toast and marmalade as an alibi, I mumbled something about falling over and hitting my face against something. As an explanation it was pathetic, but it seemed to satisfy – or did it?

'Pity Miss Locke had only just that minute come indoors. She stayed out a bit longer, she might have caught you as you fell.'

'I suppose she might,' I agreed faintly.

'Funny thing is –' the housekeeper went on relentlessly – 'she must've had a bit of a fall herself. There's a coincidence! When she came in through the french window I went into the dining-room to ask should I bring in the tea, and she was white as a sheet. And what do you think?' The old devil regarded me with an expression of the utmost innocence. 'There was blood on her hand.'

Mrs Benyon got up, the bed responding with a whinny of relief. She stood looking down at me.

'Don't you go letting those sausages get cold, now. And next time she tries to lay a hand on you, the filthy cow, take my advice an' give her back as good as you get, either on the conk or the backside, whichever is most convenient.'

To my surprise, when I went down the garden at the time I guessed Mr Betts would be taking his elevenses, I found him sitting on the bench eating a whipped cream walnut. How could that be, when only yesterday I had watched with my own eyes as he scoffed the last one?

The gardener put the chocolate down on his folded paper and got up as soon as he heard my approach. The concern that showed on his knobby face pleased me. It was all screwed up with the force of his feelings as he drew me down by both hands to sit beside him.

'Well, well! You *have* been in the wars!'

I was grateful that here was one, at least, who did not press me for details.

But then, as I quickly discovered, he had no need to. With a little help, he must have worked it out for himself.

'That young man o' yours, bin here first thing. In a dreadful hurry to get off to school, but he brought you the biscuits and the whipped cream walnuts you wanted, an' said I was to tell you there's fourpence change in the bag.' Over the last of his whipped cream walnut Mr Betts looked at me in a worried way. 'Like me t' fetch one out fer you?'

Full of my bang-up breakfast, I answered that I did not fancy one at the moment, thank you; wondering why the man still looked upset.

'It looks worse than it is,' I assured him. 'The doctor put two stitches in and once the swelling's gone down he says it'll soon dry up and I'll hardly be able to tell even where it was.'

'Tha's good! Wouldn't want yer chances ruined of ending up a star of the silver screen.'

But I could see that something was still bothering him.

'That young "wha's-his-name" –' he came out with it at last. 'He left a message for you.'

'About the fourpence, you mean? You said.'

'Not just that. He said –' There was a long pause. 'He said I were to tell you he knew he said he wouldn't tell anybody, like you made him promise, but somehow, arter he got home, he told his ma. He said it just come out like, not intending it. And his ma–' an even longer interval – 'his ma says it's better if he doesn't come again, not for a while, at any rate.' When I made no immediate comment, the gardener added, his voice gentle: 'Don't take on, gal.'

I said, more or less truthfully, that I had no intention of taking on. That it was Bagshaw I was thinking about and how Mrs Kett made Victoria sponges which weren't any good, only Bagshaw was crazy about them. I wasn't being brave, though I could see Mr Betts thought I was. Mingled with the sour taste of rejection was a sense of relief. At least I wouldn't have to rack my brains any more to remember what Robert Kett looked like. As a matter of fact, his image was already fading rapidly.

Mr Betts looked at me in admiration. He was a great patriot and I could see he thought I was keeping a stiff upper lip in the traditional English fashion, when I wasn't at all, only a stiff upper cheek, courtesy of Miss Grecian-conk Locke. So that when he went on, his rosy face rosier than ever with earnestness: 'Pretty gal like you, there's plenty more fish in the sea.' I was able to reply with sufficient honesty that, taking one thing with another, I was not dissatisfied with the way things had turned out. Boys, on the whole, were an awful bother and I had exams to think of.

For some reason, my answer only seemed cause for further disquiet. Having once been one himself, I suppose, Mr Betts insisted that boys were a good thing and I wasn't on any account to go thinking different. Living with 'them two old desiccated coconuts', which I took to mean my landlady and my co-lodger, might have given me the wrong idea.

I said it had nothing to do with the schoolmistresses. And anyway, Miss Locke wasn't old.

'They're the worst kind,' he replied darkly.

His break over, he heaved himself up on to his ex-stable boy's bowed legs and started off towards the greenhouse.

'Got to love yer and leave yer.'

I went slowly back up the garden, past all the lovely growing things. How lucky they were to have only greenfly and cuckoo-spit to worry about! I was half-way back to the house when Mr Betts overtook me.

'Head like a sieve, that's me,' he said cheerfully. 'There *were* one other thing. The young 'un asked me special to say as how he hopes the dress is OK.'

Feeling a bit low, I went indoors, got 'Pale Hands I Loved' out of the piano stool and played it loudly, hoping Mrs Benyon would hear, wherever in the house she happened to be, and come and join in. She must have been busy in the kitchen, getting the lunch ready or something. However, across the distance separating us her strange, extra-terrestrial voice sounded almost as loud as if she were in the room, her heavy hands on my shoulders, her heavy-scented breath wafting past my ear.

'Pale hands, pink-tipped, like lotus-buds that float
On those cool waters where we used to dwell,
I would have rather felt you round my throat
Crushing out life than waving me farewell.'

CHAPTER TWENTY-FIVE

Unfortunately, back at school, my fluorescent cheek and stitched wound did not attract the attention I had anticipated, but that was because it was the first day of exams, the prospect of which several of the girls in IIIa used as a pretext for histrionic displays of panic and palpitation that stole my thunder. For myself, arithmetic apart, I relished exams. They were a game that made me feel excited, stretched beyond my natural capacities. I loved the hushed ritual of coming into the classroom to find creamy ruled paper, of much better quality than our everyday stuff, laid out ready on desks which, for all their carved initials and other familiar disfigurements, had taken on a sacramental quality befitting the occasion; the inkwells fresh-filled by some unknown hand; and, face down, the examination paper, a mystery not to be divulged until the big hand on the classroom clock moved to the witching hour and the invigilator, in a voice never heard at other times, intoned, with the inevitability of fate: 'Now!'

When at last it was permissible to turn the paper over and read the questions cyclostyled on the other side, the blood pounded triumphantly through my veins at the recognition that, thanks to my good memory, none of them was beyond my powers. The delicious uncertainty of deciding which combination would best display my genius – five questions to be answered out of a total of eight – was even better than being offered a box of chocolates from which you were only allowed to select one.

My sole difficulty so far as exams were concerned was in the matter of timing. However much I began with an iron resolve to divide the time available by five and stick to it, go on to the next question once the allotted time was up, even if it meant stopping in the middle of a sentence, middle of a word even, things seldom worked out that way. There was so much I wanted to say! Invariably, for all my resolutions, the last question certainly and often the penultimate as well were scamped, to my teachers' oft-voiced despair. They constantly pointed out that since an agreed number of marks attached to any one answer, gilding the lily in the earlier part of the paper could never compensate for doing poorly in the second half.

'You'll never get Matric unless you mend your ways!' they admonished me.

The exams settled down to a lovely rhythm that left one disorientated when it stopped, buoyed up only by the thought of results. Having become accustomed to my damaged cheek and the necessity of taking extra care whenever I pulled any article of clothing over my head, I almost forgot about the injury and its cause. Almost.

At break on my first day back Miss Malahide accosted me in the north quad outside the Art Room.

'What on earth have you done to yourself, child?'

By then I was already tired of being asked that question and fudging the reply, and because it was Miss Malahide, her hairy face alight with compassion, I answered that I hadn't done anything. Somebody had done it to me. 'If you promise not to tell,' I had added, marvelling at my own audacity, 'I'll tell you who it was.'

The art mistress had looked, not angry, but alarmed. 'I think I would rather not know,' she said, and hurried away, flinging an end of her black cloak over her shoulder.

All this time, whether in school or at Chandos House, Miss Locke never so much as spoke to me. At breakfast Miss Gosse, whose doggy features had come to wear a look of permanent bewilderment, would say things like: 'I think Sylvia's face is looking a little better this morning, don't you, Helen?' or 'I'm sure the swelling's gone down. What do you think?' To which Miss Locke would make rejoinders such as 'I really couldn't say,' and go on to other matters.

For the history exam, to IIIa's surprise, she acted as invigilator, it being an unwritten law that, to avoid any suspicion of bias, mistresses did not officiate in their own subjects. Waiting for the off, I studied her straight-browed, straight-nosed profile, knowing it was quite safe to do so since she would never turn her face towards me. I came to the conclusion that, whatever writers of romantic novels might maintain, small, shell-like ears were not beautiful. They were mean, unfriendly, signifying people who did not want to listen or did not know how to. I decided, admittedly on insecure grounds, that a trumpeting elephant, charging towards you with trunk upraised, was less frightening by reason of its large ears flapping than a history mistress with her teeny-weeny shells.

And what kind of shells were like ears, when you came down to it? I could not remember a single author ever specifying. Cockles, winkles, mussels, whelks? I still hadn't decided which species they could possibly have had in mind when the big hand of the clock clicked into place and Miss Locke called out: 'Now!'

Exams over, several days of delicious lethargy followed. The mistresses were all busy marking papers and we were left more or less to our own devices. We were allowed to bring our own books to school and read them sitting outside on the grass under the trees which screened the school buildings from the roads on either side. I had brought *Antic Hay* by Aldous Huxley which I had got out of the library because I had read somewhere that he was a subtle and witty writer.

At twelve years old, the subtlety passed me by and I found precious little to laugh at; which did not entirely displease me as I was most of all in the mood to lie flat on my back, looking up through the canopy of the trees to the sky beyond, thinking of nothing special.

'Showing off as usual, Sylvia!' said Mrs Crail, smiling her crescent smile.

I scrambled to my feet, blushing and confused as I always was in her presence. The headmistress delicately put the toe of her shoe to *Antic Hay* where it lay open at my place, down-facing on the grass. 'I'm sure the librarian will be most interested to hear what care you take of the city's books.'

I wanted to shout out, 'You're doing more harm with that great fat toe of yours than I ever did leaving it open like that!' But of course I didn't say anything, and after she had opened a nasty little crack in the book's spine she sailed majestically on.

That afternoon I went down to the back gate at Chandos House for the first time in ages. Exams had been my excuse, but the unacknowledged truth was that I hadn't wanted to risk running into Robert Kett. I hoped he hadn't given up going to see Bagshaw just because he had given up coming to see me. I hoped his mother hadn't found a recipe for making Victoria sponges that rose.

I also began to feel guilty. Poor old Bagshaw! It wasn't his fault Robert Kett and I were not friends any longer.

Mrs Benyon gave me some stale bread and I went down the garden and out of the gate, both relieved and disappointed to find there was nobody there except the donkey. He was standing at the barbed wire, not looking in the least pleased to see me or my bread which as usual he swallowed as if doing me a favour. The reason was not far to seek. Lying in the middle of the path was a good-sized wedge of failed Victoria sponge, too far from the wire for even Bagshaw's scrawny stretch. Robert Kett must have chucked the cake down and run, frightened I might choose that moment to put in an appearance. A wasp was crawling about the jam filling, having a whale of a time. The sight of it on the ground out of reach must have turned Bagshaw into a raving loony. The look he gave me, and the accompanying snort! 'About time!' was definitely what he said.

Because of the wasp I didn't care actually to pick up the piece of sponge, so I found a stick in the hedge and poked at it until it was in a position for the donkey to get at unaided. He snuffled it up at a gulp, wasp and all, and still looked so plainly dissatisfied that I said I wouldn't be long, went back through the gate and up the garden as far as the bothy, where I went to the drawer which housed the custard creams. It was the first time I had been in the bothy since – I did not care to specify even to myself since when – and it made me feel peculiar. To keep my mind off the when I reminded myself that Bagshaw, a donkey of small patience, was waiting; pulled open the drawer in which I knew Mr Betts would have put the biscuits, only permitting myself tangentially to admire the workmanship of the inlay and the mitred corners, and took four custard creams out of the paper bag within. I had reemerged into the light of day when second thoughts sent me back into the gloom again to get the whole bag, every last one. I could not see myself eating a custard cream for a long time to come, probably never.

You would have thought that, with half a pound of biscuits inside him, a donkey, not an unintelligent animal whatever people might say, would have given some little intimation of gratitude – a nod, a genteel hee-haw – but not Bagshaw. He saw off the lot, one, two, three, and looked about for more. A creature mean and tricky, totally lacking in grace.

At least he didn't have small, shell-like ears like Miss Locke.

CHAPTER TWENTY-SIX

It was really weird how, in IIIa, once they were over, the memory of the examinations which a few days previously had filled our every waking moment, to say nothing of our dreams, faded into insignificance. Perhaps it was because we were still a couple of years away from the dreaded Matric; perhaps because, the term almost at its end, our minds were already on the holidays. Perhaps, most of all, it was because it was ripe and roistering summer, the blackberries already beginning to plump in the hedgerows. Whichever it was, we gave hardly a thought to results.

Consequently, when Miss Gosse came home, very happy, took both my hands into her plump little paws and began to talk about exams, it took me a moment or two to adjust to what she was on about.

'This is in strictest confidence,' she burbled. 'You're not supposed to know until marks are given out, but I simply have to tell you, if only to make that poor old cheek of yours feel better. Well! –' A pause for effect: 'You've got 62% for arithmetic. 62%!' Awaiting my reaction, eyes shining: 'What do you say to that?'

I said: 'It ought to be your mark by rights. It was all your doing.'

'Oh dear!' Miss Gosse broke into laughter in a way I hadn't heard her laugh for some time. Miss Locke seemed to have put a damper on everything and everybody. 'As the maths mistress, I ought to get 100%, surely?'

We laughed together, which actually did make my cheek feel better, I don't know why. Miss Gosse told me that as a matter of fact she herself had given me 60%, only she had asked Miss Copley, who also taught maths, to go over my paper after her, to nip in the bud any suggestion of favouritism, and Miss Copley had added another 2%. Since the marks for arithmetic, geometry and algebra were always aggregated and then divided by three to obtain the final figure which appeared under the heading of mathematics in our reports, being rotten at arithmetic had always pulled me down in the final placings. With 62% – assuming, that is, my other papers were up to scratch, which I felt pretty sure they were – I must be in the running for the Progress Prize, if not the Form Prize, which was books to the value of 7s 6d as against the Progress Prize's 5s. Not that I had any real hopes of the Form Prize which was practically certain to go to Dorothy Hopper who was not only cleverer than me but never had marks taken off for untidiness, as I always did.

Still, it was amazing how far 5s could be made to go in Jarrold's bookshop, provided you chose something Mrs Crail approved of. If she didn't, being her she never said a word, never suggested you go back to Jarrold's for a second look around. Only, when prize-giving arrived and you were all agog with the lovely anticipation of actually taking possession of the books you had chosen, you could find yourself lumbered with *A Christian Thought for Every Day of the Year*, or something equally dire.

Miss Gosse was frisking around me like Tirri the puppy who had been run over by the tram. I thought, if only I had some dog-biscuits in the nest of drawers in the bothy I could have run quickly down the garden and fetched some back for her, to say thank you for your help. I would have held one up high and told her to sit up and beg.

As it was, I said: 'It was awfully good of you to give me extra lessons when you had so much other work to do.'

Draining away most of the pleasure, Miss Gosse demurred: 'The one you really ought to thank is Miss Locke.'

It was on the last afternoon of that lovely, lazy post-examinations week that Miss Reade, the school secretary, came into the cloakroom as I was changing out of my house shoes and told me I was to go to Mrs Crail's study immediately.

From the way she spoke, with a little tremor in her voice, I could tell there was trouble ahead: so, having a little difficulty with the buttons, I changed back into my house shoes. I did not want to risk aggravating the offence, whatever it was, by walking about the school in my outdoor ones. Miss Reade quavered, 'At once!' Not young, she always wore a narrow ribbon of black velvet fastened tightly round her throat, which made her neck, full of stalky veins, look like a bundle of asparagus which would fall apart without a binding. An old girl herself from the year dot, she was, I think, as frightened of Mrs Crail as the rest of us – more probably, since her job depended on her keeping on the right side of the old battleaxe.

Heart pounding, I followed her tall, stooping figure out of the cloakroom, along the corridor to the headmistress's room, where she knocked at the door so timidly as scarcely to be heard,

I would have thought, through its thick mahogany. However – perhaps Mrs Crail had been keeping an ear out in expectation – a loud 'Come!' sounded from the other side. Miss Reade opened the door just wide enough for me to insert myself before she scuttled back to her office next door.

Everyone else I knew called out 'Come in!' when they wanted you to enter a room, and that peremptory 'Come!' froze my blood before I was well inside, where, it appeared, three persons were waiting to receive me: Mrs Crail herself, important in her important-looking chair; Miss Barton, my house-mistress, perched uneasily on the small, uncomfortable chair the headmistress normally reserved for visiting parents, and Miss Locke, who sat looking at me directly for the first time since she had hit me in the bothy. Her usually pale face was as rosy as her shell-like ears and her pale eyes were almost as bright as Miss Gosse's. The corners of her mouth were turned down in familiar, triumphant derision.

Mrs Crail lifted up her piggy snout as if to sample which way the wind was blowing and said: 'Unfortunately, Sylvia, we have had to become used to your arrogance, your chronic untidiness, and your reckless disregard for school discipline. Even so, despite all these things, we did not, until today, expect a situation to arise which would bring into question your continued attendance at this school. We did not expect to have to add cheating to the list.'

Cheating! My heart gave a leap that almost made me lose consciousness. My injured cheek sent stabs of pain up through the roof of my mouth to the top of my head. I must have swayed on my feet because Miss Barton, looking suddenly alarmed, sprang from her chair and took a step in my direction.

'Sit down, Miss Barton, if you please! I am sure Sylvia is perfectly able to answer our questions without assistance. I have never known her at a loss for words before.'

Miss Barton resumed her seat, looking upset. The wrench of producing sound scraping the soft parts of my vocal system as with a pot-scourer, I managed to croak that I hadn't cheated, I hadn't.

'Indeed?' Mrs Crail smiled her crescent smile, as if I had answered exactly as she had hoped I would. 'In that case, what are we to make of this?'

With fingers where her gold wedding-ring nestled among the ample flesh, she lifted up from her desk what I now recognized as my history examination paper, several pages stapled together in the school-approved way. She pushed them towards me, folded back so that the last but one question I had answered was uppermost.

'Take your time,' she said with dreadful kindness as I scanned the page wildly, recognizing words in my own handwriting but not taking in their sense. 'Then read it aloud. Miss Locke, Miss Barton and I are in no hurry.' She settled back, spread over her green-upholstered armchair like a basking slug. 'When you are ready.'

Miss Barton smiled at me in wan encouragement. Miss Locke I did not dare to look at, but I felt her presence: an enemy. Somehow I managed:

'*Charles I was an upright, well-meaning man, a loving husband and an affectionate father. Unfortunately, he was also very obstinate and unable to compromise, so that, whilst he patronized literature and*

the arts, he sternly repressed all political and religious opposition,
believing monarchy to be a divine right, a responsibility entrusted
to him by the Almighty, to Whom alone he was required to render
an account. In 1640, when he was forced to summon Parliament
because of the rebellion in Scotland –'

'That will do,' Mrs Crail interrupted. She sounded so gentle that I knew myself to be in deadly peril. Yet where was the cheating in what I had read? What had I done wrong?

'Now then –' Mrs Crail sounded quite jolly. She reached back into some bookshelves behind her and brought out a copy of our current IIIa history textbook, already marked in two places with paper cut into narrow strips. 'Page 39 first, I think.'

I took the book with trembling hands, opened it to page 39 and read with mounting horror: *'Charles I was an upright, well-meaning man, a loving husband and an affectionate father. Unfortunately, he was also very obstinate and unable to compromise, so that –'* my voice petered out.

The crescent smile stretching far up her cheeks, Mrs Crail ordered: 'Now the next one. Page 126.'

Page 126 dealt with the Restoration, the subject of the last question on my history paper. It also dealt with it in precisely the same terms as I had used in my answer. Surprisingly, the sight of those printed paragraphs at one fell swoop took all my nervousness away. I had long known that I possessed a good memory. I had just that moment discovered that I had a remarkable one.

Mrs Crail observed sweetly: 'Either you are not as clever as we took you for, Sylvia, or you were paying Miss Locke no compliment. You must have thought her very foolish not to have spotted what you were at.'

I protested that I had not been at anything; that I had simply fallen behind time and so, without thinking, I must have –

'Cheated?'

'No!' Reckless now of the consequences, and exhilarated by the justice of my cause, I let my voice rise. 'If you want to know, I didn't even know I was doing it! I just did. I know all my textbooks by heart and so –'

'All?'

'Yes, I do! As far as we've got in class, anyway. I don't sit down to learn them. It isn't my fault if they stick in my mind of their own accord.'

'That is remarkable!' Miss Barton put in, leaning forward in her seat and looking relieved and suddenly happy. 'I'm sure we wish we could all have memories like that,' she said to me.

'All,' Mrs Crail said again. This time she rose ponderously to look through her bookshelves, located the book she wanted and came back with it to her chair. I saw from the cover that it was *Henry V* which was our Shakespeare play for English that term.

The headmistress took her time selecting the bit out of the play she was going to test me with. Confident I was equal to whatever passage she might choose, I was beginning, in a creepy kind of way, to enjoy myself. I thought, I bet she's thinking hard cheese, it's a pity I can't make this beastly girl walk over red-hot coals to prove her innocence, the way they made them in the Middle Ages. I guessed she was turning over the pages looking for a bit that did not have any of the great set pieces in it like 'Once more unto the breach, dear friends,' which I might be expected to know anyway and wouldn't prove anything one way or the other.

At last she was ready. She didn't even tell me the scene or the act, the old devil, but never mind.

'Pistol says, *"Captain, I thee beseech to do me favours."* Go on from there.'

I braced my shoulders, screwed up my eyes in the way I knew I had when I wanted to concentrate on something, and wanted consequently to empty my mind of everything else. My luck, my God, my father, whichever it was, did not desert me. 'Act III, Scene 5,' some inner prompt instructed me, and sliding into that inner vision of which, until then, I had scarcely been aware, I saw the relevant page in my own copy of the play, even down to the two blots on the right-hand side near the bottom which looked amazingly like Corsica and Sardinia, only the other way round, with Sardinia on top of Corsica instead of vice versa. I did not, however, think to mention this interesting geographical reversal to Mrs Crail, suspecting – rightly, I felt sure – that she would not be interested.

'Pistol –' I bent to the task in hand – 'goes on to say: "The Duke of Exeter doth love thee well." Then Fluellen says, "Aye, I praise God; and I have merited some love at his hands. Pist. (Yes, I actually said, not Pistol, but Pist., just as it was printed in the book) *Bardolph, a soldier, firm and sound of heart,*

Of buxom valour, hath, by cruel fate,
And giddy Fortune's furious fickle wheel –
That goddess blind,
That stands upon the rolling, restless stone –

> *Flue. By your patience, Ancient Pistol. Fortune is painted blind,*
> *with a muffler afore her eyes, to signify to you that Fortune is*
> *blind, and she is painted also with a wheel, to signify to you,*
> *which is the moral of it, that she is turning and inconstant,*
> *and mutability, and variation: and her foot, look you, is fixed*
> *upon a spherical stone, which rolls, and rolls, and rolls. In good*
> *truth, the poet makes a most excellent description of it. Fortune*
> *is an excellent moral.*
>
> *Pist. Fortune is Bardolph's foe and frowns on him –'"*

Thank goodness, it did not frown on me. Mrs Crail let me go on to the very end of the scene – to *'And on tomorrow bid them march away'* – without my memory once letting me down. Even then, she did not say stop. I hesitated, gathering my forces and wondering if I was meant to proceed to Scene 6, when Miss Barton stood up.

'I don't think we need to prolong this further, do we?' she said to the headmistress, with what seemed to me astonishing courage.

'Probably not.' Mrs Crail seemed to have lost all her former good humour. If I had been so crazy as to expect an apology – which I wasn't – none was forthcoming. Quite the contrary, in fact.

'An interesting trick.' Mrs Crail's verdict was delivered in her sourest tone. 'However, whilst I am relieved to find that you did not, after all, cheat in the literal sense, I feel bound to say that, put into a wider context, cheating is what it undoubtedly was, and Miss Locke was quite right to bring it to our attention. The fact that, through no expenditure of time or effort, you possess a certain facility must not be taken to mean that you have any special dispensation to benefit from it above other girls who may have studied hard and long in the pursuit of knowledge. Miss Locke, I am sure, will take this into consideration in awarding her marks – or in not awarding them, as the case may be.'

As I rode home, exultant but confused, half proud of my memory, half ashamed of it as something that singled me out as being different when what I wanted above all was to be the same as everyone else; wholly uncertain as to what, if anything, I ought to do about Miss Locke, the history mistress overtook me.

'Sylvia!' she said. 'My dear child!'

That was rich, that was, coming from her. I would have ridden on if she hadn't put her hand down on the middle of my handlebars, forcing me to dismount.

'I was angry. I don't know what came over me.' Thrusting her head closer to mine than I cared for, she pleaded: 'Do you forgive me?'

Since there was no prospect of getting away without some demeaning pushing, I said, as nastily as I knew how, 'As I've forgiven you for having to have two stitches in my cheek I suppose I may as well forgive you for calling me a cheat as well. Please can I go now?'

She took her hand away, saying sadly: 'If only you loved me as much as I love you, you would understand.'

'In that case,' I snapped back, 'I'm very glad I don't!' and rode away, pleased with myself.

She was a much faster cyclist than myself, especially on the long pull-up of the Sprowston Road, so she must have stayed behind deliberately. I said aloud, triumphantly: '*That's* put you in your place!'

When I got back to Chandos House I ran straight up to my room and would have stayed there, going without tea altogether rather than risk having it with Miss Locke, if I hadn't felt so absolutely ravenous. Getting the better of Mrs Crail for once in my life had made me feel even hungrier than normal. In the end, I couldn't stand it any longer; went down to the dining-room only to find it blessedly empty and one of Mrs Benyon's bumper teas on the table. She came in with the teapot as I was tucking in and I said what a gorgeous tea it was.

She said: 'That's to celebrate another few days and I won't be having to put up with you again till summer's over.'

The tone in which she said it brought home to me how far we had come since I had first arrived at Chandos House, only a half-term ago but light-years by another reckoning. Feeling powerful and successful, I smiled up at her over my buttered scone and returned: 'You're just saying that. You know you'll miss me like anything.'

'There's a good miss and bad miss.' But she smiled back, making it not such a dusty day after all.

CHAPTER TWENTY-SEVEN

Next day being Saturday, I decided to cycle to Earlham Hall, where I hadn't been since I had gone there with my sister Maisie after my father died. First, though, I went to the post office and cashed the postal order my mother had sent me to cover my fare home, and then I went to Thorpe Station to buy my ticket. For some reason my mother had sent 28s 4d, having obviously forgotten that I was still a child, entitled to half-fare. She must have forgotten about me quite a bit to do a thing like that; but I didn't hold it against her because, to be honest, I had forgotten quite a bit about *her*, so we were quits. Actually, my mother would be getting back even more change and not only because she had made a mistake and sent the full fare. When it came to telling the man in the booking office what I wanted, I asked not for a return, but for a half single. It put off the necessity of having to make decisions.

The rockery at Earlham Hall had none of the beauty it had possessed on my previous visit. It looked drab and grey, a fit place for Quakers. Understandable, I suppose. Coming from mountainous regions where winter must often have seemed to go on for ever, what else could alpine plants do but explode into colour with the English spring, seizing the darling moment with nothing left over for afters? Who knew what summer might bring, how put any trust in it?

Who and how indeed.

To pretend to myself that my journey to the Hall had a defined purpose, I quartered the rockery paths where I had earlier clambered pierced with delight, among foliage that stuck out in sullen clumps from dustings of gravel. I shut my eyes tight in a vain attempt to resurrect remembered joy, reopening them to the even bleaker possibility that perhaps there had never been any to be resurrected in the first place: I had made it all up, peacock and all.

'Careful he doesn't peck at you!' my sister had called out, so the bird at least must have been real, those feather tips moving in the breeze. At that moment, as if my longing had conjured it out of the past, a peacock came slouching over the big stones to where I was standing – but oh dear! not the blue and the emerald and the gold nonpareil of my imagination, but a miserable moulting fowl, as out of temper with the world and its condition as I was with myself. We stared at each other and went our separate ways.

The truth was, I shouldn't have come. I wasn't feeling at all well. Not the satisfactory unwellness of being properly ill when one could, in good conscience, throw oneself upon the world's sympathy, confident of a tender response; but a niggly, drizzly sense of something being wrong in a way you could not even specify. I had intended to treat myself to one of the pêche Melba sundaes they sold in the tea-room on the ground floor of the Hall, but now the very word 'sundae' made my stomach turn over. I also jettisoned my plan of stopping on my way back through the city to replenish my stock of whipped cream walnuts at

Sullivan's sweetshop in St Giles. The thought of whipped cream walnuts was making me feel sick too.

Retrieving my bicycle from where I had left it under an oak tree, I rode slowly away down the park drive, out into Earlham Road, back towards the city centre. My head had begun to ache, an unfamiliar affliction. By the time I reached the tram terminus, outside the gates to the cemetery, I was in a mood to wonder if it wouldn't make sense and save everyone a deal of trouble to turn in there and ask if they had any space going begging; if I wasn't, like Little Nell in *The Old Curiosity Shop* or Dick in *Holiday House*, hand-picked to join the heavenly choir just when life was set to become really interesting.

Still, I pressed on, all my hopes fixed on Chandos House, the one sanctuary remaining. Struggling up the rise towards St Giles, feet pressing hard on the pedals, tears came into my eyes at the thought of how near, yet how impossibly far, was my old home. As I passed Distillery Street, a fresh horror supervened. I felt, or fancied I felt, a dampness on my thighs. It wasn't possible! I wasn't a baby, I didn't wet myself. Yet the sensation of dampness, and my consequent embarrassment, increasing, I pressed my skirt between my legs and watched unbelieving, the bicycle swaying ominously, the slow spread through its pale blue fibres of a brown – no, a red stain. I was bleeding my life away!

Lest post-war generations find it difficult to believe that a twelve-year-old girl would know nothing of the onset of menstruation, let me say that I did know something, sort of. Though the word itself was unknown to me and nobody, so far as I could remember, had ever pronounced it in my presence, I was aware – more by what people did not say than by what they did – of a mystery, of conversations begun and broken off at my approach. Girls in perfect health were excused gym or swimming on no discernible grounds. A glass case in Boots the Chemist in Goat Lane was stacked with dinky brown-paper-wrapped parcels labelled 'Sanitary Towels'. ('What are they for?' I had demanded of the omniscient Maud, only to be answered, 'What you think? For you to ask silly questions about!')

Putting the clues together, someone more determined than I, I do not doubt, could have uncovered the dread secret without too much trouble. I was too happy, too absorbed in the visible world, too untidy by nature to worry about the odd loose end. Every new day brought new knowledge, fresh excitements, hurtling my way: no need to go seeking them out. Sooner or later, once I applied my mind to it, I would find out what sanitary towels were really for.

In the meantime, nearing the top of Earlham Road appalled, beset by headache and nausea, I had no idea what to do about the blood soaking into my knickers, staining my skirt. Would I be able to reach Chandos House before I was exposed to the disgust of the populace, before it ran down my legs for everybody to see? And when I reached Chandos House, what then? How was I to keep my condition a secret from Miss Gosse and Miss Locke and Mrs Benyon? That I knew it had to be kept secret was proof that I knew *something*.

The Roman Catholic church of St John the Baptist, at the junction of Earlham and Unthank Roads and just across the way from the beginning of St Giles, is so grand that people who do not know often think it is a cathedral. I propped my bike against the wall and went up the long flight of steps to the front door awkwardly, keeping my legs pressed together just in case; fearing to hear *splash, splash!* and, looking down, see my blood – blasphemy – crimson on the grey stone. I hoped there wasn't a rule which said only Catholics were allowed in. I had to find somewhere to sit down and think, and the church was the only place handy. But what should I say if somebody stopped me and asked to see my membership card?

Nobody did, and I entered into an extraordinary amount of space, which was of itself calming; dark after the bright outdoors except for a stained-glass shaft of light coming through a great window. Only a few people were about, scattered here and there, and although one or two were on their knees praying, it did not occur to me to follow their example, to ask for a miracle to happen and take away the blood. The God of the place was not the one I was familiar with, and I felt shy of asking favours of a stranger.

Sadie and Pauline Hooper, two Roman Catholic girls I knew, had often spoken to me about praying to the Virgin Mary when they wanted something, or to one or other of the saints whose painted statues were planted along the church walls. I did not take to the statue of the Virgin Mary at all – she looked much too plump and pleased with herself – and as for the saints, I took an instant dislike to the way their eyeballs rolled up to heaven, showing off how holy they were. Strangely enough, the only ones that did not turn up like that were those of the Man on the cross, the only ones you might have expected to and could have made allowances for, considering the agony. But His eyes you could not see at all, only the downcast eyelids keeping their own counsel.

Suddenly I knew what I must do. I went over to a vast cast-iron candelabrum where candles were burning and for sale, and bought a sixpenny one which I lit and fixed on a pricket holder, feeling the heat of all the others on my face as I settled it into place. I knew from Sadie and Pauline that this was the right thing to do, even if, in the circumstances, I was the wrong person to do it. It was almost certainly the first if not the only time that anyone in the church of St John the Baptist had lit a candle to Boots the Chemist.

Mr Spencer, the manager of the Boots the Chemist shop in Goat Lane, was somebody I had known as long as I could remember knowing anybody. He had an almost completely bald head and a very bushy beard which was disconcerting, there being moments when, looking at him, one was seized with a sudden awful anxiety that he had his head on upside down. His heart was certainly in the right place. Whilst my mother, as was her custom, was trying to remember what we had come into the shop to buy, he would prepare for me, on the house, a delicious nose-tingling drink of water into which he stirred a generous spoonful of Andrews' Liver Salts. When, at my urging, my mother from time to time bought a tin of the Salts so that we could make our own at home, it never came out with anything like comparable fizz.

To call Mr Spencer manager was a bit of an overstatement because the Goat Lane Boots the Chemist was only a small shop and the only other employee was a maiden lady called Miss Meriden who came in part-time to hold the fort out front when Mr Spencer was busy in his cubbyhole behind the glass showcases, making up prescriptions. Riding down St Giles, past the markers of my former life, I kept my first and second fingers crossed all the way that it wasn't one of Miss Meriden's days.

By no stretch of the imagination could one, in Miss Meriden's hearing, mention bleeding.

Luck was with me. Mr Spencer was alone: no customers either. Relief, together with his look of unalloyed pleasure as I came through the shop door, quite unmanned me. Tears ran down my cheeks whilst, below, a bead of blood slid hatefully down my shrinking flesh.

'My dear child, what's the matter?'

Mr Spencer came out from behind the counter. He must have seen the stain on my skirt, for his expression changed to one of jolly reassurance. 'Had a little accident, have we? We'll soon fix that.' Crossing the shop floor to the case which held the little parcels he extracted one and held it out to me. 'Know somewhere you can pop in and change, do you? Or there's always the lavatory on the Market Place.'

I did not take the parcel. I stammered: 'I don't know what to do with it.'

Unaware of it as I had been at the time, a miracle had indeed occurred at the top of St Giles in the church of St John the Baptist. Mr Spencer opened the parcel and showed me what a sanitary towel looked like; with infinite tact and sweetness instructed me in the technology of its use. Out of a small cardboard container he produced a circle of elastic with, dangling fore and aft, hooks to which I was to attach the towel loops. At his bidding, I followed him behind the counter and into his dispensing cubbyhole where he left me with the cheery admonition: 'If you hear anyone come into the shop don't move a muscle till they've gone, or you'll get me into no end of trouble!'

Later, back in the shop, over a restorative glass of Andrews' Liver Salts, he continued my education, albeit looking a little troubled by the task unexpectedly thrust upon him and as if his head might really be on the wrong way round.

'You absolutely certain your mother never said a word to you? Or your sister? Or that maid of yours – what was her name? – Maud?'

I was absolutely certain. No one had ever told me anything.

By the time Mr Spencer had finished, however, my anger against all those who had left me so criminally unprepared had abated. Rightly or wrongly, I chose to interpret their silence, which had seemed such a betrayal, as only one more manifestation of their love for me. Time enough, I could imagine them reasoning, when the blow actually fell. Why blight my happy life before nature did it for me?

The good news that the Boots the Chemist manager had to impart – that the bleeding would last a few days – was quite eclipsed by the further intelligence that by 'few days' he meant a few days out of every month of my remaining life – well, until I was forty or fifty anyway, which came to the same thing. When I learned, further, that this catastrophe – there was no other word for it – was something that only befell females, my cup of wrath ran over with a slurp.

'It's not fair!'

Mr Spencer's attempted consolation – to wit, that life wasn't fair either – did nothing to make me feel any more reconciled to women's lot. I even looked at him – my saviour though he might be – with a certain jaundiced speculation. He was a man, wasn't he? Like Alfred. Like my father. One of *them*.

CHAPTER TWENTY-EIGHT

I rode home safe from public humiliation but feeling sticky and devalued as I battled the interminable gradient of Sprowston Road. My supply of sanitary towels nestled in my bicycle basket, suitably disguised in a Boots the Chemist bag. Even if they caught sight of it as I came in, nobody at Chandos House could guess what I had been shopping for.

The sanitary towels cost 1s 3d a packet. 1s 3d a month until I was fifty! The very thought of the total made me feel dizzy. Mr Spencer, really a very kind man, must have noted my consternation because he insisted upon making me a gift of the parcel I had already started, plus an additional one to prevent my needing to worry if I were running low and for some reason wasn't able to get out to the shops. He also refused payment for the elastic circle, saying that it was a privilege, on a very special occasion, to be in a position to perform some small service for an old friend.

I promised – it was the least I could do – that I would always buy my sanitary towels at a Boots the Chemist, indicating as delicately as I knew how that, as a possibly forty-year-order, it was pretty big business, not to be sneezed at. Mr Spencer said he was sure his employers would do everything in their power to prove themselves worthy of my custom, and anyway I was showing good sense because I could take it from him that I wouldn't find them for less than 1s 6d anywhere else.

I would have kissed, or at least hugged him if a man hadn't come into the shop for some senna pods just then, and I felt obliged to leave quickly before he noticed the stain on my skirt. As it was, I just said, 'Good afternoon,' and Mr Spencer said, 'Good afternoon, miss,' and gave me a wink.

All the way back to Chandos House, once I had left the city behind, I kept looking to left and to right, making a mental note of likely places for the disposal of used sanitary towels. It went without saying that I couldn't put them in the dustbin where Mrs Benyon might come upon them. I could see that I would have to ride out and, when nobody was looking, throw them over a hedge or into a ditch. The thought of all the hedges and ditches I would need to avail myself of between now and the time I was fifty depressed me beyond measure, to say nothing of what would become of the beautiful English countryside.

I reached my room safely, my skirt unseen, and would have flung myself down on the bed had not a sudden fear of staining the bedspread prevented me in the nick of time. I leaned against the chest of drawers in sheer exhaustion. 'Unclean! Unclean!' I whispered to the leaves trembling at the window.

Having aroused myself sufficiently to disinter a clean dress and knickers, I went with them to the bathroom where I stripped and washed myself as well as I could in cold water. I did not dare to light the geyser in case the noise it made brought someone to inquire the cause at such an unaccustomed hour. And besides, was it OK to take a bath at such a time? I had not thought to ask Mr Spencer and he hadn't said.

Not surprisingly, I did not make a very good job of the laundering. However much I rubbed and scrubbed with my bar of soap a shadowy outline remained. I might have made a better job of it if I hadn't begun to feel unwell again. The pink-tinged water in the wash basin made me want to throw up.

When it was clear that, try as I might, I was never going to get the stains out completely, I dressed myself in my clean clothes and, acutely aware of the unaccustomed bulk between my legs, went out of the house by the front door and round to the back to avoid running into anybody who might ask questions: hung the wet skirt and knickers on the line at the very end, close to the hedge, where I hoped they would escape attention.

In the scullery Mrs Benyon was leaning against the sink, in her hand what looked, but did not smell, like a glass of water. As I came through the door she raised the glass in salutation, spilling a little.

'So you've joined the club, have you?'

I said, blushing a deep red, that I didn't know what she meant. 'You'll get used to it,' the housekeeper observed, as if I hadn't spoken. 'We all do.'

She swigged a good half of the contents of the glass before regarding with amusement and – or was I imagining it? – some love. 'You know what it means, don't you?' And, without waiting for a reply: 'It means from now on you've got to be careful what you do, d'you understand? Bloody careful!'

As I passed the dining-room door, Miss Gosse came out and drew me inside, holding me by both hands. For the first time I realized that I had grown since coming to Chandos House, shot up so that I was just about as tall as the maths mistress on her stumpy legs. We looked at each other eye to eye. It couldn't have been the Chandos House food. It must have been all those whipped cream walnuts.

Miss Gosse did not look well. She was too dark-skinned ever to look pale, but she looked yellow, except where the flesh round her eyes had acquired a tinge of purple. She said that she had heard from Mrs Benyon that I had brought my book box out from under the bed and moved it over to my bedroom door.

'You surely aren't thinking of dragging it all the way up to London and back, just for the holidays?'

I replied, carefully not specifying what it was exactly that I still had to make up my mind about, that I hadn't decided.

A look of alarm nevertheless came over Miss Gosse's face. 'You surely aren't thinking of staying in London for good?'

Again I answered – guilt, for which I could assign no reason, making me mumble – that I hadn't made up my mind.

Speaking in a level tone which could not disguise a despair which sat oddly on her doggy features, Miss Gosse said: 'Miss Locke says, if you are going to leave Chandos House, so will she. She says she will go up to London too and try and find a position there.'

It was intolerable! Intolerable to be saddled with other people's pain, as if one didn't have enough of one's own to put up with. Two old women! What was I to them or they to me? It wasn't fair.

'*Life isn't fair,*' I could hear Mr Spencer saying.

I could also hear Miss Gosse. 'Sylvia, I beg of you. Please don't go.'

She was looking at me in exactly the way Tirri used to look at me when he wanted something. After the tram had hit him I had run out into St Giles to find, not my puppy at all, but a sack emptied of meaning, litter for the street cleaner to take away in his little cart. I looked at Miss Gosse and thought that, so far as she was concerned, the tram was still out of sight, down by the Guildhall, at the beginning of the hill. There was still time for her to get back on the pavement, out of its way. I saw that I held her happiness in my hand like a dog biscuit. If I held it high and commanded, 'Up, doggie!' she would jump for it, squealing.

Down below I could feel that I was bleeding again, my new kind of blood, but I had a sanitary towel now, I didn't need to worry. I was young and didn't need to worry about anything.

I thought. I thought about my father up there in heaven, too busy, or more likely too shy, to warn me about menstruation but still safely up there, straight up from Norwich, not forced to peer down anxiously in a vain attempt to locate me through the layers of London smoke and London people. I thought of my brother Alfred and his fiancée Phyllis and the house they were building to live in after they were married. I thought of the rest of my family, leading their busy lives in a city I should never feel at home in, not if I lived there for a hundred years. I thought of Miss Gosse and Miss Locke, to whom I was important: who loved each other and loved me, even if they had their funny ways of showing it. Of ginny Mrs Benyon and knobby Mr Betts. Of Robert Kett and Bagshaw the donkey.

At the thought of Mrs Kett and her culinary disasters my spirits lightened. Nobody was going to keep *me* down like a flat sponge. I was going to rise and rise. Never mind the bleeding, the Boots the Chemist parcels at 1s 3d a time. The way time was flying, if I didn't get on with life I'd be fifty and finished with them before I'd got properly started.

'Please go on staying with us,' Miss Gosse pleaded. 'Please come back after the holidays.'

I thought of my room, my darling room with my book box under the bed and the quivering tree outside the window. I handed Miss Gosse the biscuit without, after all, making a production of it.

'All right,' I said.